Macro-economics
an introduction
Second edition

Other books by G.F. Stanlake

Introductory Economics
Introductory Economics Workbook
Objective Tests in Economics

Macro-economics
an introduction

Second edition
G. F. Stanlake M.A., B.Sc.(Econ)

LONGMAN GROUP LIMITED
Longman House
Burnt Mill, Harlow, Essex, CM20 2JE, England

© Longman Group Limited 1974, 1979

All rights reserved. No part of this publication may be reproduced, stored in a retrieval system or transmitted in any form or by any means–electronic, mechanical, photocopying, recording or otherwise–without the prior permission of the copyright owner.

First published 1974
Second edition 1979
Fourth impression 1981

ISBN 0 582 35265 7 cased edition

ISBN 0 582 35264 9 limp edition

Printed in Hong Kong by
Wing Tai Cheung Printing Co Ltd

Preface

This book is aimed primarily at the student preparing for the A-level examination in Economics. This makes the book an appropriate text for a wide range of other students because the content and standard of the A-level course is relevant to many other examinations especially the professional examinations in such subjects as banking, accountancy and business studies. The book should also be a useful introduction to the subject matter for first-year students on degree courses.

The text assumes that the reader has some acquaintance with basic economic principles, but requires no more than the most elementary knowledge of geometrical and algebraic techniques.

Emphasis has been placed on providing a clear explanation of the theoretical basis of economics, but, throughout the text, the student will find that economic theory has been related to economic policies and there is a comprehensive account of the institutional framework in which these policies operate.

The book is based on many years experience in teaching and examining at this level and I hope that this knowledge of students' difficulties has helped me to produce a book which is both interesting and helpful.

At the appropriate intervals there are collections of essay and multiple-choice questions. As an additional aid to understanding, the text contains several worked examples of numerical problems.

This second edition contains thoroughly revised sections on Banking, the IMF and the international monetary situation, and Incomes Policy. There are several other minor changes in the text and there has been an updating of the factual material.

G.F.S.

KEY TO SOURCES OF ESSAY QUESTIONS

(AEB)	Associated Examining Board
(C)	University of Cambridge Local Examinations Syndicate
(JMB)	Joint Matriculation Board
(L)	University of London Schools Examinations Council
(O & C)	Oxford and Cambridge Schools Examination Board
(S)	Southern Universities Joint Board for School Examinations
(W)	Welsh Joint Education Committee

Acknowledgements

We are grateful to the following for permission to reproduce copyright material:

Bank of England for tables 'UK Money Supply October 1977', 'London Clearing Banks Combined Balance Sheet' from *Bank of England Quarterly Bulletin of December 1977*; Her Majesty's Stationery Office for tables 'United Kingdom National Income 1976', 'Composition of Domestic Income UK 1966–76', 'National Income and Consumer Expenditure 1966–76', 'Capital Formation UK 1976' from *National Income and Expenditure* (1966–76); a figure 'Level of unemployment and annual charge in prices UK 1957–77' from *Economic Trends*; a figure 'Unemployed and Vacancies in Great Britain' from *Department of Employment Gazette* Nov. 1977, reproduced with the permission of the Controller of Her Majesty's Stationery Office; International Monetary Fund for a table 'The Composition of World Liquidity July 1977' from *International Financial Statistics*; National Institute of Economic and Social Research for a table 'Movements of Consumer Prices 1970–77' from *National Institute Economic Review*; Times Newspapers Ltd., for a table 'UK balance of payments summary 1975–77' from *The Times* March 9 1978; and the following examining bodies for reproduction of certain questions set by them in previous examinations:

Associated Examining Board
Joint Matriculation Board
Oxford and Cambridge Schools Examination Board
Southern Universities Joint Board
University of Cambridge Local Examinations Syndicate
University of London University Entrance and School Examinations Council
Welsh Joint Education Committee

Contents

	Preface	v
1	*Scope and Methods*	1
	Micro- and macro-economics; economic policy; economic theories and models; the use of mathematical notation	
2	*The Meaning and Measurement of National Income*	11
	Output = expenditure = income; government and foreign trade; measuring the national income; real national income and money national income	
	Questions on Chapter 2	
3	*The Circular Flow of Income*	31
	Injections and leakages; planned and realised	
4	*Output, Demand and Equilibrium*	37
	Output and demand; equilibrium; real income and employment; Autonomous and induced demands	
5	*Consumption*	41
	Income and consumption; the propensities to consume and save; the consumption and savings functions	
6	*Investment*	51
	Types of investment; the basis of the investment decision; investment and income; summary	
7	*The Determination of Equilibrium*	65
	Changes in equilibrium	
8	*Output and Employment*	77
	A deficiency of aggregate demand; excess demand; an equilibrium level of employment; full employment	
9	*The Government Sector*	85
	The size of the government sector; the budgetary framework; the government and income; the government sector and the multiplier; fiscal policy	

10	*Foreign Trade and National Income*	103
	Exports and imports; equilibrium – an open economy; some worked examples	
	Questions on Chapters 3–10	
11	*Money*	119
	The nature of money; liquidity and near money; the UK money supply; the evolution of money; the creation of bank deposits; the convertibility of bank deposits	
12	*The Structure of Banking*	135
	The central bank; the London money market; the work of the discount houses; the commercial banks; other financial intermediaries	
13	*The Demand for Money – Liquidity Preference*	151
	The liquidity preference theory	
14	*The Control of the Money Supply*	159
	Open market operations; interest rate policy; funding; special deposits; quantitative and qualitative controls; monetary policy	
	Questions on Chapters 11–14	
15	*The Quantity of Money and the Price Level*	173
	The quantity theory	
16	*Output, Demand and the Price Level*	179
	An aggregate supply curve; an aggregate money demand curve	
17	*Inflation*	185
	Demand inflation; cost-push inflation; unemployment and inflation; the effects of inflation	
	Questions on Chapters 15–17	
18	*The Balance of Payments and the Rate of Exchange*	199
	The structure of the balance of payments; equilibrium in the balance of payments; exchange rates; freely fluctuating exchange rates; managed exchange rates; fixed exchange rates; devaluation and revaluation; the IMF system	
19	*Economic Growth*	221
	The meaning of economic growth; sources of economic growth; economic growth and population growth	
20	*Managing the Economy*	235
	The instruments of economic policy; the objectives of economic policy; policy problems	
	Questions on Chapters 18–20	

Appendix   Incomes Policy   254
    The problem of cost inflation; the principles of an
    incomes policy; incomes policy in the UK

Index   262

Answers to questions   266

1
Scope and Methods

Micro- and macro-economics
The subject matter of economics is divided conventionally into two branches known as micro-economics and macro-economics. This division is convenient since the problems considered in the two sections are fundamentally different as are the methods of analysis used to deal with them.

Micro-economics deals with 'parts' of the economy – it takes a sectional view rather than a general view of economic activity. In micro-economics we are largely concerned with individual markets. Analysis in this branch of economics deals with such matters as the determination of the prices of particular commodities, the incomes of particular groups, the output of individual firms and industries and the employment levels of particular industries. We assume some given level of output for all other industries and examine what causes changes in the output of a particular industry. We take the level of national income as given and then look at the question of the distribution of this income between different groups in the community. Micro-economics, then, is a kind of 'small scale' analysis which deals with prices, outputs and incomes of particular small sectors of a given framework.

Macro-economics on the other hand is concerned with the economy as a whole – it is 'large-scale' analysis. In this branch of economics we study the behaviour of the aggregates rather than the parts. We examine problems relevant to aggregates of firms and households rather than individual firms and households. Macro-economics is concerned not with the price of tea, but with prices in general; not with the output of cars, but with the level of total output; not with the individual firm or industry, but with the whole economic system.

The questions which provide the basis of macro-economics are:
(a) What determines the magnitude of the total output of a country during some given period of time?
(b) What determines the rate at which this output grows?
(c) What determines the level of prices?

(d) What determines the direction and rate of change of prices?
(e) What determines the levels of a country's exports and imports?

In attempting to answer these questions we shall be considering: the Theory of Employment; the Theory of the Price Level; and the Theory of Economic Growth. This means we shall be examining such aggregates as output, employment, consumption, investment, the supply of money, the general price level, exports and imports. In addition, of course, our study requires an appreciation of the role of government in determining the levels of these aggregates and the manner in which it uses its policy instruments for this purpose.

There is no opposition between micro- and macro-economics. It is necessary to understand the parts if one is to understand the whole. The tools of analysis (especially supply and demand analysis) developed in micro-economics are extremely useful aids to an understanding of macro-economic problems.

Economic policy

Up to the end of the last century it was generally assumed that government intervention in the working of the economic system should be kept to a minimum. Since Britain had become the world's greatest industrial power on the basis of private enterprise and free trade, it was assumed that any official intervention with the free play of market forces would only be harmful to economic development. It was also argued that the freedoms to acquire, dispose of, or utilise property, and to spend one's income, as one wished were essential aspects of human liberty.

Accordingly governments accepted no responsibility for the management of the economy. Governments were held responsible for creating a framework of rules and regulations which would assist the operation of free markets. They were required to defend the realm, maintain law and order within the country, regulate weights and measures, insist on the legal enforcement of contractual relationships and so on. It is true that they also intervened to regulate working conditions in factories and mines and to some extent controlled monopoly power in public utilities, but this kind of intervention was extremely limited.

During the course of this century there has been a remarkable change of public opinion. The successful control of national resources during two world wars, and the heavy and chronic unemployment during the inter-war period led to a rejection of the ideas that market forces should be left to work unhindered and that governments should not play an active part in determining the course of economic development. During the inter-war period the government was compelled to take some positive action to deal with unemployment. Home industry was protected by the use of tariffs, measures were adopted to reorganise depressed industries like coal and cotton, and some new industries were given assistance to establish themselves in the depressed areas. The net result of these efforts was not very great and not until the rearmament programme got under way in the later 1930s was there any significant drop in the unemployment figures.

In the post-war period things have been very different. In 1944 the British government officially acknowledged its responsibility for the overall management of the economy and in particular the responsibility for maintaining a high and stable level of employment. Since 1945 the government has exercised a much greater degree of control over the economy. A large sector of industry has been brought directly under public control. Taxation and government expenditure have been maintained at much higher levels than was the case before the war, so that budgetary policy has a much greater influence on the economy. The most important difference between the post-war and pre-war periods, however, lies in the adoption, by those in charge of economic policy, of a new set of economic principles derived from the work of Lord Keynes.[1] These ideas form the basis of the earlier sections of this book.

THE AIMS OF GOVERNMENT POLICY

There is a large measure of agreement on the broad aims of government economic policy. These aims may be classified under four headings.

Full employment

It is accepted that the main objective of government policy is to maintain a demand for labour which is great enough, in aggregate, to maintain a fully employed labour force. This does not mean that everyone willing to work will always be in employment. As we shall see later, labour is not perfectly mobile and we may have something like 2 per cent of the labour force unemployed even when the number of vacancies exceeds the numbers registered as unemployed.

Stable prices

Fluctuations in the general level of prices can cause harmful distortions in the debtor–creditor relationships, the balance of payments situation, the level of production and the distribution of real income. For example, a rapid increase in prices will reduce the purchasing power of savings; it will reduce the real burdens of debts so that debtors repay less in real terms than they borrowed; it will increase the prices of exports and make them less attractive to foreigners, and it will reduce the real income of

1. Keynes, *The General Theory of Employment, Interest, and Money*, Macmillan.

those on fixed money incomes, relative to those whose incomes are rapidly adjusted to the changing price level. Governments will be concerned to eliminate or reduce such harmful developments.

A satisfactory balance of payments equilibrium

What is a satisfactory balance of payments situation depends upon the particular circumstances in which the country finds itself. If the government has adequate foreign currency reserves and can borrow from other countries, it may allow a series of deficits to develop, while imports are rising faster than exports, as a necessary part of a policy to stimulate economic growth. In the longer run, however, a country's export earnings must balance its payments to other countries.

An acceptable rate of economic growth

'The revolution of rising expectations', as Adlai Stevenson put it, is a feature of almost every developed and developing country. The insistent demands for higher standards of living have forced governments to give a high priority to policies which will bring about a steady increase in output per head.

THE INSTRUMENTS OF GOVERNMENT ECONOMIC POLICY

The State has a variety of means available to it for the purpose of carrying out its economic policy.

Fiscal policy

This is the name given to the deliberate manipulation of government income and expenditure with a view to influencing income, output, employment and prices. The State is by far the biggest business in the country and variations in its spending will have an important influence on total demand. Similarly, changes in taxation will affect both the total of private expenditure and its distribution on various goods and services. In the type of inflationary situation, for example, where total demand exceeds total supply at current prices, the government may reduce its own spending and increase the rates of taxation on income and expenditure. The major instrument of fiscal policy is the Budget.

Monetary policy

The government, through its agent, the Bank of England, is able to control the total money supply. Total expenditure on goods and service may be increased or decreased by variations in the supply of money and in the terms on which it may be borrowed (i.e. the rate of interest). The greater part of the money supply consists of bank credit (i.e. bank deposits) and monetary policy aims to vary both the quantity and the price of such credit.

Direct controls

The State has the powers, if it wishes to use them, to institute a vast range of physical controls on the economic system. It has the political power to bring the means of production (land and capital – not labour!) into public ownership and to decide the volume and pattern of production independently of market forces. This would call for detailed central planning so that the planned outputs of the different sectors of the economy could be dovetailed together.

Alternatively it can leave all or most of the land and capital in private ownership, but by means of taxes and subsidies influence the way in which these resources are used. Most States choose some combinations of direct controls and budgetary measures (taxes and subsidies). In the UK for example, at different times, we have used tariffs and quotas to restrict imports, building licences to control the construction industry, price controls, statutory controls on wages and other incomes, as well as taxes and subsidies. Direct controls, except in emergencies, are not easy to impose on a society accustomed to a large measure of freedom of choice. Government planning, therefore, tends to be 'indicative', that is, the government prepares a list of desirable objectives and aims to achieve these by publicity, discussion, persuasion and the use of its fiscal and monetary measures.

THE INCOMPATIBILITY OF OBJECTIVES

The conduct of economic policy is a most difficult task because, so often, the principal objectives of that policy are mutually incompatible. If governments had to pursue only one of these aims without having to worry about the other targets, there would be relatively few problems of economic policy. Unfortunately this is not the case. An attempt to achieve a faster rate of economic growth, for example, might lead to a large increase in the imports of basic materials, fuel, and machinery, which might well put the balance of payments account into deficit. When there are inflationary tendencies, the pursuit of price stability might require the use of measures to reduce total demand. But these same measures could well result in a reduction of output rather than prices, so that unemployment increases. The government will find itself having to compromise – to balance one objective against another. Economic policy will have to be cast in terms of priorities, which themselves will change over time. Some degree of inflation might be the price which has to be paid for maintaining a high level of employment; some curb may have to be placed on the planned rate of economic growth in order to achieve an acceptable balance of payments equilibrium, and so on.

Economic theories and models

There are three requirements in the formation of economic policy.
1. A value judgement; that is, a statement of the objectives. This will define what the policy-makers think *ought* to be done and, as such, is a political decision.
2. A theory or model of how the economic system works.
3. A statement of the policy measures (e.g. tax changes, changes in the money supply) which, if the model works as predicted, will achieve the desired objectives.

The economist is concerned with (2) and (3), although as an individual citizen he will have his own views about (1).

Economic policy, of course, must be based upon adequate knowledge about the state of the economy. The government must be in possession of statistical information regarding the productive potential, the levels of output and employment, movements in prices, the balance of payments situation and so on. In the UK a vast amount of such data is now available and the coverage and presentation of economic statistics are being continuously improved. But factual information alone is an insufficient basis for policy decisions; the decision-takers must have some idea of the basic principles which govern the working of the economy. What is needed is a theoretical framework or model which explains how the economic system operates.

Economic theories are propositions which attempt to explain economic behaviour in terms of cause and effect; they try to explain *why* certain consequences follow certain actions. The importance of such theories lies in the fact that they help us to make predictions; they make it possible for us to say what the consequences of certain actions might be. When a theory reveals a high degree of unreliability, that is, when predictions based upon this theory are consistently wrong, it is time to discard it and seek a more satisfactory theory.

It may be objected that economics is concerned with certain aspects of human behaviour and that this is highly unpredictable, since 'everyone is different'. While this is certainly true of individuals, it is not true of the behaviour of large groups. While it is difficult to predict how any particular individual will react to a given event, it is usually possible to say with some degree of certainty how a large group will react. When Arsenal score a goal at Highbury we know that there will be a roar from the crowd although we cannot say that this or that individual will give expression to his feelings. Macro-economics is based on the assumption that there will be fairly stable behaviour patterns at the aggregate level.

The analysis of statistical data enables us to formulate economic theories and to check their validity. It also helps us to frame them in a more precise manner. For example, a particular hypothesis such as 'consumption spending is directly related to income' may be verified by checking the relevant data. Further investigation, however, might reveal that not only does such a relationship exist, but consumption spending is always equal to four-fifths of income. A complete theory of the economy will involve a whole series of relationships of this type, all fitting together and all consistent with the relevant evidence. The example above is grossly oversimplified. Consumption spending is determined not only by income, but by such factors as advertising, the stock of wealth, the availability of hire purchase facilities, expectations regarding future income and so on. But theories which try to include all possible causal relationships become extremely complicated, and, in order to obtain a clear but useful picture of the economy, it is necessary to leave out some of variables retaining only those for which there is fairly substantial evidence. This will provide a model of the economy in the form of a set of deliberately simplified relationships which should yield predictions about the way the economy works and hence help in formulating economic policy.

The aim of this book is to provide an understanding of such a model. We shall look first at the determination of the total output of goods and services. This, it will be argued, depends upon aggregate demand. It is then necessary to examine the components of aggregate demand; namely, consumption, investment, government spending and exports minus imports. There follows a discussion of the relationship between aggregate demand, output and the level of employment. Subsequent chapters look at the supply of money, the determination of the general price level, and the way in which the monetary system affects the macro-economic aggregates. The UK and most other economies are open economies – they trade with other countries. This makes it necessary to study the effects of these international relationships on the domestic economy. There is then a chapter on the manner in which the national output changes over time (i.e. economic growth). The book concludes with a discussion of the problems of managing the economy.

The use of mathematical notation

It is a great convenience in economic theory to make use of mathematical notation. People with a limited knowledge of mathematics often find the use of equations and symbols in economics rather disturbing and fear that the pages on which they appear will be beyond their comprehension. In fact, such expressions as are used in a textbook at this level amount to little more than an easily learned shorthand. For example, the statement 'consumption is determined by income' may be expressed in the form, $C = f(Y)$, where C stands for consumption and Y for the level of income. This expression may be read as 'consumption is a *function* of income'. The use of the word 'function' (f) merely indicates that some kind of systematic relationship exists between C and Y; it does not tell us what kind of relationship it is.

If there is a fixed proportionate relationship between consumption and income, it can be expressed in the form,

$$C = aY \quad \text{(where } a \text{ is a constant).}$$

For example, if consumption spending is always equal to nine-tenths of income, then $a = 0.9$ and the equation will be written,

$$C = 0.9Y.$$

Sometimes the relationship between the two variables may be more complex. There may be some consumption even when income[1] is zero (people may be spending some of their savings). In this case the equation becomes,

$$C = b + aY$$

where b represents the level of consumption when income is zero.

Most of the equations used in this text concern the rate at which one variable is changing with respect to another. The equations used above are only one way of expressing such a relationship. More commonly it is expressed in the form of a graph.

When two variables are related so that one is always changing at a constant rate with respect to the other, the relationship is said to be linear and can be represented by a straight line graph. The example used above, $C = 0.9Y$, is a linear equation since consumption always changes by £9 whenever income changes by £10.

Many of the relationships encountered in economics are non-linear; that is, one variable does not change at a constant rate with respect to the other. For example, when income rises the related increases in consumption may become progressively smaller. When income is £1m., an increase of £1 000 may cause consumption to rise by £800. When income is £2m., an increase of £1 000 may cause income to increase by only £500. When, as in this example, the proportionate relationship between changes in the variables (C and Y) is not constant, it means that the graph showing the relationship between the variables will be a curved line.

The gradient of such a curve (i.e. the tangent to the curve) at any

1. Income, here, refers to factor income; this is the income received as a reward for services rendered. (see page 13).

point measures the rate at which one variable is changing with respect to the other. For example, if C and Y are related by a curved line, the rate at which C is changing in relation to Y, at any given level of income, is given by the tangent to the curve. This rate of change might be expressed in the form

$$\frac{\Delta C}{\Delta Y}$$

where ΔY is some small change in income[1] and ΔC is the associated change in consumption. In the examples above

$$\frac{\Delta C}{\Delta Y} = \frac{800}{1\,000} = 0\cdot 8$$

$$\frac{\Delta C}{\Delta Y} = \frac{500}{1\,000} = 0\cdot 5$$

---

1. The symbol Δ (delta) is sometimes written δ. It indicates a small change in the variable it qualifies.

2
The Meaning and Measurement of National Income

Output = expenditure = income

OUTPUT = EXPENDITURE

The purpose of economic activity is the satisfaction of material wants. To this end man produces an enormous variety of goods and services. Since economic activity is continuous we can only attempt to measure its results over some given period of time, and this is invariably taken as one year. It is essential that we visualise national output as a *flow* of goods and services per unit of time and not as a stock of goods and services.

Goods and services are produced by the combined efforts of the factors of production (land, labour and capital) organised into units of production known as firms or enterprises. These enterprises may be publicly owned (e.g. British Rail), or privately owned. Where the goods and services are required for the immediate satisfaction of wants we refer to them as *consumption goods and services,* and we assume that such goods are used up at the time of purchase or very soon afterwards. Our purchases of bread, milk, entertainment and passenger transport provide examples of such consumer spending. Furniture, household electrical equipment, etc., are known as durable consumer goods because they are purchased by consumers for their own satisfaction, but yield their services over a fairly long period of time.

Part of the community's output, however, is not intended for immediate consumption. Some part of the total output will consist of *capital goods.* Capital is a man-made aid to production and consists of such things as factories, machines, roads, railways, ships, houses and schools. Such goods are demanded not because they render immediate satisfaction, but because they help in the production of consumer goods and services. Stocks of unsold consumer goods, as we shall see later, may also be regarded as capital. Since capital goods themselves are not consumable, the creation of capital requires the sacrifice of some current consumption. The resources which have been used to make the capital goods might have been used to increase the current output of consumer goods. The incentive to make this sacrifice lies in the fact that the use of capital makes possible a greater future output of consumer goods. In order to produce capital, therefore, a community must consume less than it produces – it must save.

This process of creating capital is known as *investment*. It is important to be perfectly clear on the meaning of this term in economic theory since it has a much wider meaning in everyday usage. In economics we do not describe the purchase of an existing share (or any other existing asset) as investment; the term is confined to the process of creating capital goods.

In addition to *fixed capital* (factories, machines, etc.), there will be a further part of total output which is not intended for immediate consumption. Some of the goods produced will be added to stocks of materials and finished goods. These stocks (or inventories as they are sometimes called) are held so that production can proceed smoothly when deliveries are interrupted, and so that unexpected additional orders for finished goods can be met without changing production schedules. Stocks of raw materials and finished goods are described as *circulating capital* and they are just as necessary for the efficient working of the economic system as the fixed capital.

In each year part of the output of capital goods will be required to replace worn out and obsolete assets while the remainder will be a net addition to the community's existing stock of capital. The total output of capital is defined as *gross investment* while the value of that part which is required for replacement is known as *depreciation* or *capital consumption*. The additions to the existing stock of capital comprise *net investment*. Thus:

Gross investment — *Depreciation* = *Net investment*

Our definitions of capital have made no mention of money, shares or securities of various kinds. In ordinary speech people are inclined to use the terms 'money' and 'capital' as though they were interchangeable, but money is not capital in the sense in which we are using the word. Money is not a factor of production for the nation as a whole, and increasing the amount of money in a country adds nothing directly to the country's wealth or productive capacity. Money is a claim on goods and services and the community as a whole cannot enrich itself by producing claims on itself. The only money which might be regarded as capital is the foreign currency held by residents in the home country because this represents claims on other countries' goods and services.

Although it is important, in economics, to concentrate on real output, that is the physical volume of goods and services produced, the measurement of this output can only be effectively carried out in monetary terms. All goods and services have prices, and the only feasible way of aggregating the wide variety of goods and services produced is to sum their money values. It will be seen later that this procedure gives rise to problems since the value of money itself changes over time.

We shall assume at this stage that all consumption goods and services are purchased by individuals, using the term *households* to describe these individuals, and all investment goods we assume are purchased by *firms*. We also assume that there is no government activity and no foreign trade; all economic activity is confined to households and firms.

The prices of the goods and services produced are the sums of money paid by the purchasers. In other words, one way of looking at the value of total output is from the side of expenditure. National output may be seen as the value of the total expenditure of households and firms (i.e. consumption spending and investment spending). There is one snag, however, which prevents the immediate formulation of this simple equality. That part of total output which has been described as 'additions to stocks' has not given rise to a market transaction – there is no 'expenditure' to set alongside 'output'. There has been no act of spending which creates a flow of money equal in value to the flow of goods. In order to obtain an equality between 'Expenditure' and 'Output' we have to impute a money value to the physical increase in stocks by assuming a notional expenditure by the firms themselves. We assume that firms 'buy' the output which they place in their stocks. If we take account of this imputed spending on additions to stocks we can write,

$$\text{National output} = \text{National expenditure} \left(\text{Consumption spending} + \text{Investment spending} \right) \quad (1)$$

OUTPUT = INCOME

We can now take another view of national output. Firms produce goods and services by making use of the factors of production. The payments made for the services of these factors are seen as costs by the firm, but as income by the recipients. The owners of land receive rent, the owners of capital receive interest, labour receives wages and the riskbearers (the entrepreneurs and others who have risked capital to finance the enterprise) receive profits. Wages, interest, and rent are contractual payments the amounts of which are agreed before production takes place, whereas profits are a residual item, the amount of which is unknown until the particular enterprise has been undertaken. Profits are the difference between the value of the output and the sum of wages, rent and interest. They can, of course, be negative (i.e. when a firm makes a loss).

The prices of goods and services may be regarded as 'bundles of incomes' paid out or earned during the course of production. The sum of the payments for services rendered by the factors of production (including profits) will be equal to the prices of the finished goods (assuming no taxes). This particular equality often confuses students who try to apply the principle at a particular stage in the productive process. It is quite true that all the payments made by any one firm do not take the form of direct payments to the factors of production. Some of these payments will be in respect of bought-out materials and only

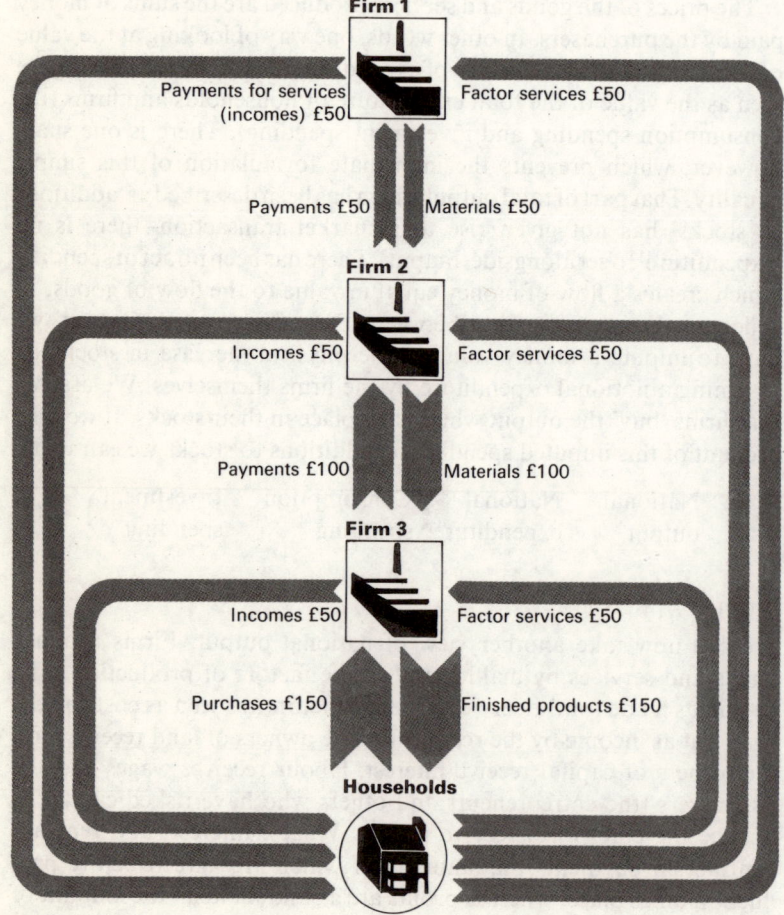

Fig. 1

part of the firm's cost payments will be made up of wages, interest, rent and profits. But if we look at the whole of the production process we can see that the prices of final goods are made up entirely of factor incomes.

Imagine there are only three stages of production, extraction, manufacturing and distribution. The output of one stage will represent the input of the next stage. The process is illustrated in Fig. 1. The output of Firm 1 is bought by Firm 2 which works on these materials, adds value to them and sells them to Firm 3. At the initial stage all the firm's payments (costs) take the form of income payments to factors of production or to the owners of factors of production (e.g. payments to the owners of forests or mineral deposits). All costs at this stage will consist of wages, interest, rent and profits. Firm 2 will increase the value of its input by the amounts which it 'pays out' as factor incomes; the value added is equal to the wages, rent, interest and profits generated at this stage of production. A similar procedure takes place in Firm 3. In Fig. 1 we can see that the value of the final product is exactly equal to the sum of the factor incomes created during the total process of production.

At each stage the individual firm buys the services of factors of production and adds value to its material inputs equal to the sum of the factor incomes paid out. We are assuming that all profits are paid out. We can write, therefore.

Value of output = Sum of incomes received by the factors of production, and in aggregate terms,

$$\text{National output} \equiv \text{National income} \qquad (2)$$

Note that the equality has been expressed as an identity ($\equiv$). We have defined the terms in such a manner that output must always equal income. Output, remember, refers to the value of the final products, and income refers to the payments made to the factors of production for services rendered. If we now combine equations (1) and (2) we have,

$$\text{National output} \equiv \text{National expenditure} \equiv \text{National income} \qquad (3)$$

Since we have defined expenditure to mean the spending on final goods and services plus an imputed spending on additions to stocks, we are in order in expressing the relationships as identities. Expression (3), in fact, is the fundamental identity of national income accounting.

INCOME AS A FLOW

Although, at this stage, we are still dealing with a highly simplified picture of the economy, it might be useful to consider a diagrammatic representation of the relationships set out in the identities developed in this section of the work. They are shown in Fig. 2, which takes the form of a conventional flow diagram.

MACRO-ECONOMICS

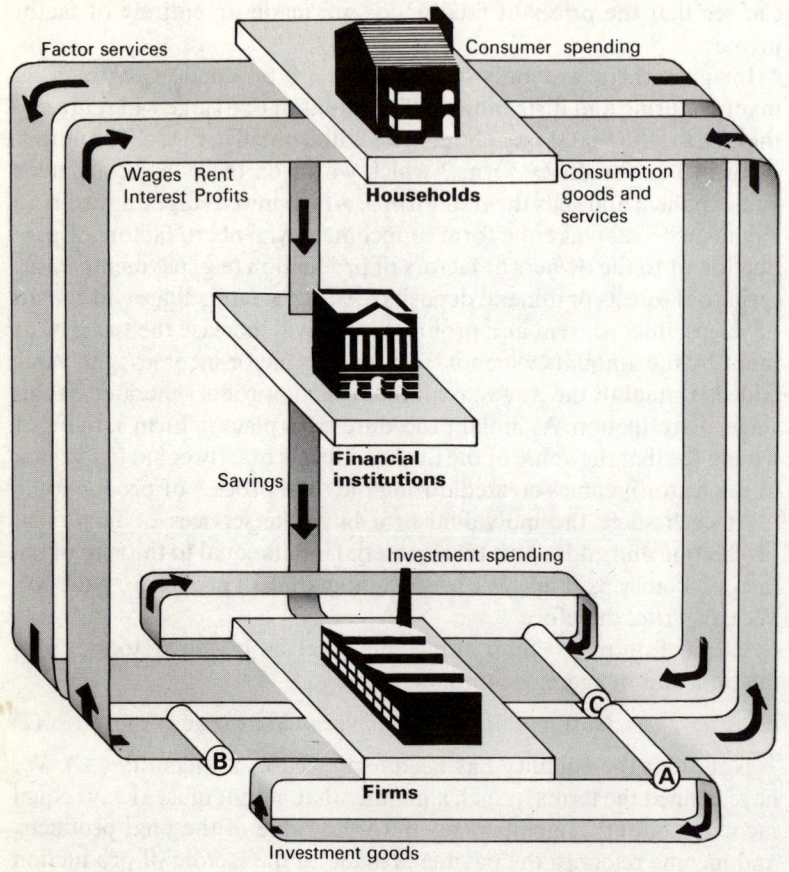

Fig. 2

On the RHS we have the flow of consumption goods and services from firms to households and the corresponding flow of payments for these items. On the LHS we have the flow of incomes from firms to households and the corresponding flow of factor services from households to firms.

Since, under present assumptions, only firms undertake investment, we have shown a flow of investment goods from firms to firms; that is, within the industry sector, together with the appropriate flow of investment spending. Households, as we know, do not usually spend all their income–part of it is saved. It is this saving which helps to finance investment.[1] In the real world the saving is usually loaned to enterprises in the capital market (banks, insurance companies, investment trusts, etc.) and it may then be borrowed by firms to finance their investment programmes. The direct path of savings from households to firms, therefore, is a very simplified picture of real events.

Our three views of national income can be clearly seen in Fig. 2. If we visualise some kind of metering device at the points A, B and C, an annual reading of the meters would give us

(a) at point A: the value of *National output*
(b) at point B: the value of *National income*
(c) at point C: the value of *National expenditure*

Government and foreign trade

For purposes of analysis and policy it is necessary to have comprehensive and reasonably accurate statistics of the national income. Before we study the ways in which national income is measured, it is necessary to relax some of the assumptions made in the previous sections, and consider the effects of government activity and foreign trade.

GOVERNMENT

The government plays a most important part in the economic affairs of the nation and its activities have a great influence on the composition and size of the national income. It comes into the picture as a direct producer by virtue of its control over the nationalised industries. The government is also a large-scale producer of services such as defence, health, education and law and order. By means of its taxation policies, the government is able to influence all kinds of economic activities. In particular, the government is able to use its taxation and spending policies to bring about significant changes in the distribution of income. A large part of national output, therefore, is accounted for directly by the public sector, while the output of the private sector may be influenced both in total and composition by means of taxes and subsidies and government spending.

A further large part of public expenditure is devoted to social security benefits such as pensions, unemployment pay, sickness benefits and supplementary allowances. Although these payments make up part of or the whole of the income of the recipients they do not form part of the national income, since they are not payments to factors of production for services rendered. There is no real output corresponding to these payments. Such items are known as *transfer payments*.

---

1. Saving does not *cause* investment, it makes it possible.

FOREIGN TRADE

Britain, like most other countries, is an open economy; that is, it takes part in international trade. This affects the composition and size of the national income in several ways. Part of the national output is not bought by domestic households and firms, but by foreigners, and some part of national expenditure will be devoted to the output of foreign firms. In other words, total domestic expenditure need not equal national output. Exports diminish the supply of goods and services available on the home market while imports augment these supplies. The effect on domestic incomes, however, is exactly the opposite. Exports generate income at home, but imports generate income abroad.

While the terms 'exports' and 'imports' may be clearly understood in relation to the movements of physical goods, confusion often arises when international trade in services is being considered. Britain earns a considerable income from foreigners by providing them with banking, insurance, shipping, tourist and other services. She also receives a substantial income in the form of interest and dividends on her investments in other countries. Transactions which result in the receipt of such income from foreign firms and households are invisible exports and they provide us with foreign currencies and therefore claims on foreign goods and services. Similar transactions in the opposite direction (e.g. a British citizen taking a holiday abroad) are invisible imports and provide foreigners with claims on our national output. In calculating the national income, account must be taken of both visible and invisible items of foreign trade.

Measuring the national income

Earlier we identified three different ways of looking at national income. They are:

1. Output – the total output of goods and services becoming available to the nation in the course of one year
2. Income – the sum of the factor incomes paid out for services rendered in producing the national output
3. Expenditure – the sum of the expenditures on consumption goods and services and investment goods (including net additions to stocks).

The measurement of the national income may be undertaken from each of these viewpoints.

THE OUTPUT APPROACH

Value added or final products

There are one or two pitfalls to be avoided in using this method. If we add the values of the outputs of all productive enterprises, our final total will greatly exceed the national income. For example, the sum of the values of the outputs of iron ore producers, steel producers and motor car producers would contain the value of the iron ore content of the motor car three times and the value of the steel content twice. This problem is usually described as *double counting*. We have already shown in Fig. 1 that the value of a final product 'embodies' the values of the outputs of the intermediate stages. In Fig. 1 the value of the final product is £150, but adding together the sales of all three firms would give us a total value of £300. There are two possible solutions to this problem. We must either

(a) *take the sum of the values added at each stage*, or
(b) *take the values of the final products*.

Both methods must result in the same total, as the simple example below demonstrates.

Stages of production	Sales	Purchases	Value added
Landowner (sells trees)	50	0	50
Timber producer	100	50	50
Furniture producer	200	100	100
Furniture retailer	250	200	50
			250

Stock appreciation

It has already been noted that any additions to stocks must be included in the value of total output. A problem arises when the prices at which the stocks are valued vary during the course of the year. When this happens it is necessary to make an adjustment known as 'the adjustment for stock appreciation' in order to obtain a true measure of the value of the physical change in stocks.

For example, at the beginning of the year a firm may be holding 100 tons of copper at a prevailing price of £100 per ton. At the end of the year the stocks may have increased to 120 tons, but, at the same time, the market price may have risen to £120 per ton. This problem may be dealt with by assuming an average annual value of £110 per ton and making a *deduction* of £2 200 for stock appreciation. If prices have been falling, of course, the adjustment for stock appreciation will raise the value of total output.

Imports

Some part of the value of total output is made up of imported materials and a deduction must be made for the value of the import content if the value of output is to be the same as the value of factor incomes. The official statistics of output usually show the various categories of output with this correction already made. The values of output recorded are net of intermediate output and of the import content.

The sum of the values of final outputs of domestic industries when adjusted for stock appreciation and import content will give us the *Gross Domestic Product* (See Table 1.). G.D.P., however, does not give us 'the final total of goods and services becoming available', since income is also earned by British citizens in the form of interest, rent and dividends on property owned abroad. Similarly some of the factor payments on domestic output have accrued to foreign citizens. These two items are offset so that an item 'Net property income from abroad' appears in the official statistics. Hence:

$$\textit{Gross Domestic Product} + \textit{net property income from abroad} = \textit{Gross National Product}$$

There remains one further adjustment concerning depreciation, which we have defined as that part of output required for replacement purposes. A sum equal to the estimated annual depreciation (or capital consumption) must be deducted from G.N.P. in order to obtain *Net National Product* or National Income.

$$\textit{Gross National Product} - \textit{Depreciation} = \textit{Net National Product (National Income)}$$

THE INCOME APPROACH

To measure national income (national output) by the income method it is necessary to obtain an aggregate which is equal to the sum of the rewards paid to the factors of production for services rendered in producing the national output. This aggregate will *not* be equal to the sum of all personal incomes for these will include a fairly large element of transfer payments (see page 17). On the other hand there are some payments to factors of production which do not enter into the total of personal incomes. Items such as undistributed profits of companies and the trading surpluses of publicly owned bodies (such as the nationalised industries) are factor incomes which do not find their way into the incomes of households. Corporate income of this nature must be included in the national income since it represents payments to factors of production.

It should be noted that it is the gross value of factor incomes which is relevant (i.e. before tax deductions) because it is the gross income which indicates the contribution of the factor to the value of output. Table 1 (ii) shows the official presentation of the income approach. The gross domestic factor income is adjusted for stock appreciation and net income from abroad in order to arrive at gross national product.

Stock appreciation must be deducted from the total of incomes since through accounting conventions it tends to get included in company profits. A deduction for depreciation then leaves us with national income.

THE EXPENDITURE APPROACH

This method depends upon the fact that incomes are earned only when someone spends – 'one man's spending is another man's income'. Adding together all expenditures by households and firms will not, however, provide a measure of the national income since it is only expenditures on final goods which is relevant. All intermediate spending must be excluded. In the case of the public sector, only public spending on goods and services can be included – we must not include that part of public spending which takes the form of pension payments and other transfer payments.

If expenditures are recorded at market prices, it will be necessary to make a deduction equal to the value of the taxes levied on goods and services. Indirect taxes (taxes on expenditure) inflate the money values of goods and services and in order to arrive at a factor cost evaluation it is necessary to deduct such taxes from the market price values. Some items such as food and housing are sold at prices which are lower than factor cost values, because they are subject to government subsidies. The value of subsidies should, therefore, be added to total expenditure in order to obtain the factor cost values of national output.

It is also necessary to take account of the value of the physical increase in stocks, and an imputed expenditure is included for this item (see page 13).

The spending by foreigners on home produced goods (i.e. exports) must be added to total domestic spending. Correspondingly a deduction must be made for that part of domestic spending which is devoted to imports. The total expenditure account must also be adjusted in respect of property income earned abroad and property income paid abroad since the expenditure items will not include this income and we must finish with a total which is equal to national income. Table 1 (iii) shows the UK national income as seen from the expenditure viewpoint.

Real national income and money national income

The measurement of the national income must be carried out in terms of money values. The flow of output is measured by multiplying the volume of goods and services produced by their prices and this gives us the total money value of output. But using money as a measuring device gives rise to serious problems when the value of money itself changes, that is, when prices change. When measuring changes in the

Table 1. *United Kingdom–national income–1976 (£ million)*

OUTPUT (i)		INCOME (ii)		EXPENDITURE (iii)	
Agriculture, forestry, fishing	3 116	Income from employment	78 639	Consumers' expenditure	73 656
Mining and quarrying	2 458	Income from self-employment	10 208	General government final consumption	26 562
Manufacturing	30 464	Gross trading profits of companies	12 445	Gross domestic fixed capital formation	23 427
Construction	7 793				
Gas, electricity, water	3 905	Gross trading surpluses of public corporations	4 460	Value of physical increase in stocks and work in progress	359
Transport	6 624				
Communication	3 691	Gross trading surpluses of other public bodies	120		
Distributive trades	10 379	Rent	8 783	Total domestic expenditure at market prices	124 004
Insurance, banking, finance	3 015				
Ownership of dwellings	6 723	*Less* stock appreciation	−6 557		
Public administration and defence	8 458			Exports	34 837
Health and educational services	8 055			*Less* imports	−36 564
Other services	13 417			*Less* taxes on expenditure	−16 660
Residual error	982	Residual error*	982	Subsidies	3 463
Gross Domestic Product at factor cost	109 080	Gross Domestic Product at factor cost	109 080	Gross Domestic Product at factor cost	109 080
Net property income from abroad	1 179	Net property income from abroad	1 179	Net property income from abroad	1 179
Gross National Product	110 259	Gross National Product	110 259	Gross National Product	110 259
Less capital consumption	−13 583	*Less* capital consumption	−13 583	*Less* capital consumption	−13 583
NATIONAL INCOME	96 676	NATIONAL INCOME	96 676	NATIONAL INCOME	96 676

*Note: Two estimates of Gross Domestic Product are built up from largely independent data on incomes and final expenditure. The residual error is the difference between these two estimates. It is placed in the income and output tables purely as a matter of convenience—it does not imply that expenditure estimates are superior in accuracy.

Source: *National Income and Expenditure* (Blue Book) HMSO 1966–1976.

Fig. 3

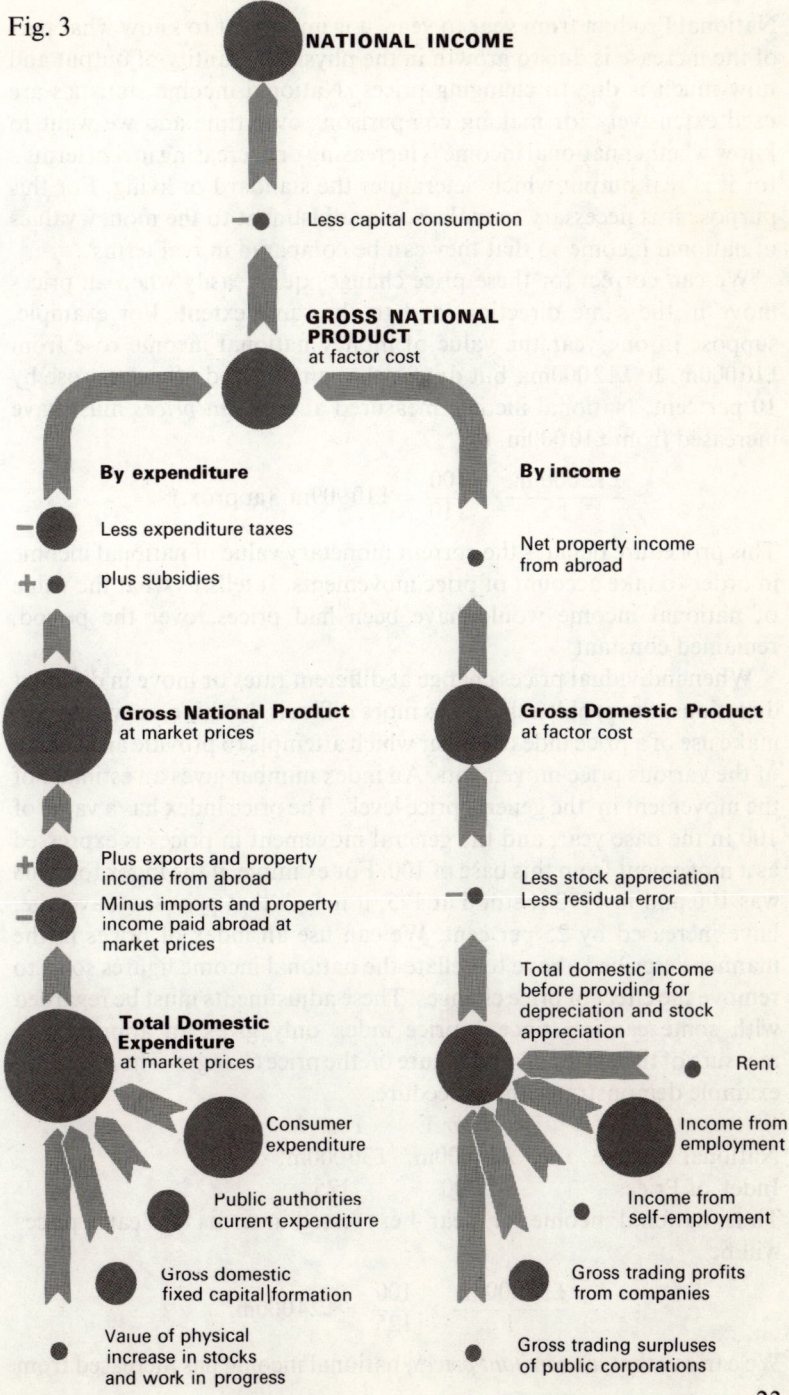

National Product from year to year, it is important to know what part of the increase is due to growth in the physical quantity of output and how much is due to changing prices. National income statistics are used extensively for making comparisons over time and we want to know whether national income is increasing or decreasing in *real* terms – for it is real output which determines the standard of living. For this purpose it is necessary to make some adjustment to the money values of national income so that they can be compared in real terms.

We can correct for these price changes quite easily when all prices move in the same direction, and to the same extent. For example, suppose in one year the value of money national income rose from £10000m. to £12000m., but during the same period *all* prices rose by 10 per cent. National income measured at *constant prices* must have increased from £10000m. to

$$\frac{£12000m.}{1} \times \frac{100}{110} = £10909m. \text{ (approx.)}.$$

This procedure deflates the current monetary value of national income in order to take account of price movements. It tells us what the value of national income would have been had prices, over the period, remained constant.

When individual prices change at different rates or move in different directions, the problem becomes more difficult. In this case we have to make use of a price index number which attempts to provide an average of the various price movements. An index number gives an estimate of the movement in 'the general price level'. The price index has a value of 100 in the base year, and the general movement in prices is expressed as a movement from this base of 100. For example, if the index for 1968 was 100 and in 1972 it stood at 125, it means that prices, on average, have increased by 25 per cent. We can use an index of prices in the manner described above to deflate the national income figures so as to remove the effect of price changes. These adjustments must be regarded with some caution since a price index only gives an approximate measure of the extent of, and nature of, the price changes. The following example demonstrates the procedure.

	Year 1	Year 4
National Income	£20000m.	£30000m.
Index of Prices	100	125

Thus, national income for Year 4 expressed in terms of Year 1 prices will be

$$\frac{£30000m.}{1} \times \frac{100}{125} = £24000m.$$

We can say that, at *constant prices,* national income has increased from

THE MEANING AND MEASUREMENT OF NATIONAL INCOME

£20000m. to £24000m., an increase of 20 per cent.

To summarise some of the more important relationships developed in this chapter,

1. $\dfrac{\text{Gross Domestic}}{\text{Product}} + \dfrac{\text{Net income from}}{\text{abroad}} = \dfrac{\text{Gross National}}{\text{Product}}$

2. $\dfrac{\text{Net National Product}}{(\textit{National Income})} = \dfrac{\text{Gross National}}{\text{Product}} - \dfrac{\text{Depreciation}}{(\textit{Capital consumption})}$

3. Gross Investment = Net Investment + Depreciation

4. Gross National Product (at factor cost) = Gross National Product (at market prices) − Indirect Taxes + Subsidies

INTERPRETING AND USING THE STATISTICS

Interest in measuring the national income arose from attempts to obtain some indicator of economic welfare. National income is, in fact, the main index of such welfare since it attempts to assess the extent to which goods and services are becoming available to the nation over some given period of time. But one must recognise its limitations as a measuring rod of economic wellbeing.

The basic indicator of the standard of living is *national income per head,* not simply national income. A rapidly rising population could be contributing to a rising national income, but income per head may be static or falling. The standard of living also depends upon the way in which the national income is distributed. Two countries may have the same income per head, but if in one the income is fairly evenly distributed, while in the other there are very few, very rich people and large numbers of very poor, the standards of living will be very different in the two countries.

The problem of price movements has already been discussed – it is real income per head, or movements in real income per head, which are relevant to the standard of living. In order to draw any conclusions about the standard of living one must examine the composition and distribution of the national income. The products which make up the national income must be those things which relate directly to economic welfare, if income is to be meaningfully associated with the standard of living. If national income increases due to large-scale military expenditures, it would be misleading to take this increase in income as reflecting a corresponding increase in welfare.

Material output and consumption is only one (although a very important one) aspect of wellbeing. Leisure is also important. A higher national income may be achieved by long hours of work and whether

MACRO-ECONOMICS

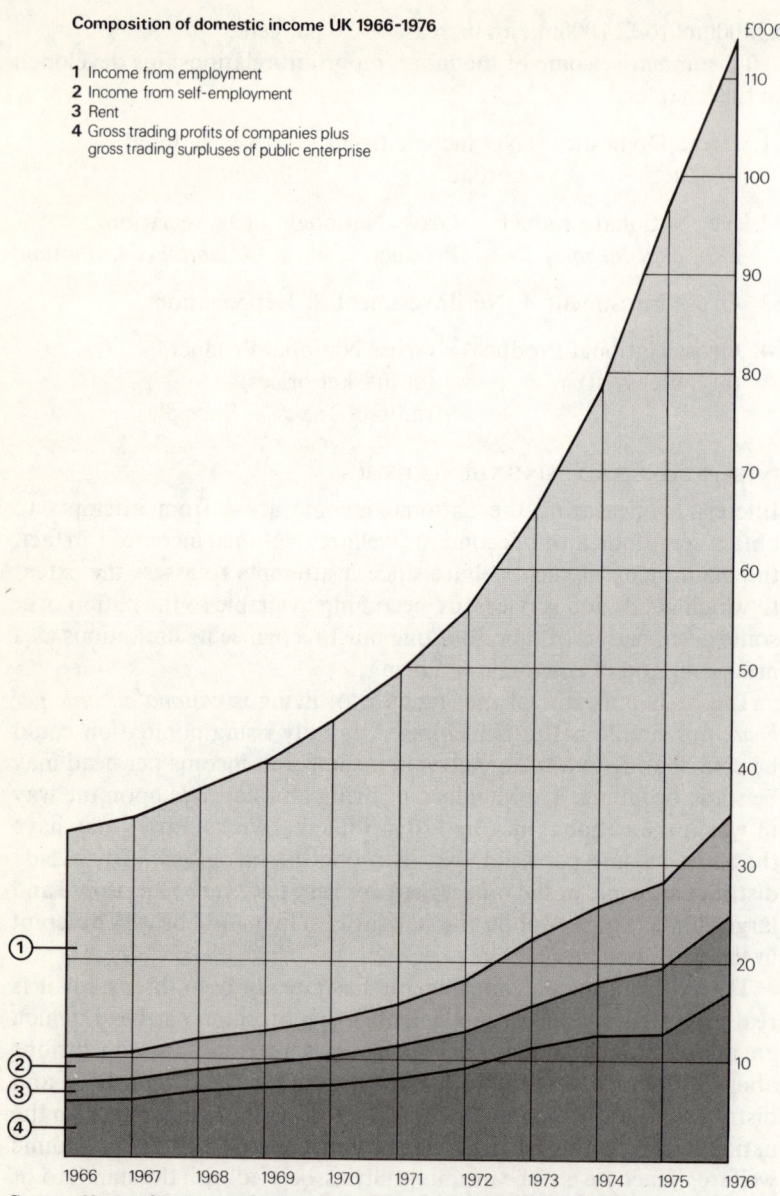

Composition of domestic income UK 1966-1976

1. Income from employment
2. Income from self-employment
3. Rent
4. Gross trading profits of companies plus gross trading surpluses of public enterprise

Source: National Income and Expenditure (Blue Book) HMSO, 1966–1976.
Fig. 4

this represents an improvement in welfare depends upon the community's valuation of leisure as compared with material consumption.

These difficulties of interpretation are particularly important when the national income statistics are used for purposes of international comparison. In this case there are additional problems. National income statistics can only take account of market transactions—'do it yourself' output is not recorded. In some countries, particularly the less developed countries, families tend to be far more self sufficient, providing for themselves those goods and services which are purchased in the market in the more advanced countries. The differences in the figures for national income per head, therefore, tend to exaggerate the differences in economic welfare. Since different countries use different currencies, a further problem arises when international comparisons are attempted. Such comparisons can only be made in terms of a common currency so that it is necessary to use the existing rate of exchange to convert the national income of one country into the currency of another. The rate of exchange, however, is determined largely by the goods and services traded internationally and it does not necessarily provide a good indicator of the relative domestic purchasing powers (e.g. for food and clothes) of the two currencies in question.

The national income statistics are presented in considerable detail in the official publication *National Income and Expenditure* published annually. The various aggregates are broken down in a variety of ways in order to facilitate analysis and provide essential data for the formulation of policy. Since governments are increasingly held responsible for the performance of the economy their policy decisions must be based on such comprehensive data.

Later in this book we shall see how government policies may influence output, income and employment. Details of changes in the national income, the distribution of the national income, changes in the industry composition of total output, movements in gross investment and the degree of dependence on foreign trade are some of the essential data provided by the national income statistics. It is this type of information which helps the government formulate its policies on such matters as employment, investment, savings, inflation and the balance of payments. The remainder of this book, in fact, is devoted largely to an analysis of the relationships between these important phenomena.

Questions on Chapter 2

ESSAY QUESTIONS

1. State and explain the various methods that are used to measure the size of the national income. Apart from the practical problems of estimation, what are the main complications of principle involved in the measurement? **(W)**

2. 'Money national income is a measure of the money value of goods and services produced in an economy in a year'. Explain and discuss. **(L)**

3. Define money national income and explain how it is measured. **(L)**

4. How do economists estimate the level of a country's national income? **(AEB)**

5. Define the term 'national income'. Outline the problems involved in measuring national income and discuss two methods by which it is measured. **(JMB)**

6. (*a*) In 1960 total domestic expenditure at market prices in the UK was £25491m. Exports and income received from abroad totalled £6475m., imports and property income paid abroad was £6734m. Taxes on spending amounted to £3405m. and subsidies totalled £489m.
    1. What was the Gross National Expenditure at market prices? Say how you arrived at your figure.
    2. What was the Gross National Product at factor cost? Show how you arrived at your figure.
    3. What other information is required to enable Net National Product at factor cost to be calculated?
    (*b*) Discuss the principal reasons why the government tries to evaluate the various aggregates of income in an economy. **(JMB)**

7. According to published figures, the British National Income went up by nearly 80 per cent between 1958 and 1968. Prices rose by nearly 50 per cent, the total population by 7 per cent and the working population by 5 per cent. Write an economic commentary on these figures. **(W)**

MULTIPLE CHOICE QUESTIONS

1. Gross National Product *minus*
    Gross Domestic Product *equals* (*a*) Depreciation
                                                    (*b*) Net Investment

(c) Net National Product
(d) Net income from abroad.

2. Gross National Product at factor cost *plus* indirect taxes *minus* subsidies *equals* (a) G.D.P. at market prices
(b) N.N.P. at market prices
(c) G.N.P. at market prices
(d) National Income

3. Which of the following items would *not* be included in the national income accounts?
1. A pension from an overseas government
2. The total market price of a second-hand car
3. A policeman's pay
4. Unemployment benefits

(a) 2 and 4.
(b) 1 and 3.
(c) 1, 2 and 4
(d) 1, 2, 3 and 4.

Questions 4 and 5 are based on the following data:

	£
Gross National Product at market prices	1 000
Net property income from abroad	20
Taxes on expenditure	40
Subsidies	10
Capital Stock	4 000
Depreciation at a rate of 5 per cent per annum	

4. Gross Domestic Product at market prices *equals*
(a) £980
(b) £990
(c) £1 020
(d) £1 050

5. National Income *equals*
(a) £770
(b) £800
(c) £830
(d) £970

6. In the simple economy described below there are only three enterprises and only the transactions indicated take place:
A sells to B for £500 and to C for £300.
B sells to private consumption for £400 and to exports for £800.
C sells to capital formation for £500.

What is the Gross National Product?
(use either value added or final expenditure approaches):
(a) £1300
(b) £1600
(c) £1700
(d) £2500

Problem

Although the following table contains only a selection of items from the national accounts of Country X for a particular year, there is sufficient information to derive the national income for that year. There was no residual error in the accounts and prices were constant throughout the year. What was the national income?

	£
Personal consumption expenditure	500
Pension and family allowances	100
Value of stocks, 31 December 1971	100
Exports of goods and services	200
Wages and Salaries	750
Incomes of self-employed	50
Gross domestic fixed capital formation	250
Income tax revenue	150
Public authorities' current spending on goods and services	200
Value of stocks, 1 January 1971	80
Imports of goods and services	120
Net domestic fixed capital formation	150
Net property income from abroad	35
Indirect taxes	60
Dividends received by persons	90
Subsidies	10

3
The Circular Flow of Income

Injections and leakages

National income may be viewed as a flow of final goods and services, or as a flow of factor incomes generated in the production of the national output. These incomes flow back to producers in the form of expenditures on the national product. This idea of a circular flow of income is a very useful analytical device. The simplest possible model of such a flow would take the form of a closed circuit in a two-sector economy where payments for factor services flow from firms to households and the whole of this income is returned to firms in the form of consumer spending. Such a model would continue in equilibrium indefinitely as long as nothing is added to it or taken away from it – as long, that is, as there are no leakages from the circular flow of income and no injections into it. It would, however, be a very unrealistic model since even the simplest real-world economy has at least one leakage (saving) and one injection (investment).

An injection is an addition to the circular flow which does not arise from consumers' current income. Income which is derived from exporting goods and services constitutes an injection; it is spending which is additional to that arising from the spending of domestic households.

A leakage consists of any part of the income generated in producing the national output which is not passed on within the system. Saving constitutes such a leakage since it means that some part of the incomes paid out by firms is not being returned in the form of spending on current output.

It should be apparent that leakages will tend to diminish the flow of income while injections will increase it. Where leakages exceed injections the flow of planned expenditure will be less than the total value of factor incomes being paid out – firms will not be receiving revenues to cover the value of current output (= income). Stocks will accumulate and firms will cut back output and income. The reverse will apply when injections are greater than leakages. When injections

MACRO-ECONOMICS

balance leakages the economy is said to be in *equilibrium;* planned expenditures = total factor incomes.

SAVINGS AND INVESTMENT

In a simple two-sector economy where there is no government and no foreign trade, incomes are received by households which dispose of them in two ways. They either spend the income on consumer goods and services or save it. The only part of total income not received by households will be that part of profits which firms retain as reserves. These undistributed profits belong to shareholders and are clearly part of total savings. Thus:

$$Y = C + S$$

(where Y = income, C = consumption and S = saving).

Investment is defined as the process of capital formation plus any additions to stocks. It is therefore that part of total output which is not currently consumed. Thus:

$$Y = C + I$$

(where I = investment).

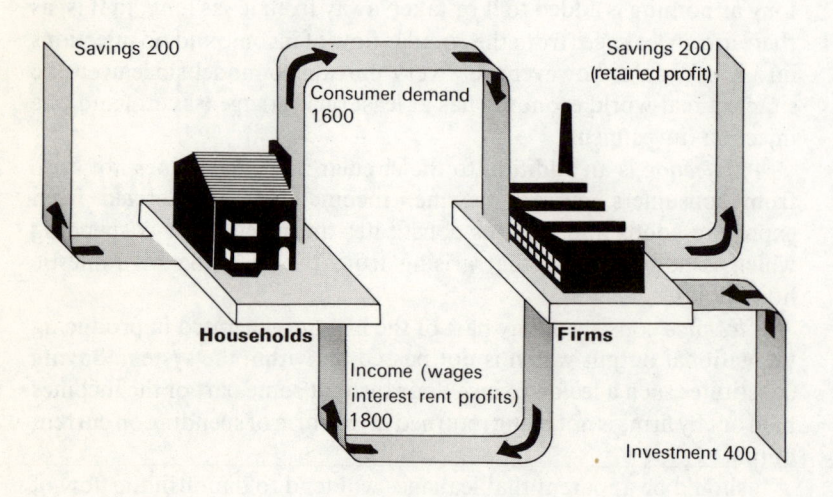

Fig. 5

Fig. 5 provides a very simplified model of the flow of income and spending in a two-sector economy. The model is in equilibrium since $S = I = 400$. More fully,

Expenditure	Income = Output	Disposal of Income
Consumer spending 1 600	(Y)	Purchases of consumer goods 1 600
Investment spending 400	2 000	Savings by firms 200
		Saving by households 200

Stating the equilibrium condition in terms of an equality between saving and investment may be rather misleading unless the meanings of the terms are clearly specified. The next section deals with this question which often causes difficulties for beginning students.

Planned and realised values[1]

There is a sense in which 'saving is always equal to investment'. This equality may be derived directly from our national income identities. If saving is defined as that part of income which is not spent on consumption,

$$\text{Gross National Income} = \text{Consumption} + \text{Saving}$$

If investment is defined as that part of total output not consumed,

$$\text{Gross National Product} = \text{Consumption} + \text{Investment}$$

Since total output is equal to total income, these equations can be combined to produce the equality,

$$\text{Saving} \equiv \text{Investment}$$

The expression is presented as an identity since the terms have been defined in such a way as to make them identically equal. If expenditure on consumption goods exceeds the value of the current output of such goods, there will be changes in stocks corresponding to the discrepancy. These changes in stocks represent changes in investment. The identity $S \equiv I$ does not tell us anything about *causes,* it simply demonstrates that the amount of saving which *has taken place* over a period of time must be equal to the amount of investment which *has taken place* during the same period of time. In more precise terms we say that,

$$\text{Realised saving} \equiv \text{Realised investment}$$

In seeking answers to questions about the behaviour of income, output and employment it is necessary to look at the intentions of producers and consumers, because we need to know *why* the realised values are

---

[1]. In some textbooks the terms *ex ante* and *ex post* are used for *planned* and *realised.*

what they are. The important relationships are those between *planned or intended* levels of saving and investment.

There is no good reason why planned investment should be equal to planned saving. Saving is carried out by individuals who have chosen not to consume the whole of their income. Investment represents the decisions of firms to acquire new machinery, new buildings, additions to stocks and other capital assets. The two sets of people making saving and investment decisions are not the same neither are the motives which cause them to make their decisions. There is no reason why their intentions should coincide in such a way that the part of total output not demanded by consumers should be exactly equal to the amount demanded for investment purposes. In other words,

$$\text{Planned saving} \gtreqless \text{Planned investment}[1]$$

This statement has important implications. If planned I and planned S are not equal, injections will not be equal to leakages and the circular flow of income will not be in equilibrium, although at any given moment realised S and realised I will be equal due to unplanned movements in stocks. This distinction between what is planned and what is realised will be an important feature of subsequent analysis; for the moment we can state that *the equilibrium condition for a two-sector economy requires that Planned S = Planned I.*

EXPORTS AND IMPORTS

It is difficult to envisage any economy which is completely self-sufficient – all economies to some extent take part in international trade. When a country exchanges goods and services with other countries, its circular flow of income is affected by additional injections and leakages.

Imports (M)

Some part of total expenditure is now devoted to the purchase of goods and services produced by foreigners. This expenditure constitutes a leakage from the flow of income. All the income generated in economic activity at home is not being returned in the form of expenditure on the national output. Total leakages now consist of $S + M$.

Exports (X)

The sales of goods and services abroad constitute an injection, since these expenditures by foreigners generate sales receipts and incomes to domestic firms and households. When a British car firm sells its products to foreign buyers there is an increase in the circular flow of income in the UK which does not arise from any change in the spending of British households. Total injections now consist of $I + X$.

[1]. The sign $\gtreqless$ means 'may be greater than, equal to, or less than'.

THE CIRCULAR FLOW OF INCOME

TAXES (T) AND GOVERNMENT EXPENDITURE (G)

The public authorities (for which we use the term 'government') can influence the level of income in two ways. Through its ability to levy taxes the government can withdraw income from the circular flow, and by means of its expenditure it can increase the flow of income. Taxation, therefore, is a leakage, and government spending is an injection.

Taxes act in the same way as savings and imports. If the taxes are levied on firms, part of their receipts from sales will not be passed on to households. Taxes on households reduce the amounts they can pass back to firms in the form of consumer spending. Total leakages now consist of $S + T + M$.

Government expenditure may be divided into three main types. There is the expenditure on the production of goods and services which are sold to households. The nationalised industries (electricity, gas, railways, etc.) carry out such activities. These commercial operations by the government are best dealt with by including them in the sector we have designated 'Firms'. A second category of government spending has already been classified as transfer payments (see page 17). These will not appear in our picture of the circular flow of income since they are not factor payments and do not increase total output. The third type of government expenditure covers the spending on a wide range of activities and covers the provision of roads, education and health services, administration and so on. These payments are made for services rendered and there are corresponding additions to national output.

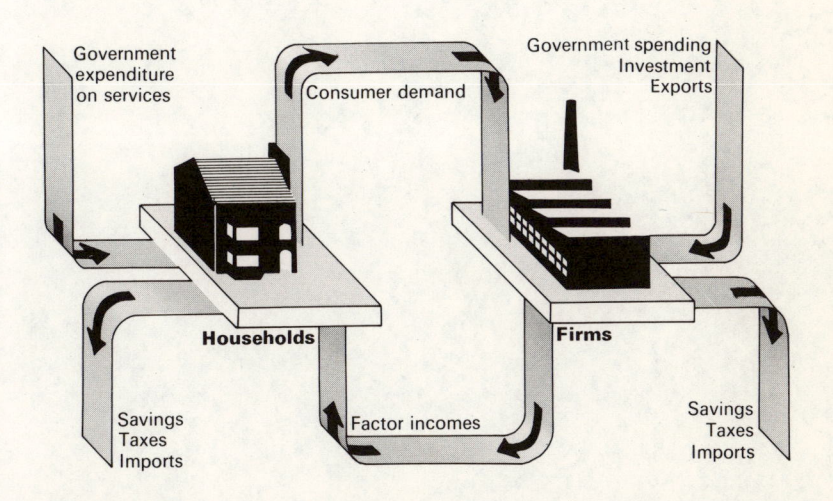

Fig. 6

Government spending on goods and services therefore is an injection. Total injections will now consist of $I + G + X$. Fig. 6 shows our model of the flow of income and expenditure modified to take account of government activities and foreign trade.

Total leakages and total injections

Injections and leakages are not entirely unrelated. We know that some part of saving finances investment, and taxation may be used to finance all or part of government expenditure. It is also true that some of the expenditure on imports provides foreigners with the means to purchase our exports. But each of these activities arises from decisions made, in the main, by entirely different groups of people. The decisions to import are not made by the same people who decide to export; the decisions to save are usually made by different groups from those taking investment decisions. In the government sector, budget revenues and expenditures do not have to be balanced. Although the leakages may eventually finance the injection spending they do not *cause* it. There is no reason why planned S should equal planned I, planned X equal planned M, or planned G equal planned T. Fig. 6 demonstrates that the equilibrium condition, planned S = planned I, appropriate to the two sector economy now needs to be modified. It should be clear that *the equilibrium condition for the open economy with a government sector is,*

$$\begin{array}{c} \text{Total planned injections} \\ G + I + X \end{array} = \begin{array}{c} \text{Total planned leakages} \\ S + T + M \end{array}$$

4
Output, Demand and Equilibrium

It has been shown that the process of producing the national output generates a flow of factor incomes (wages, profits, etc.) which is equal in value to the national product. The flow of output is also equal in value to that flow of spending on goods and services which is defined as national expenditure. Hence the very important national income identities, $NP \equiv NI \equiv NE$.

These identities tell us that, whatever the level of total output, the national income will always be sufficient to buy all the final goods and services produced. An economy always generates sufficient income to buy its total output. The national income identities, however, provide no clues as to the size of the national product, they simply demonstrate three ways of looking at some given level of output. A central problem of macro-economics is 'What determines the level of national income?'

Since the national income is measured in monetary terms, its size is a function of both the general price level and the physical volume of output. Any attempt to explain the value of the national income must, therefore, explain why the volume of output is what it is, and why prices are at their present levels. We have to deal with these problems one at a time; first a theory of output and then a theory of prices.

For the time being we are assuming that the total values of output are expressed at constant prices. If consumption expenditure rises by 10 per cent it means that people are buying 10 per cent more in volume terms. If investment expenditure falls by 5 per cent it means that real capital formation has fallen by 5 per cent. In other words all movements in money values represent corresponding changes in physical terms; any change in *money* national income is equivalent to the same change in *real* national income.

Output and demand

At any given moment of time there is obviously some upper limit to the physical output of an economy. With the existing stock of resources (labour, land and capital), and existing techniques of production, this upper limit will be reached when all resources are fully employed. We shall make great use of this concept of 'full employment output'. In the longer run, better methods of production, improved machinery, increased stocks of capital and more technical knowledge will enable full employment output itself to increase. This is a question of economic growth which is discussed later in the book. At this stage we are concerned with the short run – a period of time during which the level of full employment output is governed by the existing resources and existing techniques of production.

We all know that an economy does not, at all times, keep all its resources fully employed. We assume that firms try to maximise their profits so that they will only produce what they can sell. What is produced is determined by what is demanded. If total demand is such that firms and households are prepared to buy £1m. worth of goods and services per week, then production will adjust itself to this level of demand. If firms overestimate this demand and produce say, £1·2m. worth of output per week, stocks will accumulate and output will be adjusted downwards. If firms underestimate demand, stocks will run down and output will be expanded.

This type of adjustment is not possible when demand is greater than the current value of full employment output. In this case there will be a shortage which will show itself in the form of waiting lists and queues, or, more likely, in the form of rising prices. An increase in the level of prices, however, means higher money incomes so that the excess money demand could well persist and inflationary conditions develop. This subject is discussed later (Chapter 17). For the moment we shall be concerned mainly with an economy having some spare capacity so that output is determined by the level of aggregate demand.

Equilibrium

It is most important that the distinction between aggregate demand and national expenditure be fully understood.

Aggregate demand refers to the planned expenditures of households and firms. It is the value of the goods and services which households and firms are trying to buy.

National expenditure is the money value of the goods and services actually sold plus an imputed spending on additions to stocks.

For example, suppose that firms produced and planned to sell an output of £2m. worth of goods and services, but firms and households were only demanding £1·8m. of output.

Aggregate demand = £1·8m.

National expenditure = £1·8m. (market sales) + £0·2m. (additions to stocks).

Aggregate demand therefore is less than national expenditure. Similarly if firms and households plan to buy more than the current output, aggregate demand will exceed national expenditure. In both cases there is a situation of disequilibrium with total output too small or too great to satisfy total demand.

Aggregate demand can be subdivided into its separate components in exactly the same way as national expenditure is subdivided in Chapter 2. These components are consumption, investment, government current spending, exports and imports. The important distinction is that these components of aggregate demand refer to *planned* expenditures, not realised expenditures. Thus consumption in the National Expenditure tables refers to realised consumption, but, in the context of aggregate demand, consumption refers to the plans of consumers. They may or may not realise these plans. Aggregate demand may be expressed as $C + I + G + X - M$ and the equilibrium situation, when producers have adjusted their output to the level of aggregate demand, will be,

(Output) $Y = C + I + G + X - M$ (Aggregate demand)

Real income and employment

The important equilibrium equation given above refers to *real* quantities. Apart from the need to simplify the analysis this concentration on the determinants of real income is important from the point of view of employment. Although the relationship may not be a very simple one, there is clearly a strong connection between the volume of goods and services produced and the level of employment. It should be noted that the equilibrium equation given above does not imply a full employment situation – an economy can be in equilibrium when a substantial part of its resources is unemployed. Equilibrium, as such, should not be regarded as a necessarily desirable state of affairs, but merely as a position of balance between sets of forces.

Autonomous and induced demands

All that we have said so far is that the volume of output will depend upon the level of aggregate demand. The problem now is 'What determines the level of aggregate demand?' The answer to this question involves a study of each of the components, C, I, G, X and M. This will be our task in the next few chapters, but it might be useful before proceeding further to note the distinction between *induced* and *autonomous* demands.

Some components of demand are influenced directly by the level of income – they change as income changes and the change in income is the causal factor (but not necessarily the only one). Those elements of aggregate demand which are influenced by income in some way will be described as induced demands. Other components of demand are said to be autonomous (or independent). They are obviously influenced by certain factors, but changes in income are not causes of changes in these elements of demand. We shall see later that most of the variables we deal with have both an induced and an autonomous element.

5
Consumption

Consumption expenditure makes up by far the greater part of total expenditure. In the UK it accounts for about 75 per cent [1] of Gross National Expenditure. Consumer spending divides itself into three main streams. The largest part is the expenditure on *non-durable goods* such as food, clothing, heating, lighting – all those items whose economic life is relatively short. The second category is the expenditure on *services* such as transport, entertainment, banking, insurance, health and education. The third stream of spending is devoted to *durable consumer goods* which includes such items as motor cars, washing machines and refrigerators whose economic life may be many years.

Expenditure on non-durable consumer goods tends to be very stable since this group includes many of the necessities of life, but spending on durable consumer goods tends to be more volatile. Expectations regarding future income, advertising and variations in hire purchase terms all play a significant part in determining the level of expenditure on durable consumer goods. As incomes rise the proportion of consumers' expenditure devoted to services and durable goods tends to rise. Higher standards of living mean better food and clothing, but the *proportion* of income spent on these things tends to fall. More and more of the additional income is spent on services (holidays abroad, 'eating out', etc.) and durable consumer goods (colour televisions, motor cars, etc.)

Income and consumption

The most obvious limitation on consumption is the level of income; in the long run most people cannot consume more than their income. Since both wealth and income can be consumed, it is possible for a rich person's consumption to exceed his income, but most people have relatively little wealth. In the short run there is the possibility of supplementing one's income by borrowing, but such debts have to be

[1] *Public and private consumption. Fig. 7 refers to private consumption only*

repaid so that a borrower, in the future, must underspend while the debt is repaid. In the long run, therefore, income provides the upper limitation on the ability to consume.

If we take the UK figures for consumer spending and national income (both at constant prices) and plot them against each other as in Fig. 7 we notice a fairly close direct relationship between C and Y. It does not, of course, necessarily imply any causal relationship–it does not prove that the movement in Y is *causing* the movement in C or vice versa. Nevertheless available evidence suggests that consumption spending is determined in a definite way by the level of national income.

National Income and Consumer Expenditure 1966-76
Figures in thousand million pounds at 1970 prices

National Income
Consumer Expenditure

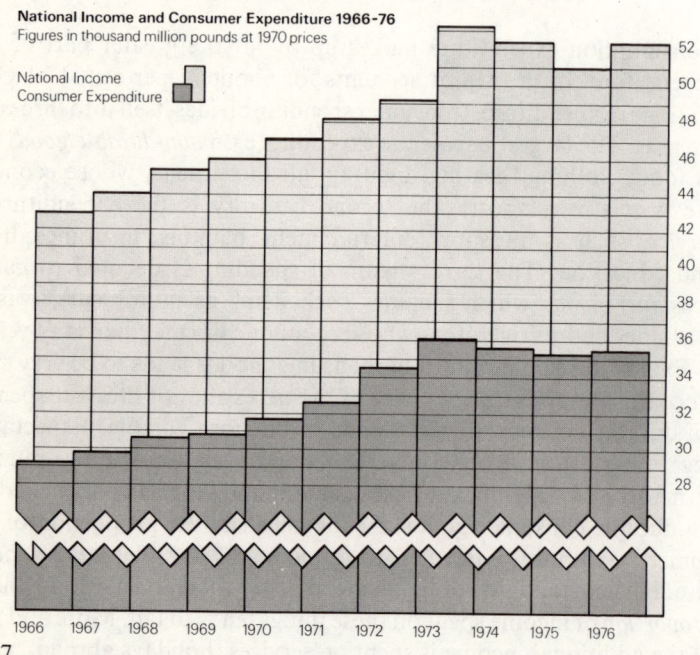

Fig. 7

Source: National Income and Expenditure (Blue Book) HMSO, 1966–1976.

The reader may now think we have gone round in a circle. We began by seeking the determinants of national income and postulated that it was determined by aggregate demand of which consumption was a major component. C was then seen as a determinant of Y. But we have now said that C itself is determined by Y. Consumption appears to determining, and determined by, income. Yet there is nothing odd in this kind of two-way causality. It is quite common to find this 'feedback' mechanism in economics. It arises here because of the *induced* element in consumer demand. An increase in C will cause an increase in Y, but the increase in Y will then cause a further increase in C.

The propensities to consume and save

The relationship between changes in income and the related changes in consumption and saving are very important for purposes of macro-economic analysis. The relationship between C and Y^1 is described as the *propensity to consume* or the *consumption function*. It tells us what consumers plan to spend at any given level of income. Consumers may be prevented from carrying out their plans, in which case realised expenditure will not be the same as the level of consumer demand. C refers to the planned or intended consumption in real terms. There are two ways of measuring the relationship between Y and C.

THE AVERAGE PROPENSITY TO CONSUME (APC)

One method is to take any given level of income and simply compute consumption as a proportion of that income. For example if $Y = £10m$. and $C = £9m$., the average propensity to consume is 0·9. Thus:

$$\text{APC} = \frac{C}{Y}$$

THE MARGINAL PROPENSITY TO CONSUME (MPC)

Another way of measuring the relationship between C and Y is to concentrate on the relative changes in the two variables. Much of our analysis is concerned with the rate at which one quantity changes with respect to another. The marginal propensity to consume is a measure of the rate at which consumption changes as income changes. For example, if an increase of £1 in Y leads to an increase of 60p in C, the marginal propensity to consume is 0·6. Thus:

$$\text{MPC} = \frac{\Delta C}{\Delta Y}$$

MPC is the proportion of any small increment of income which is spent on consumption.

A consumption function implies a savings function since saving is defined, at this stage, as that part of income which is not spent. The relationships between Y and S are measured in a similar manner to those between Y and C.

THE AVERAGE PROPENSITY TO SAVE (APS)

That proportion of total income which is saved is described as the average propensity to save. If $Y = £10m$. and $S = £1m$., then $APS = 0·1$:

---

1. At this stage we assume all income is 'paid out' and becomes available for spending or saving, that is, total income = disposable income. Later we shall see that disposable income usually differs from total income.

$$\text{APS} = \frac{S}{Y}$$

Since income is either saved or consumed, we can write, APC + APS = 1.

THE MARGINAL PROPENSITY TO SAVE (MPS)

That part of any small increment of income which is saved is defined as the marginal propensity to save. If, when Y increases by £1, S increases by 40p, the marginal propensity to save is 0·4:

$$\text{MPS} = \frac{\Delta S}{\Delta Y}$$

Since any increment in income must be either spent or saved, MPC + MPS = 1.

Table 2 provides some hypothetical figures to help in clarifying the meanings of the terms just introduced.

Table 2. *The propensities to consume and save*

Y	C	APC	MPC	S	APS	MPS
100	90	0·9	–	10	0·1	–
120	108	0·9	0·9	12	0·1	0·1
140	124	0·89	0·8	16	0·11	0·2
160	139	0·87	0·75	21	0·13	0·25
180	153	0·85	0·7	27	0·15	0·3
200	167	0·83	0·7	33	0·17	0·3

The reader should have little difficulty in working his way through this table. Only the MPC and MPS columns are likely to cause any difficulty. The MPC is obtained by taking the increase in C and expressing it as a proportion of the increase in Y. For example, as Y increases from 140 to 160, C increases from 124 to 139. An increase of 20 in Y is associated with an increase of 15 in C.

$$\frac{\Delta C}{\Delta Y} \text{ therefore, is } \frac{15}{20} = 0\cdot75$$

Another way of looking at this is to say that each unit increase in Y is associated with an increase of 0·75 units in C. The relationships

shown in this table may be expressed algebraically as follows,
$C = f(Y)$ consumption is a function of income
$S = f(Y)$ saving is a function of income

Graphical representations

THE CONSUMPTION FUNCTION

Consumption functions are most often presented in diagrammatic form, and for this purpose we make use of a conventional 45° diagram.

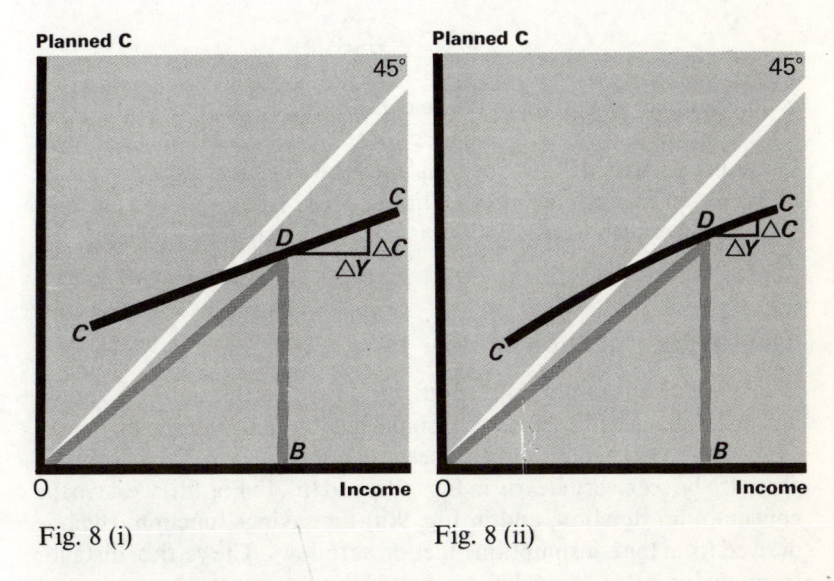

Fig. 8 (i)   Fig. 8 (ii)

In the Figs. 8(i) and 8(ii) income is measured along the horizontal axis and consumption along the vertical axis. Both axes are drawn to the same scale so that the 45° line drawn through the origin represents a consumption schedule where consumption is always equal to income. If consumption took a path along this 45° line, the whole of income would be spent, whatever the level of income, and there would be no savings and no dissaving (i.e. spending financed from past savings).

In both diagrams, however, the consumption functions (labelled C) have gentler slopes than 45° so that C increases less than proportionately as Y increases. The diagrams can be used to illustrate the average and marginal propensities to consume.

$$APC = \frac{C}{Y}$$

so that when income is *OB*,

$$\text{APC} = \frac{BD}{OB}$$

which, in turn, is a measure of the gradient of the line *OD*. Note that, although the consumption function in 8(i) is a straight line, APC is *not* constant. Only if the consumption function takes the form of a straight line passing through the origin will APC be constant.

The MPC is illustrated by assuming that *Y* increases by some small amount (ΔY) and then expressing the resulting small increase in *C* (ΔC) as a proportion of the change in *Y*. We can see, therefore, that

$$\text{MPC} = \frac{\Delta C}{\Delta Y}$$

is a measure of the gradient of the consumption function at any given level of income. Note that when the consumption function is a straight line as in Fig. 8(i), MPC will be constant since consumption is increasing at *a constant rate* against income. In Fig. 8(ii) MPC is falling as income increases because consumption is increasing against income at *a decreasing rate*.

The savings function

If we have a consumption function, it follows that this tells us not only how much households plan to consume, but how much they plan to save ($Y = C + S$). This has already been demonstrated in Table 2, but it may also be seen very clearly in Figs. 9(i) and (ii). In Fig. 9(i) we have the consumption function, and in Fig. 9(ii) the savings function which is derived from the consumption function as follows. The vertical distance from any point on the *C* line to the 45° line represents the amount of planned saving at that level of income. For example, when income is *OD*, consumption is *BD* and saving equals *AB*. This must be so since the 45° line makes *OD* = *AD*. This saving of *AB* is shown as *FG* in Fig. 9 (ii). The savings line, or savings function, therefore, is obtained by plotting the differences between the *C* line and the 45° line, as positive or negative amounts of saving.

When income is *OE*, households plan to spend the whole of current income, and saving will be zero. At levels of income below *OE*, consumer spending plans exceed income so that dissaving will take place. When income is greater than *OE*, income exceeds planned consumption so that saving is positive.

The APS and MPS can also be demonstrated graphically. The APS will be equal to the gradient of a line drawn from the origin to any point

CONSUMPTION

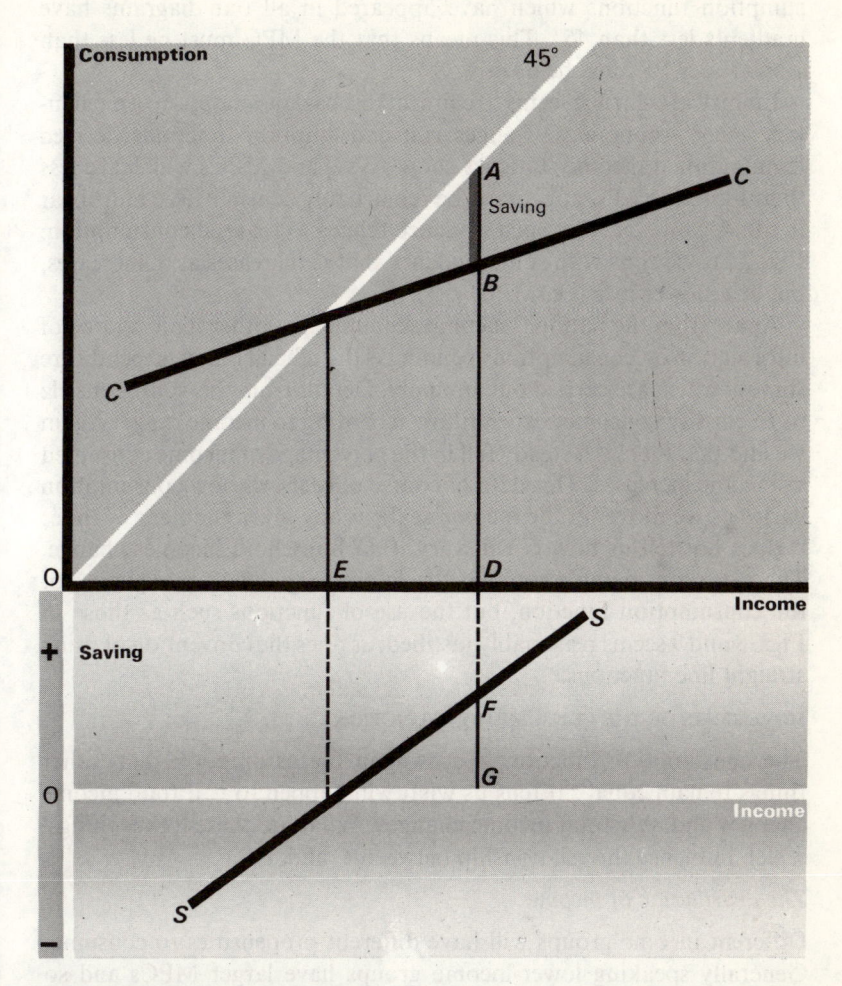

Fig. 9 (i) top and 9 (ii) bottom

on the savings line. At income level OG,

$$\text{APS} = \frac{FG}{OG}$$

which is the gradient of the line OF. The MPS is the gradient of the savings function at any given level of income.

EMPIRICAL CONSUMPTION FUNCTIONS

If the consumption function has a gradient of 45°, MPC must be equal to 1, since the MPC is equal to the gradient of the C line. The con-

47

sumption functions which have appeared in all our diagrams have gradients less than 45°. This means that the MPC must be less than 1 and the MPS must be positive.

Empirical evidence seems to confirm this basic assumption of elementary macro-economics. Longer run consumption functions derived from national income statistics show APCs and MPCs which are less than 1 and the APC appears to be remarkably constant. We must bear in mind, however, that such evidence relates to realised consumption. Fig. 7 provides us with some evidence that C increases as Y increases, but at a slower rate (i.e. MPC < 1).

Apart from the national income accounts, the other main source of information on consumption spending is the official family expenditure surveys which are carried out annually. Details from this source enable us to classify consumer expenditure according to income range. Again we find that there is a steady fall in the percentage of income consumed as income increases. This data of course only shows how consumption varies as we move up the income scale at any given moment of time; it does not tell us how C will vary if *all* household incomes change. There are considerable complexities in deriving an accurate picture of the consumption function, but the use of functions such as those in Figs. 8 and 9 seems reasonably justified, as does the convention of using straight line functions.

MOVEMENTS OF THE CONSUMPTION FUNCTION

The consumption function is drawn on the assumption that 'other things remain equal'. It tells us what will happen to C if total income changes and *only* total income changes. What are these 'other things' which influence the relationship between C and Y?

The distribution of income

Different income groups will have different propensities to consume. Generally speaking lower-income groups have larger MPCs and so spend proportionately more of their incomes on consumption than do higher income groups. Any change in the distribution of income, therefore, will affect consumption spending although total income might be unchanged. A more equal distribution of income would tend to raise the average propensity to consume.

Availability of credit

Many consumer goods, and especially durable consumer goods such as motor cars and domestic appliances, are purchased with borrowed funds, either bank loans or hire purchase credit. Changes in the terms on which such funds are made available will affect these sectors of consumer spending independently of any changes in income.

Consumers' expectations

Current spending on consumer goods is influenced by expectations regarding future movements in income and prices. If prices are expected to rise, consumer spending will be stimulated while expectations of falling prices will cause consumers to postpone their purchases. When rises in wages and salaries are confidently expected, consumers might anticipate them by increasing their spending now. A change in expectations, therefore, might cause a change in the propensity to consume out of a given income.

The distribution of wealth

The ability to consume is related to wealth as well as income. Changes in the distribution of wealth, like changes in the distribution of income, will affect consumer spending.

These are probably the main factors influencing the level of consumption spending from a given real disposable income, although we have to consider later the important effects of taxation which will affect the levels of *disposable* income itself. Changes in the determinants of consumption such as those set out above will affect the propensity to consume – the whole consumption function is changed, and the C line will move upwards or downwards.

We must be careful to distinguish between *a change in consumption* (a movement along the C line) and *a change in the propensity to consume* (a movement of the whole C line). The former is due to a change in income, while the latter will be due to changes such as those discussed above.

Most of the forces which affect the propensity to consume change relatively slowly over time, others are likely to have slight influence in the short run. For purposes of our analysis, which is concerned with the short run, we can justify a given consumption function.

6
Investment

Investment is the second of the elements of aggregate demand represented in the equilibrium equation $Y = C + I + G + X - M$. In the context of this equation, investment is similar to the other components of demand in that it represents a demand for part of the nation's current output. There is, however, an important difference in that, if the investment is more than sufficient to replace worn out or obsolete equipment, the nation's total productive capacity is increased.

Investment in macro-economic analysis has very little to do with the type of 'investing' familiar to us—the purchase of shares or bonds. The purchase of an existing share merely transfers the ownership of an existing asset and in no way alters the real capital of a country. Even when the share is a newly issued one, the transaction does not represent investment. Only when the company uses the funds to acquire *new* capital equipment has investment taken place. Investment must be interpreted very strictly to mean the purchase of new machines, buildings and other 'produced means of production', including additions to stocks.

Types of investment

It is useful to classify investment into different categories since the investment decisions will be determined by different factors according to the type of investment.

STOCKS

Net additions to stocks during any given period of time count as part of total investment. They are treated as capital goods although they need not be additions to capital goods and are likely to include food stocks and durable consumer goods added to stocks. Additions to stocks rank as investment since they are part of current output which is not consumed. The important point about this type of investment is that it can be rapidly increased or diminished—it is a volatile element in total investment.

PLANT AND MACHINERY

This is a more familiar type of investment and includes such things as lathes, generators, computers, lorries and so on. The total includes both replacement items (depreciation) and additions to the capital stock (net investment). The estimate given for depreciation in the official statistics should be used with some caution because it is very difficult to obtain accurate figures for this item. Machines are often replaced with more advanced and efficient models. If such replacement machines are purchased for the same prices as the originals, there has been some net addition to the productive capacity of the country although there has been no apparent addition to capital stock. It is also likely, under inflationary conditions, that a replacement machine will cost far more than the original, even though they are identical. In this case there will be no real addition to capital stock although expenditure statistics will indicate such an addition. In making allowances for these features there is obviously a margin for a fairly substantial error.

CONSTRUCTION

A large part of the expenditure under this heading will be outlays on houses. There are special factors which influence the demand for houses such as population changes, the availability of building society mortgages, and movements in personal income. Other activities under this heading will include the construction of factories, offices, shops, etc.

PUBLIC INVESTMENT

A large part of total investment in the UK is accounted for by the public sector. Investment by the central government, local authorities and public corporations makes up about 45 per cent of total investment. This has important policy implications since it means that investment demand can be strongly and directly influenced by government policy. The motivations for capital accumulation in the public and private sectors tend to be very different. Profit expectations largely determine the investment decisions of the private firm whereas political and social factors are very important in determining the amount of public investment. Nevertheless, as we shall see later, techniques such as cost-benefit analysis enable us to apply similar principles to the analysis of public and private investment. Table 3 gives an indication of the nature of investment in the UK.

Table 3. *Capital Formation* UK 1976 (£million)

Sector		Type	
Personal sector	3 546	Vehicles, ships, aircraft	2 368
Companies:		Plant and machinery	8 116
Industrial & Commercial	7 745	Dwellings	4 632
Financial	2 024	Other construction	8 311
Public corporations	4 730		
Central government	1 388		
Local authorities	3 994	Gross domestic fixed capital formation	23 427
Gross domestic fixed capital formation	23 427		
		Net additions to stocks	6 916
		Net investment abroad	−1 405
		Gross Investment	28 938

Source: *National Income and Expenditure* 1966–1976

Note: Although the purchase of stocks and shares have been excluded in our definition of investment, this does not apply to the acquisition of shares in foreign enterprises. These represent additions to the nation's total assets. Net investment abroad includes both the acquisition of physical assets abroad and paper claims on other countries.

THE MOTIVES FOR INVESTMENT

In the private sector, where our basic assumption is that firms aim to maximise their profits, it is clear that expected profitability will be the main motive for investment. Businessmen will invest if they anticipate a satisfactory net return on the project under consideration. How they might arrive at this decision is discussed later. An expectation of a growth in sales will be a major factor but only if the increased demand is expected have permanent features. If firms are operating below full capacity it is unlikely that they will expand their capital stock to meet an increased demand. Current trends in demand will undoubtedly provide an important indicator for businessmen trying to assess future prospects. Investment in housing is also closely linked to the growth prospects of the economy both in terms of income and population.

But certain types of investment (i.e. autonomous investment) may not need any growth in sales to justify them. The replacement of worn out capital will go ahead if sales are expected to remain at their present level. Innovations and inventions provide a real stimulus to investment. The introduction of new products, new techniques and significant improvements in machinery will provide the prospects of new markets or cost reductions in existing markets. The container revolution, for example, has provided the incentive for large-scale investment in transport.

Investment might also be encouraged where labour costs are rising relative to capital costs and there are possibilities of substituting a capital-intensive process for a labour-intensive process.

In the public sector profit maximisation is not a basis for policy decisions. Some projects such as roads, schools, hospitals and defence establishments provide services for which no prices are charged so that it is not possible to compare revenues with costs. In others, such as the nationalised industries, which do sell goods and services, it is argued that they should do no more than 'break even'. Most of these industries, in fact, have now been given investment guide lines and they are expected to earn a target rate of return on their investment.

Even in the public sector there has to be some decision made on the desirable total level of investment and the distribution of these resources among alternative uses. All the desirable projects cannot be undertaken and it is necessary to come to some decision on which projects are most worth while. To this end cost–benefit techniques are now being used to evaluate public investment. Essentially these techniques attempt to assess the *social profitability* of proposed investments. In addition to the 'paid out' costs and the revenues actually received, money values are attributed to the social costs and social benefits of the proposed investment. *Social costs* are the sacrifices, in terms of the alternative satisfactions foregone, imposed upon the community but which do not appear in the 'paid out' costs of the enterprise imposing the social burdens. For example, the commercial costing of the erection of unsightly pylons to carry electricity will not reveal the sacrifice of amenities (rural beauty) which the construction entails. The commercial costing of a new factory will not indicate any increased incidence of pollution or traffic congestion which might develop as a consequence. In a similar manner *social benefits* refer to satisfactions enjoyed by the community which are not fully revealed in the revenues earned by an enterprise. The revenues of a new underground transport system will provide no measure of the social benefits it creates in the form of reduced congestion, noise and pollution in the city streets.

The techniques of cost–benefit analysis are not fully developed, but the point to note is that an assessment of whether a project is worth while (in the public sector) might use similar procedures to those used in the private sector – expected returns (social) may be compared to expected costs (social).

The basis of the investment decision

When contemplating a particular investment project the firm will have

(1) an estimated expected stream of net earnings (expected revenues minus expected variable costs) and (2) a supply price (the current costs of the capital). These two elements must now be related to each other in some way so as to assess the likely profitability. This will involve using another important factor, (3) the rate of interest.

The investment decision is very complex since the entrepreneur is dealing with very few 'knowns' and many 'unknowns'. He knows the current price of the capital goods (the supply price) and he knows the current price of any loans[1] he may need. In other words he knows (2) and (3) above. He does not know and cannot know, since it lies in the future, the yield or returns he may obtain on his investment. In order to arrive at some estimate of (1) above, he has to forecast the demand for his final product over the years which lie ahead.

The future demand for his product can be affected by such things as changes in government policy, the development of new competing products, changes in the level of economic activity, changes in world trading conditions, changes in consumer tastes and fashions and so on. There is also another area of uncertainty relating to his future costs. He cannot be certain of the life of any new capital equipment since this will depend upon technical progress. He will not be able to foresee with any degree of accuracy changes in the prices of other factors of production such as labour and raw materials.

His investment decision, therefore, is fraught with uncertainty. Even with the help of the best and most up-to-date statistics and the most thorough market research, investment decisions still contain a large element of guesswork and are often no more than good hunches. All this helps us to understand why private investment can be so volatile.

PRESENT VALUE

An investment decision is based upon a comparison between the expected net profitability of a project and its current cost. If the expected future returns are expressed as an annual percentage yield, we have what is known as the *marginal productivity of capital*. Note that it is the net returns from the capital goods which is relevant. The estimated additional variable costs incurred in operating the new equipment must be deducted from the estimated additional revenue in order to get the net revenue from the proposed investment.

This procedure will provide a series of estimated annual returns stretching away into the future and covering the expected life of the

---

1. Where the firm does not borrow but uses its own funds, the market rate of interest is still a 'cost' in the sense that it represents income foregone. It measures the income the firm could have received had it loaned the funds to someone else.

capital assets. Something like this,

Estimated net income (expected life of asset, 5 years)

Purchase price of Capital	Year 1	Year 2	Year 3	Year 4	Year 5
£3 000	£1 000	£1 000	£1 000	£850	£700

The problem which now arises is how to evaluate the expected future stream of income. Would it be sensible to add these expected receipts and compare the total revenue with the purchase price of the machine? Alternatively the annual returns might be averaged and the result expressed as an average profit per annum. If this annual average profit were then expressed as a percentage of the supply price, would it give us a true measure of the yield on the investment?

In fact neither of these approaches would provide a true measure of the earning potential of the investment, because neither approach takes into account the fact that a sum of money due in the future has a lower *present value* than the same sum of money due now. In order to estimate the earning potential of the capital it is necessary to find the present value of the expected receipts and then compare this with the current supply price of the assets. In this way we are comparing current costs with current values of the expected profits. The procedure for obtaining present values is known as *discounting* and it requires the use of compound interest calculations 'in reverse'; that is, we know the Amount, we have to find the Principal.

Example

Compound interest. Assume rate of interest is 5 per cent, then

£100 deposited now will be worth £100 + 5% of £100 = £105 in 1 year's time

£100 deposited now will be worth £105 + 5% of £105 = £110·25 in 2 years' time

and so on.

Expressing this more precisely we can say that to find *the future value* of a sum of money loaned at 5 per cent,

(a) for 1 year we multiply the Principal (P) by $(1 + \frac{5}{100}) = P(1\cdot05)$

(b) for 2 years we multiply the Principal (P) by $(1 + \frac{5}{100})^2 = P(1\cdot05)^2$

(c) for 3 years we multiply the Principal (P) by $(1 + \frac{5}{100})^3 = P(1\cdot05)^3$

INVESTMENT

In general terms, if the rate of interest is r per cent, the final amount (A) is found by the formula

$$A = P(1 + \frac{r}{100})^n,$$

where n is the number of years.

Discounting. Assume the rate of interest is 5 per cent, then from the above it can be seen that £105 (i.e. A) due in 1 year's time has a present value (P) of £100, and £110·25 due in 2 years' time has a present value of £100, and so on. More precisely,

For 1 year, $A = P(1·05)$; i.e. $P = \dfrac{A}{1·05}$

For 2 years, $A = P(1·05)^2$; i.e. $P = \dfrac{A}{(1·05)^2}$

For 3 years, $A = P(1·05)^3$; i.e. $P = \dfrac{A}{(1·05)^3}$

In general terms, for n years, at a rate of interest of r per cent, the present value

$$P = \frac{A}{(1 + \frac{r}{100})^n}$$

If we continue to assume a market rate of interest of 5 per cent, the present value of the expected returns from the £3000 machine, in the earlier example, would be

$$\frac{£1\,000}{(1·05)} + \frac{£1\,000}{(1·05)^2} + \frac{£1\,000}{(1·05)^3} + \frac{£850}{(1·05)^4} + \frac{£700}{(1·05)^5}$$

Such a series is known as a *discounted cash flow* and the idea is shown diagrammatically in Fig. 10.

In using this particular technique, the businessman has two possible methods to choose from:

(1) He can use the market rate of interest to discount the expected net profits in the manner shown above. He can then compare the present values of these returns with the supply price of the capital goods. If this present value exceeds the supply price, the investment would be profitable.

(2) This approach is slightly different. In this case it is necessary to find the rate (x) at which the future stream of income must be discounted in order to make the present value of the expected profits exactly equal to the supply price of the capital. Returning to our example of the machinery with a supply price of £3000, we have to discover the rate

57

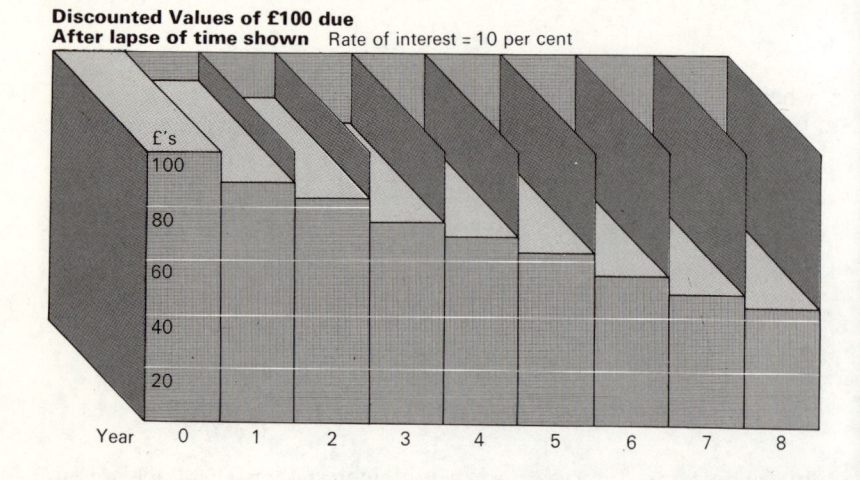

Discounted Values of £100 due
After lapse of time shown   Rate of interest = 10 per cent

Fig. 10

(x) at which the expected returns £1 000 + £1 000, etc., must be discounted so that the sum of the present values is exactly equal to £3 000. The problem looks like this,

$$£3\,000 = \frac{£1\,000}{(1 + \frac{x}{100})} + \frac{£1\,000}{(1 + \frac{x}{100})^2} + \frac{£1\,000}{(1 + \frac{x}{100})^3} + \frac{£850}{(1 + \frac{x}{100})^4} + \frac{£700}{(1 + \frac{x}{100})^5}$$

The student should not be disturbed by an inability to solve this equation; it is a difficult task. Approximate values of x can be obtained from appropriate statistical tables. All we need to know is that the value of x (i.e. the rate of discount) can be ascertained. If this rate exceeds the current market rate of interest, the project will be profitable. The rate of discount (x) in the equation above was defined by Keynes as the *marginal efficiency of capital,* and it is this concept which we shall use in explaining how the level of investment is determined. Keynes' precise definition is, 'The marginal efficiency of capital is that rate of discount which makes the present value of the series of annual returns from the capital assets, over its life, exactly equal to its supply price'.

The mathematical formulae used above might, perhaps, give a rather misleading idea of precision and accuracy. While this might be true of the calculations themselves, we must remember that they are based on estimates which may be little better than intelligent guesswork.

INVESTMENT AND THE RATE OF INTEREST

Both the approaches just outlined make the level of planned investment dependent upon the rate of interest. An increase in the capital stock will be proceeded with if its potential earning power, as measured by the marginal efficiency of capital (MEC), is greater than the cost of the funds required to finance the project (i.e. the rate of interest). A demand curve for capital, therefore, will relate the rate of interest to the quantity of capital demanded. What will be the shape of this demand curve?

Other things being equal, increasing investment in any one type of capital will tend to reduce the marginal efficiency of that capital for several reasons.

(a) The marginal productivity of capital, that is, the extra output resulting from successive small increments in the capital stock, will tend to diminish as more and more capital is combined with some fixed amount of the other factors of production.

(b) The increased output of the goods being produced with the capital will tend to drive down their prices.

(c) The increased demand for capital might raise its supply price. All these developments would tend to reduce the net revenues expected from further investment.

Marginal Efficiency of Capital and Rate of Interest
Per cent per annum

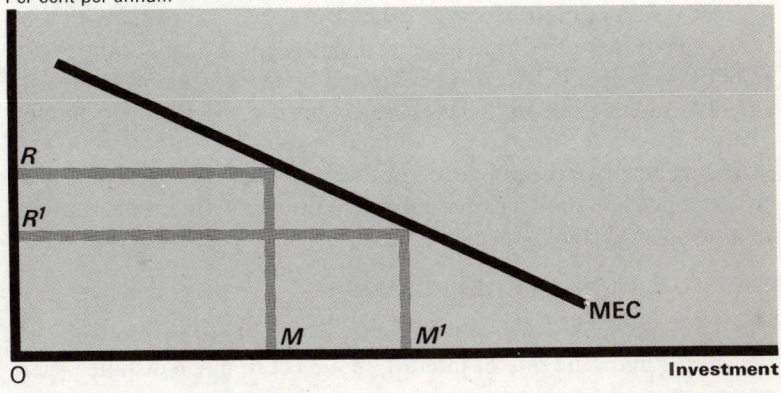

Fig. 11

It is to be expected, therefore, that the demand curve for capital will be of the normal shape, sloping downwards from left to right. Such a demand curve is illustrated in Fig. 11. It is, in fact a curve representing the marginal efficiency of capital (MEC). The quantity of capital demanded depends upon the relationship between the MEC and the market rate of interest. We take the MEC curve in Fig. 11 to represent the aggregate demand for capital. Although the MEC for different types of capital assets will be different at any given time, we are assuming profit maximisation determines investment behaviour so that the MEC schedule of capital will be the aggregate of the MEC schedules in different industries.

The equilibrium level of private investment can now be determined. It is that level at which the market rate of interest is equal to the marginal efficiency of capital. In Fig. 11 when the rate of interest is OR the level of investment will be OM. If the rate of interest falls to OR', investment will increase to OM'. If the rate of interest is very high only a few projects will appear profitable. If the rate of interest falls, projects with lower expected returns will now offer the prospects of profits. The equilibrium situation is the familiar one; businessmen will purchase capital up to the point where the marginal productivity of capital is equal to its cost (i.e. where the MEC curve cuts the interest rate line). According to this theory, the investment function will be $I = f(r)$, where r is the rate of interest.

Much of this analysis can be applied to the public sector. Investment in the nationalised industries is now evaluated on a commercial basis which makes use of the discounted cash flow techniques described above. Many investment proposals in the public sector are subject to cost–benefit analysis. The net social benefits are discounted and the present values of these expected benefits are then compared with their costs. Even where this kind of assessment is not thought appropriate, public investment is likely to be affected by movements in the rate of interest, more especially, those longer term projects where interest charges form a substantial part of total costs.

The inclusion of the public sector does not alter the basic conclusion that planned investment can be related to the rate of interest in the form of a downward sloping demand curve.

THE INFLUENCE OF THE RATE OF INTEREST

The basis of this theory, which holds that the level of investment is dependent upon the rate of interest, is subject to much dispute. There are some good reasons for supposing that investment decisions may not be so sensitive to interest changes as the theory seems to imply.
1. The degree of uncertainty surrounding the investment decision makes it impossible to obtain precise estimates of the MEC which can be compared with the rate of interest. The businessman is likely to work with estimates which give a fairly wide range of possible returns, a

range, perhaps, of some 10 or 15 per cent. This will mean that relatively small changes in interest rates will not make much difference to his calculations. While this may be true of short-term projects, longer-life investments such as buildings are affected to a much greater extent by changes in the rate of interest.

2. Large enterprises usually engage on long-range planning which calls for an investment programme spread over many years. Short-term movements in interest rates are not likely to disturb these plans to any serious extent.

3. The rate of interest, in certain circumstances, may not be viewed as a major item in the firm's costs. Interest charges may be claimed as costs for purposes of taxation so that the burden of interest payments is offset to some extent by reductions in tax payments. In times of inflation the *real* burden of interest charges is reduced by rising prices. If prices are rising at 5 per cent per annum, and the rate of interest is 8 per cent, the real rate of interest is about 3 per cent.

4. Even when interest rates are low, firms may be unable to borrow as much as they would like. If the government is operating a 'credit squeeze' funds will be difficult to obtain because of quantitative restrictions. The amount of planned investment would then be more influenced by the availability of credit than by its cost.

5. Investment in stocks, at least in the manufacturing sector, does not seem to be seriously affected by changes in the rate of interest. Interest charges are normally a small part of total costs, and, in any case, much stock holding is financed by trade credit, the charges on which do not usually move with market rates of interest. Where stock holding is a major function as in retailing and wholesaling, firms may be more sensitive to interest rate changes, although when prices are rising, stock appreciation could offset any interest rate effects.

EXPECTATIONS

One of the difficulties in using the Keynesian theory as a tool of economic policy is the fact that the MEC is likely to be very unstable. The calculation of the MEC is very much a matter of forecasts, expectations, hunches and guesses. Business expectations are bound to be strongly influenced by current optimism and pessimism and hence will be subject to sudden shifts as confidence rises or falls. Changes in expectations alter the whole basis of the MEC. Rising hopes will mean higher expected returns and the MEC curve will shift to the right. A sudden collapse of business confidence will cause a downward revision of the estimates of future returns and the MEC curve will move bodily to the left. With an unstable demand curve, therefore, it is extremely difficult to predict just what will be the demand for investment goods at any given rate of interest. Keynes himself was well aware of this problem and he stressed the importance of expectations in the determination of the rate of planned investment.

Investment and income

Of all those factors which are most likely to influence investment, the one most susceptible to short-term variations is the expectation of profit. Expectations are most closely related to movements in current income. Investment which stems from the desire of firms to meet an increase in the demand for their product is known as *induced investment*. This type of investment is related to movements in current income, or, more accurately, it is related to *the rate of change* of income. Investment which is determined independently of current income is known as *autonomous investment*, some examples of which are given on page 53. Induced investment is the basis for a theory of investment known as the acceleration principle.

THE ACCELERATION PRINCIPLE

This theory assumes that firms try to maintain some constant relationship between the level of output and the stock of capital required to produce that output. In other words, we assume a constant *capital–output ratio* which can either be expressed in physical terms or in money terms. The accelerator helps us to understand how small increases in demand in one sector can be magnified and spread throughout the economy. It can best be explained by using a simple arithmetical example.

Assume a given manufacturing industry, producing consumer goods, which has,

(*a*) a capital–output ratio of 2, i.e. £1 000 worth of capital is required to produce £500 worth of consumer goods per annum,
(*b*) machines whose average life is 10 years, and
(*c*) a capital stock which has been built up evenly over time so that 10 per cent of the capital stock becomes due for replacement each year.

Table 4 now provides us with the data necessary for an understanding of the accelerator.

In Year 1 we find that the industry is in equilibrium with sales of £10 000, a capital stock of £20 000 and a regular replacement demand valued at £2 000. We now assume that sales rise to £12 000. In order to meet this demand the industry requires £24 000 worth of capital equipment. Its annual demand for capital now increases from £2 000 to £6 000 (replacements plus additional units). A rise of 20 per cent in

INVESTMENT

consumer demand has led to a rise of 200 per cent in investment demand. In Year 3 consumption demand rises again to a figure of £13 000. How does this affect the industry's demand for capital goods? Its replacement demand is still £2 000 worth of equipment (the machines bought ten years earlier) and it will require an additional £2 000 worth of capital to meet the increased demand for its output. In fact total investment demand falls from £6 000 to £4 000.

Table 4.

Year	Sales	Existing capital	Required capital	Replacement demand	Net investment	Total investment
1	£10 000	£20 000	£20 000	£2 000	–	£2 000
2	12 000	20 000	24 000	2 000	£4 000	6 000
3	13 000	24 000	26 000	2 000	2 000	4 000
4	13 500	26 000	27 000	2 000	1 000	3 000
5	13 800	27 000	27 600	2 000	600	2 600
6	14 000	27 600	28 000	2 000	400	2 400
7	14 000	28 000	28 000	2 000	–	2 000
8	13 000	28 000	26 000	–	–	–
9	13 000	26 000	26 000	2 000	–	2 000

Note that a simple increase in consumer demand is not sufficient to maintain the level of investment. In order to hold the level of investment to the amount achieved in Year 2, consumer demand would have to *increase at the same rate* (i.e. £2 000 per annum). It is *the rate of change* in consumption which determines the amount of induced investment. A slow-down in the rate of growth of consumer spending can cause an absolute decline in the orders to the capital goods industries.

The reader can verify this by noting the effects in Years 3, 4, 5 and 6. Note what happens in Year 8 when consumption declines from £14 000 to £13 000. The demand for new equipment falls to zero although sales are 30 per cent higher than they were at the beginning of the sequence. The example provides us with some ideas on why the swings in the level of activity in the capital goods industries are much greater than those experienced by the consumer goods industries.

The extent of the accelerator effect depends largely upon the durability of the capital equipment. If the life of the machines in our example had been 5 years instead of 10 the accelerator effect would have been much smaller.

SOME QUALIFICATIONS

It is important to bear in mind that the upward leverage effect of the accelerator only takes effect if the industry is operating at or near full

63

capacity. If the industry has excess capacity it can meet a larger demand by increasing output on its underutilised equipment.

Additional machines will only be ordered when the increased demand is believed to be permanent otherwise firms will deal with the additional orders by running down stocks or operating waiting lists.

If the rise in the demand for investment comes at a time when the capital goods industries are fully employed, it could well lead to an increase in the prices of capital goods. This may lead to some reduction in the demand for capital and encourage the adoption of more capital-saving techniques. If this is so the accelerator effect will be reduced.

Nevertheless, in spite of these qualifications, there is empirical evidence to support the accelerator theory both in the USA and in the UK.

Summary

We have now considered a number of influences on investment demand. It is clear that there are several determining factors affecting the rate of planned investment, and there is no conclusive evidence in favour of any one particular theory of investment.

It appears that a large part of investment is autonomous (i.e. independent of the level of income). This will be true of a substantial part of public investment as well as that part of private investment stimulated by technical progress, growth in foreign trade and the long term plans of large corporations. Accelerator investment is induced investment in so far as it is related to the rate of change of current income, but if there is a time lag in the process, current income may not be the determining influence.

Expectations are a major determinant of short-term movements in the rate of private investment and these will be subject to a wide range of influences.

The rate of interest also plays a part, although the extent of its influence on the level of investment is subject to much dispute. More is said on this point in the chapter on monetary policy.

7
The Determination of Equilibrium

We are now ready to show how the equilibrium level of income can be determined for a simple economy where there are only two sectors—households and firms. Before proceeding with the analysis we should restate the assumptions on which it is based:

(*a*) There are unemployed resources
(*b*) The techniques of production remain unchanged
(*c*) The hours worked by each worker remain unchanged
(*d*) Prices remain constant

Output, income, and employment, therefore will be determined by aggregate demand.

Our simple model has only one injection—investment, and one leakage—savings. Equilibrium, we know, requires that leakages should equal injections and in our model that means that planned savings should equal planned investment. Since there is no government sector, there will be no taxation. We also assume that firms pay out all their profits. Personal disposable income, therefore, is equal to national income. The whole of factor income is received by households who can either spend it or save it. There are two approaches to the problem of equilibrium. We can ask:

1. *What level of income will generate sufficient planned saving to equal planned investment?* or
2. *What level of income will generate sufficient planned consumption plus planned investment to buy the whole of current output?*

We shall take each approach in turn, beginning with an explanation of equilibrium in terms of saving and investment.

Income is equal to output so that saving may be regarded as that part of output which consumers are prepared to forgo; that is, to leave for purposes other than consumption. If the amount of total output forgone by consumers is exactly equal to the demands by firms for capital formation (including additions to stocks) then planned saving is equal to planned investment, total demand is equal to total supply and equilibrium will exist. But if consumers plan to save more or less than firms plan to invest there will be a situation of disequilibrium. Table 5 and Fig. 12 should help us to get the picture more clearly.

Table 5.

(1)	(2)	(3)	(4)	(5)	(6)	(7)
Planned output (=income)	Planned consumption	Planned saving	Planned investment	Total planned expenditure	Realised investment	Tendency of income
1000	1000	0	200	1200	0	Expand
1200	1100	100	200	1300	100	Expand
1400	1200	200	200	1400	200	Equilibrium
1600	1300	300	200	1500	300	Contract
1800	1400	400	200	1600	400	Contract

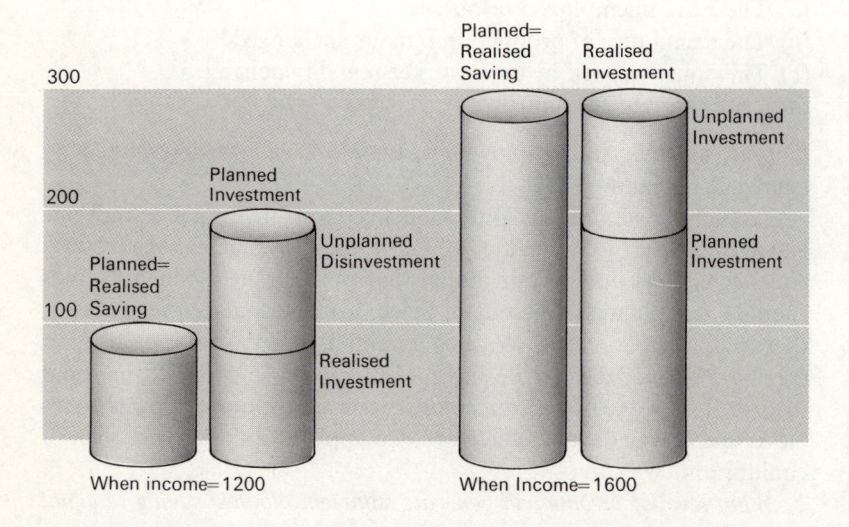

Fig. 12

The table shows us (*a*) the plans of households and firms at different levels of income, (*b*) the realised situation which results from the interaction of households' and firms' spending plans, (*c*) the effects on output and income. We assume that households' plans to spend and save are realised.

In Table 5, column 1 indicates possible levels of total output (= income). Column 2 shows the levels of planned consumption appropriate to the different levels of income. Column 3 gives details of the saving planned at each level of income—these details are derived from columns 1 and 2. In column 4 we have the investment intentions of firms and, for the purpose of this exercise, we assume investment to be autonomous.

Total planned expenditure is obtained by summing the amounts in columns 2 and 4 (i.e. $C + I$) and is shown in column 5. The amount of investment which actually takes place (realised investment) is given in column 6 and will consist of unplanned plus planned investment. For example, when income is at the level 1 600, planned investment is 200 and unplanned investment amounts to 100 (expenditure falls short of output by 100 so that there is an unplanned increase in stocks). Note that only when income is 1 400 are investment plans realised. At higher levels of income expenditure falls short of planned output and there will be unplanned investment. At lower levels of income, expenditure exceeds the value of current output and there will be unplanned disinvestment (stocks will run down). These effects are seen in Fig. 12.

The equilibrium level of income, therefore, is 1 400. This is the only situation where total demand is equal to total supply, where the plans of producers are in harmony with the plans of spenders and there are no forces at work tending to change the level of output. It is, of course, the level of income at which planned saving is equal to planned investment.

Table 5 can be used in the second approach. Column 5 ($= 2 + 4$) provides us with details of the level of aggregate demand at each level of income. Column 1 indicates the level of planned output. Equilibrium requires that

$$\frac{\text{Total value of planned expenditure}}{\text{(Aggregate demand)}} = \frac{\text{Total value of planned output}}{\text{(Aggregate supply)}}$$

Only at the income level 1 400 does Planned Output (Column 1) = Planned Expenditure (column 5). At higher levels of income firms will be paying out more in factor incomes than they are receiving back in the form of sales receipts—they will reduce output. At lower levels of income they will be receiving more in sales receipts than they are paying out in the form of factor incomes—they will expand output. The short-term adjustments will take the form of changes in the levels of stocks (i.e. unplanned investment or disinvestment).

These same relationships may be seen very clearly in Fig. 13. In Fig. 13(i) expenditure is marked on the vertical axis and income is shown on the horizontal axis. We use the same conventions as developed earlier so that the 45° line shows all points of equality, Expenditure = Income. The line CC represents consumption spending at different levels of income, while the $C + I$ line shows total expenditure in a two-sector

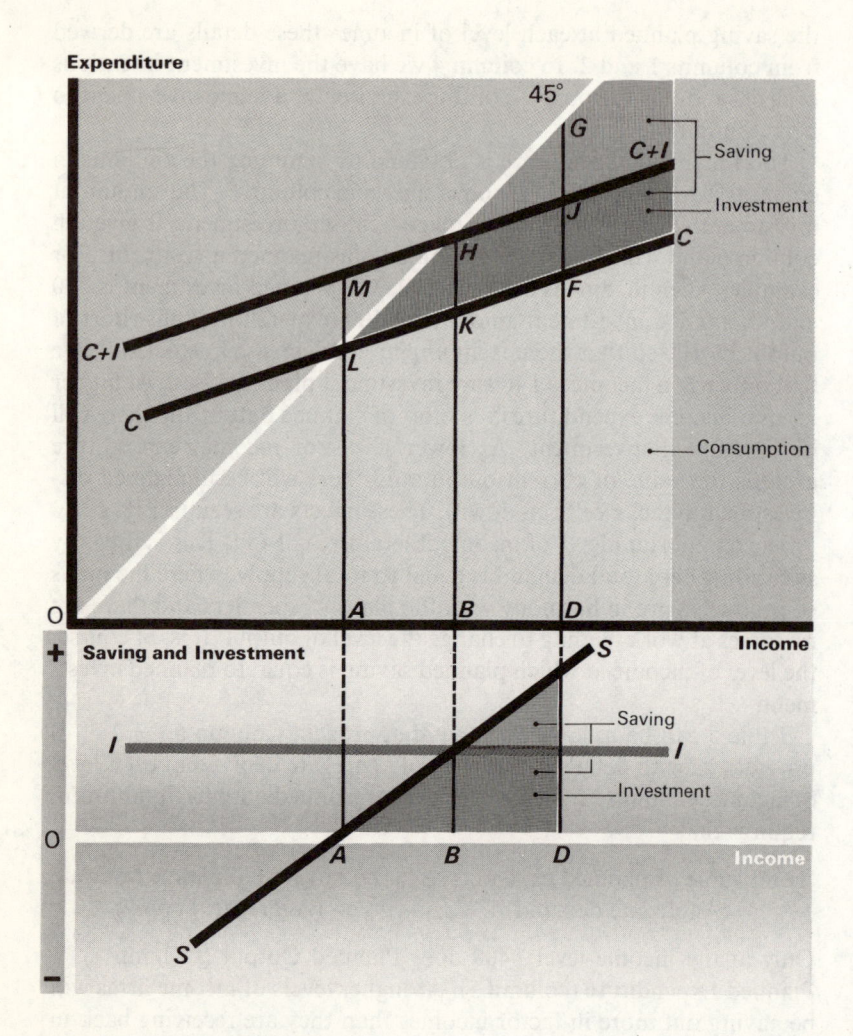

Figs. 13 (i) top and 13 (ii) bottom

economy. Investment amounts to the vertical distance between the CC line and the $C + I$ line. Since we are assuming investment is autonomous the two lines are parallel; investment is the same at all levels of income.

Now the vertical distance between the CC line and the 45° line must indicate the amount of saving at any given level of income. For example, when income is OD, consumption will be FD and saving amounts to FG. At this level of income, investment is FJ. Income is equal to output and it can be seen that only when income is at OB do we have an

THE DETERMINATION OF EQUILIBRIUM

equilibrium situation where total supply (OB) = total demand ($BK + HK$). At this level of income planned savings = planned investment since both are equal to HK.

At higher levels of income such as OD we note that total expenditure DJ is less than the value of output ($GD = OD$). This is because planned savings (GF) is greater than planned investment (FJ). Output (= income) will be reduced and will tend to fall to OB.

At lower levels of income such as OA, total expenditure (AM) is greater than the value of planned output ($OA = AL$). Planned saving is zero, while planned investment is ML. Injections exceed leakages and income will tend to expand to OB.

Fig. 13(ii) looks at the same situation but concentrates the view taken in our first approach; that is, the relationships between planned I and planned S. The savings line is derived from Fig. 13(i), as explained earlier. The investment line is parallel to the horizontal axis since I is constant. Again it can be seen that OB is the only equilibrium level of income. At higher or lower levels of income, divergencies between planned S and planned I will set up changes in production plans which will cause income and output to move towards OB.

Changes in equilibrium

Given the investment and propensity to consume schedules there is one and only one equilibrium level at which income tends to settle. Diagrammatically it has been shown to be determined where the $C + I$ cuts the 45° line. In this position firms will find that they have made the correct output decisions since they will be able to sell all their planned output and there will be no unplanned changes in their stocks.

By taking: Y to mean current planned output (= income),
C to mean current planned consumption spending and
I to mean current planned investment spending,

the equilibrium condition is $Y = C + I$ and any disequilibrium situation will tend to correct itself by changes in output plans.

But what will happen if there is a change in planned investment? The investment schedule will move and, assuming no change in the savings schedule, a new equilibrium will be established where planned S = planned I. Alternatively we can say that the aggregate demand schedule ($C + I$) will move and a new equilibrium situation will arise when aggregate demand again equals planned output. These changes are illustrated in Fig. 14.

The original aggregate demand function is $C + I$ so that the equilibrium level of income is OA where planned expenditure ($C + I$)

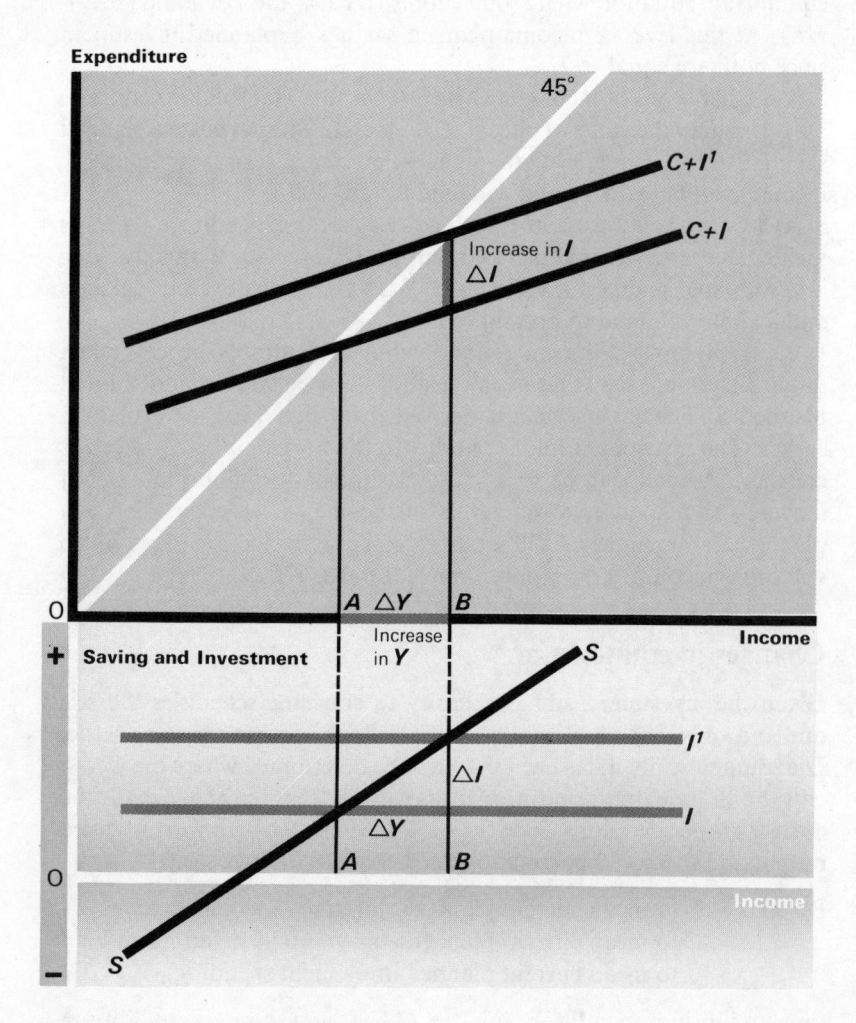

Figs. 14 (i) top and 14 (ii) bottom

equals planned output (OA). Another view of the same situation is presented in Fig. 14(ii) where equilibrium income is established by the equality of planned S and planned I.

Now assume that planned investment, at all levels of income, increases by an amount ΔI. The demand curve shifts to $C + I'$ (Fig. 14(i)) and the investment line from I to I' (Fig. 14(ii)). Income and output will now increase by an amount ΔY to the new equilibrium level OB. As one would expect, an increase in planned investment has led to an increase in output and income, but the interesting feature is that the resulting change in income is much greater than the change in investment ($\Delta Y > \Delta I$). The nature of the relationship between ΔY and ΔI is explained by one of the most important concepts in economics–the multiplier.

THE MULTIPLIER

The multiplier describes the fact that *changes in spending have an impact on income that is greater than the original change in spending*. Since we are dealing with a two-sector economy, we shall explain the multiplier process by means of a change in investment spending. Later we shall see that there is a multiplier effect whenever there is an autonomous increase in the other components of aggregate demand.

Beginning from a position of equilibrium we can suppose that investment spending is increased due to a substantial increase in the programme of housebuilding. Assume that the rate of investment in housing has been fairly stable for some time at £1 000m. per month and it now increases to £1 100m. per month. Hence $\Delta I = £100$m. The immediate effect of this increase in investment will be an increase in the incomes received by construction workers, who, we assume, had been previously unemployed. Incomes in this industry will rise by £100m. per month. If the MPC of the community is constant at 0·8 then £80m. of this additional income will be spent and £20m. saved. But this is not the end of the matter, because the producers of the goods and services bought by these construction workers will find their incomes increased by £80m. This particular group will proceed to spend £64m. and save £16m. And so it will go on–each round of spending will create additional income, part of which will be passed on. Setting out the sequence more formally we have,

Increase in Investment (ΔI)	generates	Increases in Income (ΔY)
£100m.		£100m. + £80m. + £64m. + £51·2m. + +

These rounds of spending will continue until the amounts have become infinitely small. It must be noted that we are equating each round of spending with a corresponding increase in income. This means that we are assuming that businessmen react immediately to changes in spending by changing their production plans.

The eventual increase in income is the sum of the successive rounds of spending generated by the increase in investment. It is, in fact, a geometric series diminishing to infinity. There is a simple formula for summing such a series:

$$\text{Sum of the series} = \frac{\text{First term}}{1 - \text{the common ratio}}$$

The common ratio of the series we are dealing with is 0·8; it is the factor by which each term is multiplied in order to obtain the succeeding term. Hence:

$$S = \frac{£100\text{m.}}{1 - 0·8}$$
$$= \frac{£100\text{m.}}{0·2}$$
$$= £500\text{m.}$$

As a result of the multiplier process, income has increased by an amount 5 times greater than the change in investment.

$$\text{The Multiplier} = \frac{\text{Eventual change in income}}{\text{Change in investment}} = \frac{\Delta Y}{\Delta I} = \frac{£500\text{m.}}{£100\text{m.}} = 5$$

But we can put it in more precise terms than this. The common ratio (0·8) used in the formula above is the MPC of the community. The sum of the series might therefore be written,

$$S = \frac{£100\text{m.}}{1 - \text{MPC}} = £100\text{m.} \left(\frac{1}{1 - \text{MPC}}\right)$$

The expression in the brackets is the multiplier.

$$\text{The Multiplier} = \frac{1}{1 - \text{MPC}} = \frac{1}{\text{MPS}} \text{ (Since MPC + MPS = 1)}$$

The size of the multiplier obviously depends upon the size of the MPC. The larger the MPC (the smaller the MPS) the larger is the multiplier. All we are saying is that the greater the amount of income passed on at each stage, the larger will be each term in the series and hence the larger will be the eventual rise in total income.

SAVINGS AND THE MULTIPLIER

We have seen how an increase in one of the injections (investment) will cause income to expand by a multiple of the change in the level of spending. It will be seen later than any change in either a leakage or an injection will cause income to change until leakages are once again equal to injections. In a two-sector economy a change in investment will cause income to change until planned savings are once again equal to planned investment. We can develop the earlier example to show the change in savings as well as in income.

The increase of £100m. in planned investment generates expenditure and income as follows:

Increase in Y	Increase in C	Increase in S
100	80	20
80	64	16
64	51·2	12·8
51·2	40·96	10·24
,	,	,
,	,	,
,	,	,
,	,	,
,	,	,
500	400	100

We have used the formula

$$\frac{\text{First term}}{1-\text{common ratio}}$$

to sum the first column to a total of £500m. Exactly the same procedure enables us to obtain the sum of the series for consumption spending and saving. Note that the expansion of income continues until planned saving is again equal to planned investment – both increase by £100m. The economy is now in equilibrium. The process is presented diagrammatically in Fig. 15.

If there is a change in the level of S or I so that planned S is not equal to planned I then income will change until these planned aggregates are once again equal to one another.

Worked Example

National Income = 1000, Consumption = 600, APC = MPC = 0·6
There is no government or foreign trade; the economy is in equilibrium. What would be the effect on income if planned investment increased by 50?

Initially,
$$Y = C + S$$
$$1000 = 600 + S$$
$$S = 400 \text{ (therefore } I = 400)$$

Therefore, APS = MPS = 0·4 and the Multiplier = $\frac{1}{0·4} = 2\frac{1}{2}$

Investment now increases to 450.
$$\Delta Y = \Delta I \times 2\frac{1}{2}$$
$$= 50 \times 2\frac{1}{2}$$
$$= 125$$

The Multiplier Process

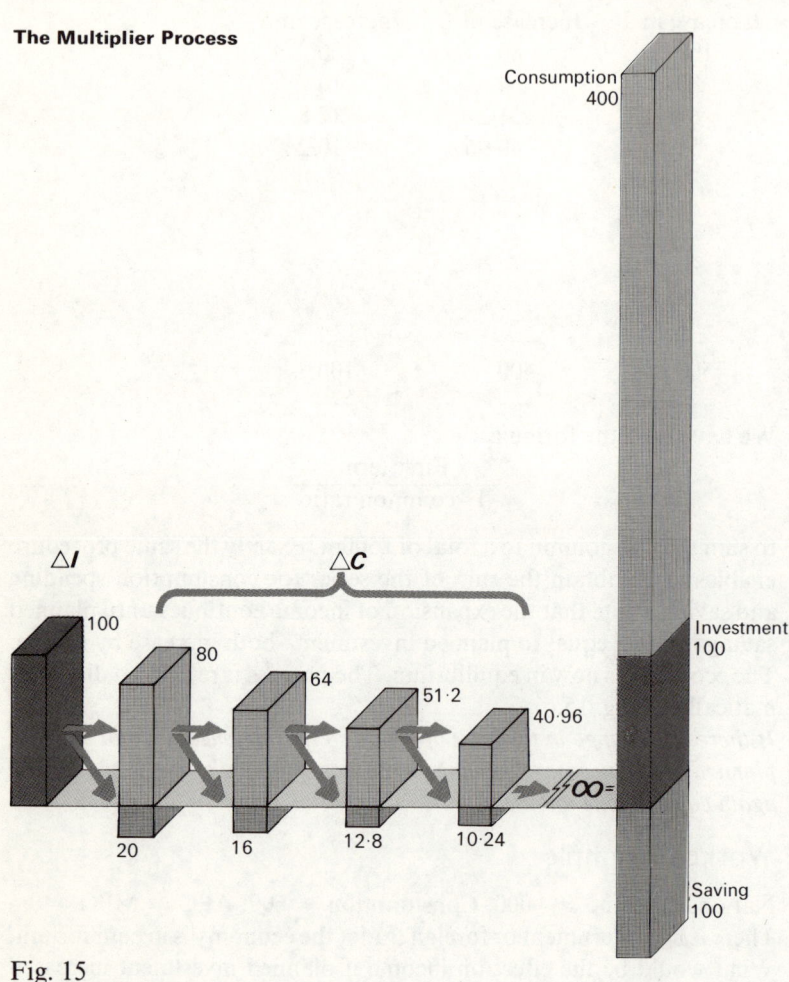

Fig. 15

New level of national income = 1 125
Note that saving at this level of income will be $0.4 \times 1\,125 = 450$ (= Investment).
Income has increased until planned S = planned I.

THE DOWNWARD MULTIPLIER

The multiplier is a most important key to an understanding of economic fluctuations. Not only does it explain how relatively small increases in spending plans can exert considerable upward pressure on income, it

THE DETERMINATION OF EQUILIBRIUM

also helps to explain why relatively small decreases in the rate of spending might lead to serious falls in income and employment.

The multiplier is a two-edged weapon – it cuts both ways. Just as additional income is respent to create still further income, so any cut in spending will reduce income which, in turn, will lead to further cuts in spending and income in a cumulative manner. It should be easy for the reader to recast our arithmetical example (page 71) to show the effects when planned investment falls by £100m. The terms in the geometric series will now have negative signs and the ultimate effect will be that national income falls by £500m. Income will fall until planned saving is again equal to planned investment.

THE PARADOX OF THRIFT

The fact that income must always move to the level where the flows of saving and investment are equal leads to one of the most important paradoxes in economics. The paradox of thrift explains how, under

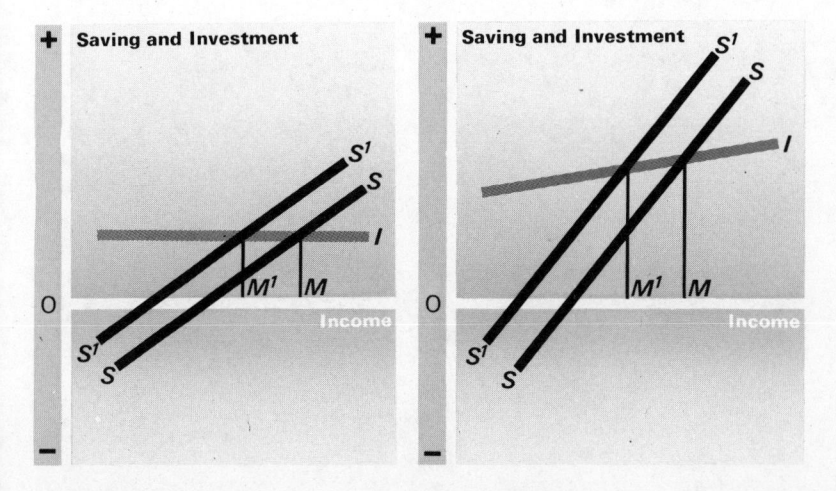

Fig. 16 (i)

Fig. 16 (ii)

certain circumstances, *an attempt to increase saving may lead to a fall in total savings.* Any attempt to save more which is not matched by an equal willingness to invest more will create a deficiency of demand. Leakages will exceed injections and income will fall to a new equilibrium level. Fig. 16 illustrates the effects of an increase in the propensity to save. In Fig. 16(i) we have only autonomous investment and the savings line giving an initial equilibrium level of income OM. An increase in the propensity to save (i.e. people attempt to save more at all levels of income) raises the savings curve to $S'S'$. Income falls to OM' and the level of saving remains unchanged.

In Fig. 16(ii) investment includes both autonomous and induced elements. In this case an increase in the propensity to save reduce income from OM to OM', but the level of saving itself falls. The attempt to save more has meant that *less* is saved. The explanation for this, of course, is that an increase in the propensity to save is the same thing as a fall in the propensity to consume. This is an autonomous fall in one of the components of aggregate demand which will have downward multiplier effects on income.

8
Output and Employment

The simplifying assumptions on which the present analysis is based enable us to relate changes in output and income directly to changes in employment. We have seen how the equilibrium level of output is determined by aggregate demand and we known that the level of output determines the level of employment.

Ever since the Keynesian 'revolution', full employment has ranked highly amongst the goals of government policy. This leads us, therefore, to the idea of a 'desired' level of output – that output which will provide full employment for the labour force. Equilibrium in the market for goods and services obtains when aggregate demand is just sufficient to absorb current output at constant prices. Now it does not follow that an equilibrium situation in the markets for goods and services will produce the desired equilibrium in the market for labour (i.e. full employment). This is one of the most important points to emerge from the Keynesian analysis of income determination.

A deficiency of aggregate demand

Suppose we have a given aggregate demand function $(C + I)$ as in Fig. 17(i). This will produce an equilibrium level of output OB. The output of goods and services required to maintain a full employment situation, however, may be OD. In this case, at the full employment level of income (OD) there is a deficiency of aggregate demand equal to the vertical distance between the $C + I$ line and the 45° line. This deficiency is known as a *deflationary gap*. If firms were to produce an output equal in value to OD, the deflationary gap measures the value of output which would remain unsold. With the given aggregate demand schedule the economy would settle in equilibrium at OB and this level of income would be associated with unemployment of labour and under-capacity operation of capital equipment. This situation will persist unless there is an increase in planned C or planned I or both. In the two-sector economy, the deflationary gap represents an excess of

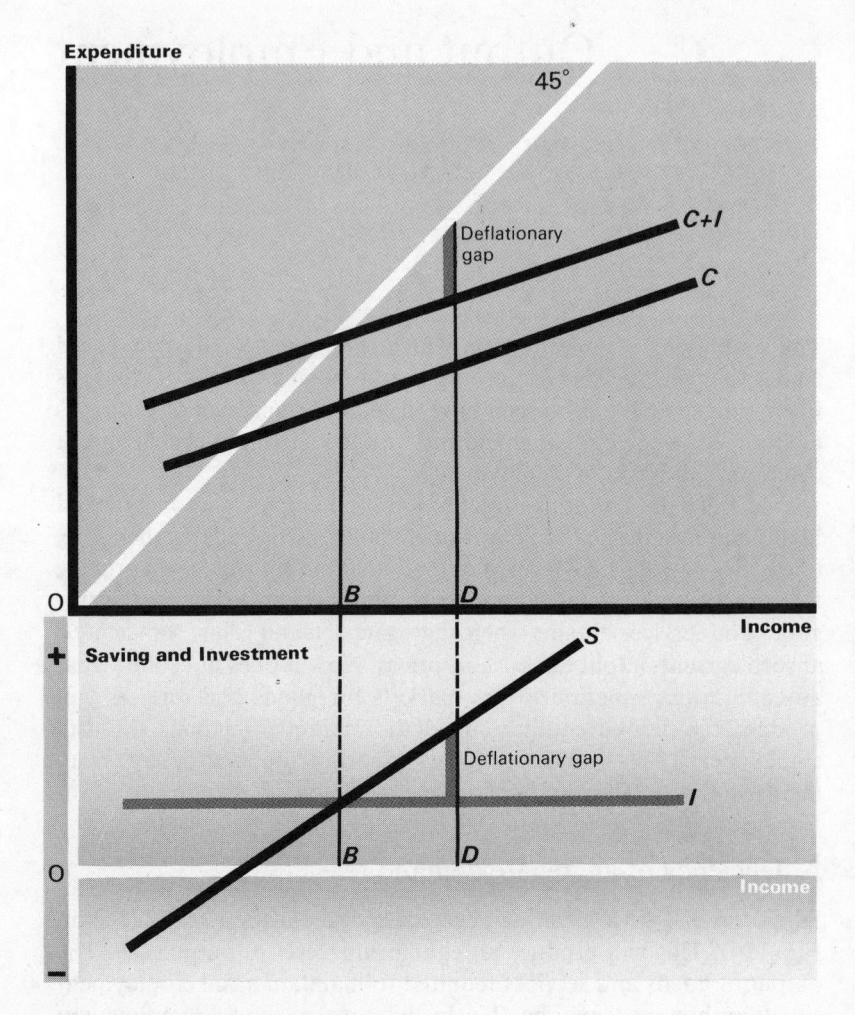

Figs. 17 (i) top and 17 (ii) bottom

planned S over planned I at the full employment level of income. This is clearly seen in Fig. 17(ii).

The important point to grasp is that there is no guarantee that equilibrium output will be large enough to ensure the full employment of labour and capital. If the propensities to spend by the private sector are insufficient to generate the required level of output, the deflationary gap must be closed by the appropriate public policy. This is discussed in Chapters 9 and 20.

OUTPUT AND EMPLOYMENT

Excess demand

It is possible that planned consumption and planned investment might produce a level of aggregate demand greater than that required to produce the full employment output at constant prices. Such a situation is illustrated in Fig. 18(i). Equilibrium output is OY, determined at the intersection of the $C + I$ line and the 45° line. Suppose, however, that OX, represents a full employment level of output. At this output, planned spending exceeds the value of output by the amount identified as the *inflationary gap* in the diagram. This gap measures the extent of

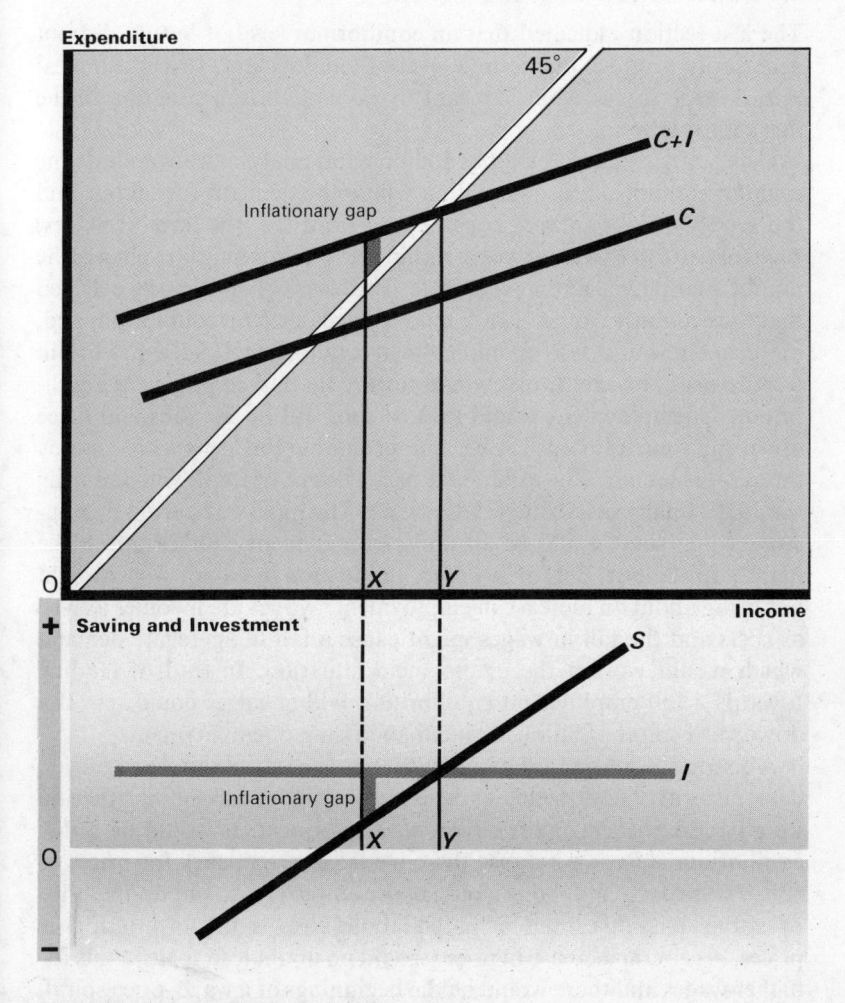

Figs. 18 (i) top and 18 (ii) bottom

the excess demand over the maximum output at constant prices. Spending plans in real terms cannot be realised and inflationary pressures will be present in the economy. This excess demand must be eliminated by a cut in C or I or both. Again, it will probably require some deliberate act of public policy to bring about the required changes in spending (see Chapter 20). As in the previous example, the inflationary gap may be seen in terms of injections and withdrawals. Fig. 18(ii) shows the inflationary gap as an excess of investment over savings at the full employment level of income.

AN EQUILIBRIUM LEVEL OF EMPLOYMENT

The last section indicated that an equilibrium level of output did not necessarily produce the desired level of employment. It seems logical at this stage to ask what is meant by an equilibrium situation in the market for labour.

Using the traditional supply and demand analysis we would define such an equilibrium as a situation where the demand for labour and the supply of labour were equated at a price (i.e. the level of wages) such that no forces were at work, within the system, tending to change the numbers employed at that wage rate. The classical economists believed that the economy would always tend towards such an equilibrium and, moreover, it would be a full employment equilibrium. If a disequilibrium were to arise, market forces would restore the full employment equilibrium. Unemployment would lead to competition for jobs and force down the wage rate until it became profitable for firms to re-employ the surplus labour. The experience of persistent unemployment during the 1930s finally discredited these views. The inter-war period demonstrated that there could be an under-employment equilibrium in the market for labour. But, in any case, a reduction in money wages might not bring about an increase in employment. Wages are incomes as well as costs and the fall in wages might cause a fall in aggregate demand which would worsen the employment situation. Instead of tending towards a full employment equilibrium, falling wages could set off a downward spiral of falling demand and rising unemployment.

A disequilibrium in the labour market is also possible where aggregate demand is at a level which exceeds the supply of labour – a situation usually described as one of *over-full employment*. It would be a disequilibrium situation because there would be a tendency for prices to rise. The scarcity of labour would cause employers to bid up the price of labour, passing on the increased labour costs in the form of higher prices. A general increase in prices would no doubt lead to demands for higher wages and there would be the beginnings of a wage–price spiral. (See Chapter 17.)

The policy aim of governments is a full employment equilibrium, but it is difficult, if not impossible, to provide a precise and meaningful definition of full employment. Whatever meaning is given to the term it clearly relates to some particular relationship between the demand for and supply of labour. It is the interpretations given to these terms, especially the supply of labour, which makes it so difficult to be precise about the meaning and measurement of full employment.

THE SUPPLY OF LABOUR

Strictly speaking this should be defined in terms of the number of man-hours of labour supplied at any given wage rate over some given period of time. The amount of labour supplied can be varied without any change in the numbers of people employed. Existing workers may work longer hours (e.g. overtime) or they may be placed on 'short-time' (i.e. working three or four days each week). Over the longer period the aggregate supply of labour from any given labour force will tend to fall if there are pressures for a shorter working week and longer holidays.

In discussions of employment and unemployment, however, it is usual to refer to the supply of labour in terms of the number of persons seeking work. Since there are limits to the amount of overtime the labour force will accept, and limits to the amount of short-time working which can be offered, it is reasonable to expect that the numbers employed will vary with total output.

The level of employment will depend, at least in part, on how many of a given population *want* to work. In the UK this appears to be about 60 per cent of those over the age of 16. This *participation rate*,[1] as it is called, is an important concept since it is subject to short-term variation. In other words, there is a degree of elasticity in the aggregate supply of labour even in the short term, and this causes difficulties when we attempt to measure the true extent of unemployment (i.e. the amount of surplus labour).

The participation rate is influenced by the current demand for labour. When the unemployment level is high more married women may try to enter the labour force in order to supplement the family income. Similar conditions in the labour market may persuade many young people to stay on in further education in order to acquire better qualifications or to postpone entry to the labour market until conditions are more favourable. On the other hand, in good times when jobs are plentiful more people, especially married women and retired people seeking part-time work, will be tempted to enter the labour force. Thus, the participation rate will vary with the state of the economy.

In the UK the extent of unemployment is measured by reference to

1. It may also be described as the activity rate.

MACRO-ECONOMICS

the number of persons who are formally registered as unemployed. This figure will understate the amount of surplus labour since registration is also a requirement for obtaining unemployment benefits. People seeking work, but not entitled to such benefits do not have the same incentive to register. This group will include married women who do not pay the full rate of national insurance, young people who have not yet paid the qualifying amount of national insurance, and a fairly large number of people who will take part-time jobs when the labour market is favourable, but will not register as being available for work at other times.

In some countries the extent of unemployment is measured by means of household surveys in which people are asked if they are actually looking for work. If the sample of households is adequate this method probably gives a better indication of unemployment in the sense of the numbers actively seeking work but unable to find it. If this number is then added to the number in employment we have one indication of the aggregate supply of labour measured in terms of the potential labour force.

THE DEMAND FOR LABOUR

The demand for labour is a derived demand. Labour is not demanded for its own sake, but for the goods and services it can produce. Just as there are problems in trying to measure the supply of labour so there are similar problems in trying to assess the demand. The number of persons actually in employment is one indicator of the current demand for

Fig. 19
Source: Department of Employment Gazette, November 1977

labour. Movements in the numbers at work give some idea of the direction in which the demand for labour is moving. A further useful statistic is the number of unfilled vacancies. The official register of unfilled vacancies, however, is likely to understate the demand for labour since not all employers register their vacancies and those who do may not register all their vacancies. We do not know, therefore, the full extent of the demand for labour.

The official statistics of registered unemployed and unfilled vacancies help to give us a picture of trends. An increase in one is invariably accompanied by a decrease in the other as Fig. 19 shows.

A major problem in trying to apply the elementary techniques of supply and demand to the total labour market is that demand and supply may not refer to the same thing. Employers may be demanding labour of a different type to that which is available. The demand for labour is derived from the demands for a great variety of goods and services and the nature of these demands is always changing. The supply of labour comprises a wide variety of skills and abilities. The changing demands for goods and services give rise to a continually changing pattern of demand for labour. Given the real world immobilities, both occupational and geographical, in the labour force it is apparent that there will always be some unemployed people while, at the same time, some employers are looking for labour. This feature of the labour market is known as *frictional unemployment*.

FULL EMPLOYMENT

The difficulties associated with the interpretation and measurement of the supply of and demand for labour should serve to remind us that economics, as a science, is still in its early stages of development. The fact that many economic terms have come into common use should not delude us into thinking that we know all there is to know about such things. Full employment is one such term. What does it mean?

On the simplest level it could mean that the total available supply of labour was completely absorbed into gainful employment. We have already noted that, in the real world, this cannot possibly be achieved. Since labour is not perfectly mobile between places and occupations, there are many separate labour markets each with its own supply and demand conditions. A definition of full employment which requires that the demand for and supply of labour be equated in each and every labour market is not tenable.

An alternative definition would require the sum of the demands in all the labour markets to be equal to the sum of the supplies, even though in several of these markets there may be an excess of demand over supply or supply over demand. This is the meaning usually given to full employment. It is a definition which accepts the existence of some unrequited demand and some unused supply. The unemployment which is consistent with a state of full employment will be frictional unemployment.

Although we have a definition of full employment it is a very different matter to say when such a situation exists. Some authorities would say that full employment exists when there is a balance between the unfilled vacancies and the numbers unemployed. Unfortunately these statistics do not provide an accurate picture of the supply and demand situation. In any case these concepts are aggregates which could mask uneven occupational and geographical distributions of unemployment. A balance between the numbers looking for work and the number of jobs available to them is not in itself sufficient evidence of full employment since it is conceivable that a situation might arise where there were, say, two million out of work and two million vacancies. This could hardly be described a full employment. Any acceptable definition of full employment demands that the existing amount of unemployment be relatively small.

Another way of assessing the employment situation is to calculate the probable amount of frictional unemployment and then compare it with the number of workers unemployed. Lord Beveridge in his classic work *Full Employment in a Free Society* (1944) used this technique and estimated that something like 3 per cent of the working population might be unemployed at any one time for 'frictional' reasons. In fact this figure is well above the average unemployment figure for the UK over the greater part of the post-war period. From 1945 to 1969 the average rate was rather less than 2 per cent. Beveridge, of course, based his estimates on studies carried out before the war and he lacked adequate statistics on unfilled vacancies. Given the possible variations in the participation rate and the inadequacy of data on the demand for labour it is very difficult to obtain a precise measure of frictional unemployment. Some guide as to the nature of the unemployment problem might be obtained from the statistics showing the length of time which unemployed persons have been on the register. If the average duration of unemployment is fairly short this might be taken as an indication that the unemployment is largely of the frictional type.

In practice the authorities must use the available evidence of registered unemployed, unfilled vacancies and the duration of unemployment as rough guides in assessing whether there is an excess supply or excess demand for labour. Full employment, however, is such an important aspect of policy that political judgements must also be considered. It seems that for the UK an unemployment rate above 2 per cent is not regarded as politically acceptable. Employment policy is discussed in Chapter 20.

9
The Government Sector

Up to this point we have worked with a very simple model of a two-sector economy. The aim of this chapter is to introduce a government sector into the model and examine the manner in which government income and expenditure affect the national income. The government can expand total demand through its purchases of goods and services, or by stimulating private spending by means of tax reductions. Similarly it can reduce total demand by decreasing its own spending or by increasing taxation, or both. Government spending may be treated in the same way as investment – it is an injection into the circular flow of income. Taxation may be regarded as a leakage from that circular flow.

The size of the government sector

The government sector, which includes both central and local authorities, is a major part of the UK and most other economies. The size of the public sector may be defined in various ways. If we take the role of government and publicly owned bodies as employers of labour, the public sector accounts for well over 25 per cent of the nation's labour force. Another way of measuring the importance of the public sector is to take the value of the output of publicly owned institutions and add it to the value of the purchases by public authorities from the private sector. For the UK this measure indicates that 35–40 per cent of economic activity is either under public ownership or dependent upon public sector activities.

Perhaps the most widely used indicator of the importance of the public sector is the figure for total public expenditure. In the UK this amounts to about 50 per cent of the Gross National Product. Total public spending may be usefully divided into the following categories:

(*a*) Public authorities' consumption spending
(*b*) Public authorities' investment spending
(*c*) Transfer payments (pensions, family allowances, interest on debt, and so on).

MACRO-ECONOMICS

This is an important breakdown since as Fig. 20 shows, in the UK about two fifths of public expenditure is devoted to the third category – transfer payments. These consist of transfers of money which are spent privately by households and firms. Thus a large part of total public spending does not take the form of direct spending on goods and services. To the extent that these transfers are financed from taxation, they simply amount to a redistribution of income.

Only the first two categories constitute demands by the public sector on the real resources available to the economy. In other words, the proportion of national output devoted to collective rather than private purchases amounts to about 30 per cent of the GNP. This is the part of public spending which affects aggregate demand *directly*. We must bear in mind, however, that transfer payments have an important influence on the distribution of disposable income. They will affect the consumption function and hence have some influence on aggregate demand.

UK Public Expenditure 1976

- 45.5% Current Spending on Goods and Services
- 13.5% Public Investment
- 41% Transfer Payments

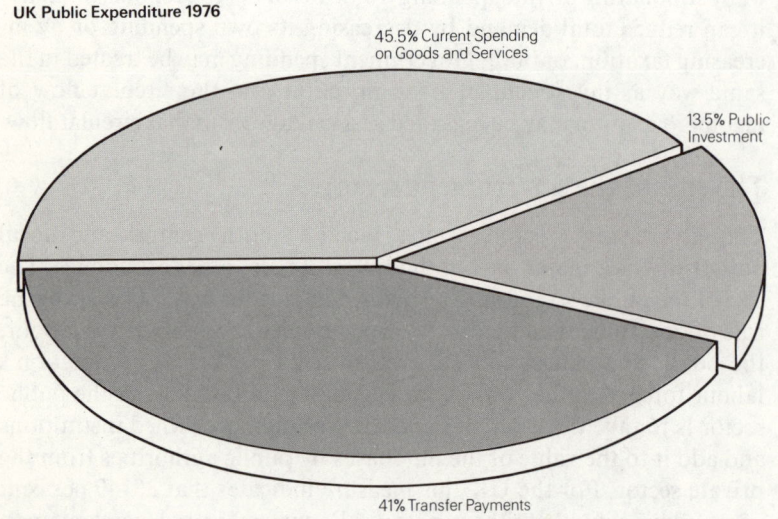

Fig. 20

Quite apart from its sheer size another reason for differentiating the public sector from the private sector is that the motivations for spending are different. In the private sector we assume that the motives for spending are the maximisation of personal satisfactions in the case of households, and the maximisation of profits in the case of firms. The expenditures in the public sector are not determined by habits, personal preferences or profit expectations, but by political decision. They are subject to the collective will of the people expressed through their central and local legislatures. How large should the public sector be? The answer to this question is political rather than economic. Even when there is broad agreement on the range of goods and services which should be provided collectively there is still room for wide disagreement on the proportion of the nation's resources which should be devoted to the public sector.

The budgetary framework

The annual Budget sets out the planned income and expenditure of the government for the year ahead together with a statement of the revenue and expenditure for the past financial year. The original purpose of the Budget was to raise just sufficient revenue to cover public expenditure; it was regarded as most desirable that the Budget should be balanced. Nowadays, the Budget is used as the major instrument of economic policy and a budget surplus or deficit may be deliberately planned in order to bring about economic changes. This deliberate manipulation of G and T is known as *fiscal policy* which may be formally defined as 'the policy that government receipts and expenditures should be consciously planned, particularly in their aggregate amounts so as to effect beneficial changes in the overall level of incomes, prices, and employment'. We shall look at the use of fiscal policy later in this chapter; for the moment, we shall be concerned with the instruments of that policy, one aspect of which – public expenditure – has already been discussed.

TAXATION

Taxes may be structured in various ways. A *proportional tax* requires all taxpayers to pay the same percentage of their income, wealth, or expenditure in taxation. A person with a large income would pay more than a person with a small income, but each would have the same percentage of income taken in taxation. In the UK, Corporation Tax and Value Added Tax are examples of proportional taxes.

A *progressive tax* is one which removes a greater proportion of income or wealth from the better-off members of the community. The highly paid person might pay 50 to 60 per cent of his income in tax whereas the person in the lower income groups might only pay 5 per cent of his income in taxation. Such a tax is held to be more equitable than a proportional tax because it bears a closer relationship to the ability to pay. Income Tax and Capital Transfer Tax are examples of progressive taxes.

A *regressive tax* is one in which the proportion of income or wealth taken in taxation decreases as the amount of income or wealth increases. In the UK there are no taxes structured in this manner.

A *flat-rate tax* imposes the same monetary burden on all taxpayers. The motor vehicle duty in the UK is the same for all car owners whether they be rich or poor. This type of tax is widely used as the basis for expenditure taxes. In the UK the excise duties on petrol, tobacco and alcoholic drinks are all levied on a flat-rate basis.

Taxes are usually divided into two categories, direct and indirect. *Direct taxes* are those levied on income and wealth and the burden of such taxes is borne by those upon whom they are levied. Income tax, corporation tax and capital transfer tax are examples of direct taxes and, as such, they are collected by the Inland Revenue Department. *Indirect taxes* are imposed on items of expenditure and, in this case, it is possible for the person on whom the tax is levied to pass on the burden, or part of it, in the form of higher prices. Just how much of the tax burden can be transferred in this way depends upon the elasticities of supply and demand. If the commodity on which the tax is imposed has a demand which is very inelastic with respect to price (consumers have very strong preferences for it) it will be possible for the seller to embody most of the tax in an increased price. Customs and excise duties and the value added tax provide examples of indirect taxes. They are collected by the Customs and Excise Department. Indirect taxes are said to be regressive in their effects since they are usually of the flat-rate type. The tax paid on any particular purchase represents a greater burden to the poor man than to the rich man.

The State also has a substantial source of income in the form of compulsory levies on employers and employees in the form of National Insurance contributions. Although these are not collected by the taxation departments they are, in effect, a form of taxation. The revenues from these contributions are paid into the National Insurance Fund and must be spent on specified social security benefits.

The public sector also raises revenue by means of local rates. These are taxes levied by the local authorities on the owners of buildings in their administrative areas.

The government and income

The introduction of government calls for a substantial modification of our simple model of the economy. Government expenditure (G) is treated as being autonomously determined since it is subject to political decision. We regard it, therefore, as being independent of income. Thus, our model now has two injections into the circular flow of income, I and G.

Taxation (T), both direct and indirect, represents a leakage from the system. Taxes, unlike government spending, cannot be treated as autonomous since the revenue from taxation bears a direct relationship to income, and tax revenue is a function of income.

Indirect taxes cause spending at market prices to exceed spending at factor cost so that the whole of current spending does not go on to generate incomes. Direct taxes are a compulsory withdrawal of income from firms and households. Our model now has two leakages, S and T. It is necessary to take account of subsidies which, since they cause the market price to be less than factor cost, can be regarded as negative taxes. We use T_i to stand for net indirect taxation (i.e. indirect taxes–subsidies) and T_d to stand for direct taxes. The expression for aggregate demand, therefore, is

$$C + I + G - T_i$$

Equilibrium obtains when this planned expenditure at factor cost is equal to the value of planned output at factor cost. This planned output may be expressed in terms of the factor incomes which it will generate. These incomes may be disposed of in three ways:

1. Part will be spent on consumption (C).
2. Part will be saved (S).
3. Part will be taken in direct taxation (T_d).

Planned output (= income), therefore, may be expressed in the form,

$$C + S + T_d$$

Equilibrium requires,

$$C + I + G - T_i = C + S + T_d;$$
i.e. $\quad I + G \quad = \quad S + T_d + T_i$
(Planned injections) (Planned leakages)

The introduction of a government sector means that an equality between planned S and planned I is no longer a necessary condition for equilibrium. A discrepancy between S and I can be offset by an equal discrepancy between G and T (where $T = T_d + T_i$). It must also be noted that a balanced budget is not a necessary condition for equilibrium; all that is required is that planned injections = planned leakages. This is illustrated in Fig. 21, where the equilibrium level of income is seen to be OY.

The existence of the public sector also calls for a modification of the consumption function. Consumption expenditure is clearly related to *disposable income* (Y_d)–the income available to households for saving or spending. In the two-sector economy Y_d is the same thing as national income (Y) since all income is paid out and there is no taxation leakage. In our present model the situation is

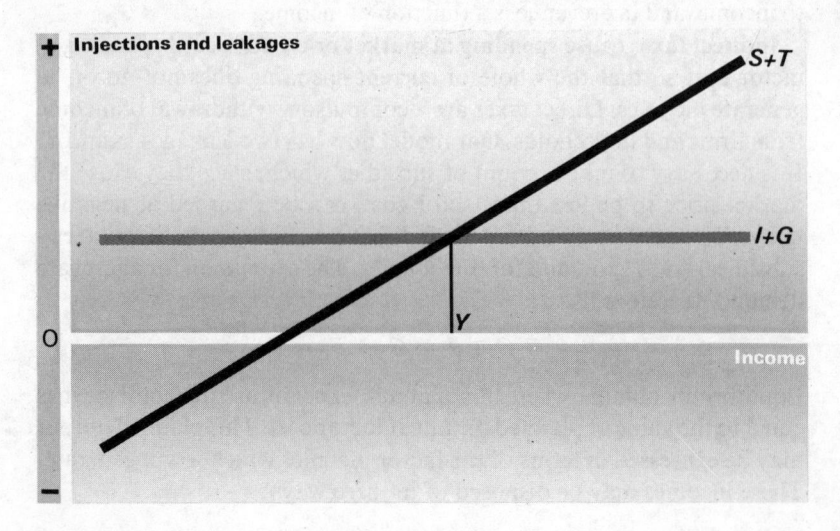

Fig. 21

Disposable Income (Y_d) = National Income (Y) − Direct Taxes (T_d)[1]
+ Transfer Payments − Undistributed profits
and $C = f(Y_d)$

Nevertheless it is necessary to express C as a function of Y for purposes of analysis. We wish to know how much planned consumption spending will be generated by any particular level of planned output. For example, if we know that $C = \frac{3}{4}$ of disposable income, and disposable income is $\frac{2}{3}$ of national income we have,

$C = \frac{3}{4} \times \frac{2}{3}Y = \frac{1}{2}Y$ (i.e. APC = $\frac{1}{2}$)
and $S = \frac{1}{4} \times \frac{2}{3}Y = \frac{1}{6}Y$ (i.e. APS = $\frac{1}{6}$)

It is also necessary to express the marginal propensities to consume and save as proportions of changes in national income. This is made clear in the worked examples later in this chapter.

The government sector and the multiplier

Changes in government expenditure and in *rates* of taxation will have multiplier effects since they will cause changes in aggregate spending which are not related to changes in income.

EFFECTS OF CHANGES IN GOVERNMENT SPENDING

The government may alter the level of income by changing its own

[1] Including national insurance contributions.

THE GOVERNMENT SECTOR

spending on goods and services, that is by changing the level of G in the equilibrium equation. In order to simplify the analysis of these changes we must make some assumptions:

(a) We assume that the rates of taxation (both direct and indirect) are unchanged. In other words, the marginal rate of taxation (t) is constant.
(b) Changes in G are assumed to have no influence on I.
(c) MPC (c) and MPS (s) are constant.
(d) There are no transfer payments.

Now if government expenditure is increased by an amount ΔG it will give rise to a multiple expansion of income equal to ΔY. It will, in fact, have exactly the same effect as the increase in investment described on pages 71/72. The series of increments in income generated by the increase in G will be

$$\Delta G + \Delta G(k) + \Delta G(k)^2 + \Delta G(k)^3 + \Delta G(k)^4 + + + + +$$

where k is the proportion of each increment of income which is spent. The sum of the series ($= \Delta Y$) is

$$\frac{\Delta G}{1-k} = \Delta G \left(\frac{1}{1-k}\right)$$

so that $\left(\frac{1}{1-k}\right)$ is the multiplier.

Now $k = 1 - $ marginal rate of leakage $= 1 - (s + t)$. The multiplier, therefore, is

$$\frac{1}{1-(1-(s+t))} = \frac{1}{s+t} = \frac{1}{\text{marginal rate of leakage}}$$

Hence

$$\Delta Y = \Delta G \left(\frac{1}{s+t}\right)$$

In fact, it is not likely that tax rates will remain unchanged. Direct taxes are progressive so that the rate of tax leakage will increase as income increases. The multiplier therefore will become smaller as income increases.

Worked example

An economy is in equilibrium and national income $= 1000$. Rates of taxation are constant and equal to $\frac{1}{4}$ of gross income. MPC $=$ APC $= \frac{2}{3}$ of disposable income. What would be the effect on national income of an increase of 100 in government spending on goods and services?

Saving = $\frac{1}{3} \times \frac{3}{4}Y = \frac{1}{4}Y$
Therefore, APS = MPS = $\frac{1}{4}$; marginal rate of taxation = $\frac{1}{4}$.

$$\therefore \text{Multiplier} = \frac{1}{s+t} = \frac{1}{\frac{1}{4}+\frac{1}{4}} = 2$$

$\Delta Y = 2 \times \Delta G$
$= 2 \times 100$
$= \underline{200}$ Income will increase by 200

EFFECTS OF CHANGES IN RATES OF TAXATION

Changes in the rates of taxation may also be used as a means of influencing aggregate demand. The effects of such changes are subject to much uncertainty. An increase in direct taxation will reduce disposable income but the eventual effect on spending depends upon the extent to which people are prepared to maintain their expenditures by reducing their savings. An increase in the rates of taxation may alter the propensity to consume and hence the multiplier. The effects also depend upon the nature of the tax increase. If it falls mainly on the less prosperous section of the community, where the margin of saving is smaller, it will obviously have a much greater effect on spending than would be the case if the more affluent groups were to bear the main brunt of the increase in taxation. A reduction in taxation will also have uncertain effects for similar reasons. Changes in direct taxes may also have effects upon investment—this is discussed later.

Changes in indirect taxation will also affect consumption. The effects will depend upon the elasticities of demand for the goods in question and on whether the changes in tax rates affect the propensity to consume. If the taxes on goods such as petrol or tobacco are increased, expenditures on these goods tends to increase since the demands are very inelastic. This may reduce spending on other goods and services so that aggregate demand is reduced. But consumers may decide to maintain their spending in real terms by cutting back their saving.

If we again make simplifying assumptions by specifying constant I and G and a constant marginal propensity to consume, it is possible to derive the multiplier effects of changes in the rate of taxation. The first point to note is that the given change in tax revenues will have a smaller multiplier effect than the same change in G or I. The reason is that a change in taxation will lead to a corresponding change in disposable income, but, since part of disposable income is saved, the full extent of the change in taxation does not fall on spending. For example, if $\frac{3}{4}$ of disposable income is spent, a reduction of the tax burden of £1m. will lead to an initial change in spending of only £750 000.

The second problem in dealing with the multiplier effects of tax changes is that the value of the multiplier itself will be affected. The

THE GOVERNMENT SECTOR

value of t in the denominator alters when we change the rates of taxation.

The effects of changes in the rates of taxation may be illustrated by means of a fairly simple arithmetical example. We shall assume that changes in taxation leave G unaffected, that MPC remains constant, and that rates of taxation are the same at all levels of income. We must further assume that the only tax is an income tax and that there are no transfer payments.

Worked example

$Y = 1000$
Planned $I = 300$
Planned $G = 100$
Planned $T = 200$ i.e. MPT $= 0.2$ and $Y_d = 0.8Y$
Planned $S = 200$ i.e. APS $= 0.25Y_d$ or $0.2Y$ MPS $= 0.2$
Planned $C = 600$ i.e. APC $= 0.75Y_d$ or $0.6Y$ MPC $= 0.6$

This is an equilibrium situation because,

Planned injections = Planned leakages
$I + G$ $S + T$

Now assume that the government increases the rates of taxation to $0.4Y$. What will be the effects on income?

1. Disposable income now equals $0.6Y$ and since APS is constant $S = 0.25 \times 0.6Y = 0.15Y$.

    In equilibrium $I + G = S + T$
    $$300 + 100 = 0.15Y + 0.4Y$$
    $$0.55Y = 400$$
    $$Y = 727.27$$

    Therefore Income will fall by approximately 272.7.

2. Alternatively, we can say that the initial effects of the increase in taxation will be to reduce disposable income from $0.8Y$ to $0.6Y$; that is, from 800 to 600. Therefore, initially, C would fall from 600 to $0.75 \times 600 = 450$. The multiplier effects of this fall in C can now be calculated.

    $$\Delta Y = \text{Change in } C \times \text{the multiplier}$$
    $$= -150 \times \frac{1}{s + t}$$
    $$= -150 \times \frac{1}{0.15 + 0.4}$$
    $$= -272.7 \text{ approx.}$$

TRANSFER PAYMENTS

For purposes of simplification transfer payments have been assumed to be zero in the preceding analysis, but it was made clear in the introduction to this chapter that they are an important element in disposable income. Transfer payments financed from taxation are clearly a means of redistributing income. They are not factor incomes and do not contribute directly to national income. Nevertheless they do influence national income since, via their impact on disposable income, they affect the propensity to consume. They may be regarded as negative direct taxes. Even when transfer payments are financed wholly by direct taxes they may still have an expansionary effect on aggregate demand if the MPCs of the recipients are greater than those of the taxpayers from whom the revenue is raised.

Fiscal policy

The deliberate use of government income and expenditure as an active instrument of economic policy is a relatively new concept. It stems essentially from the work of John Maynard Keynes during the Great Depression. Until the 1930s the traditional argument had been that the State, like the individual, could not afford to spend more than it received (through taxation). A deficit Budget, it was held, would lead to inflation and increase the National Debt; both regarded as most undesirable developments. These views were attacked by Keynes and others who argued that a deficit Budget will create demand, but, where the economy is operating at less than full employment, this extra demand will call forth extra output rather than increase prices. In the 1930s unemployment rates were more than 20 per cent so that fears of inflation seemed very inappropriate.

The basic idea behind modern fiscal policy is simple enough. We have seen that in a two-sector economy an excess of planned saving over planned investment will lead to a cumulative downward movement of income. Where planned leakages are greater than planned injections at the full employment level of output, the economy will settle at an equilibrium with men and machines lying idle. But it is also possible that planned injections might be greater than planned leakages when resources are fully employed so that there would be strong upward pressures on prices.

Modern fiscal policy aims to use G and T as *compensating* devices to deal with situations where aggregate demand is either excessive or deficient at the full employment level of income. It is helpful to divide fiscal measures into two types, *automatic* and *discretionary*.

AUTOMATIC STABILISERS

There are some propensities in government spending and income that play a compensating role in the economy quite independently of any direct political intervention. The reason for this is that taxation revenues and a large part of public expenditure are both closely related to activity in the private sector.

(*a*) *Taxation revenue* at given tax rates is a function of national income and will tend to rise as income rises and fall as income falls. Where direct taxes are progressive, the tax yield will rise faster than income, and, as income falls, tax yields will fall even faster. Assuming that the government does not change its own spending, progressive taxes will act as a stabilising influence, slowing down the growth of aggregate demand when income is rising, and reducing the fall in aggregate demand when income is falling.

(*b*) *Transfer payments* can also serve as stabilising devices. Some transfer payments such as family allowances and sickness benefits are not affected when income changes, but others such as unemployment benefits and supplementary benefits tend to vary inversely with income and output. When output is falling and unemployment rising these payments prevent disposable incomes falling as fast as factor incomes. Similarly when income and output are rising these payments will decline and national insurance contributions will increase so that aggregate demand does not rise as fast as factor incomes. Where the State supports farm incomes with such schemes as guaranteed price supports there will also be an automatic stabilising effect since farm incomes will not fall proportionately with farm prices, neither will they rise to the same extent as farm prices.

The advantage of automatic stabilisers is that, since they are built into the economic system, they require no legislative approval before they can take effect and no new administrative machinery is needed which might delay their implementation. Their effect is to counter autonomous changes whether the authorities are aware of them or not. The disadvantages of these built-in stabilisers is that they do not come into effect until some de-stabilising change has actually taken place – they cannot prevent the initial change and, although they do have some stabilising influence, they could stabilise the economy at a high unemployment level. They work both ways so that they could operate to delay a much needed recovery from a depression.

Automatic stabilisers partially compensate autonomous changes in GNP, but it may be necessary to fully compensate such changes if price stability and full employment are to be achieved. This will require public action of a discretionary nature.

DISCRETIONARY FISCAL POLICY

Let us suppose that national income is in equilibrium at a level which is not providing for the full employment of the nation's labour force; there is a deficiency of aggregate demand at constant prices.

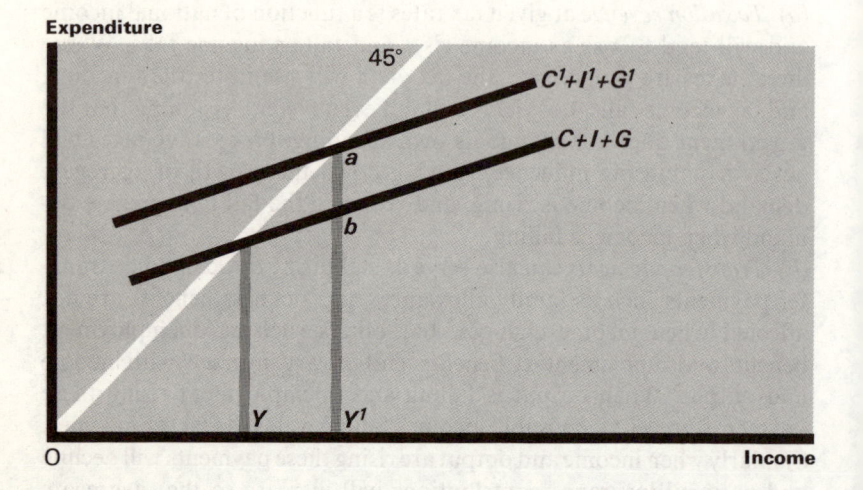

Fig. 22

In Fig. 22 equilibrium income is at OY where the aggregate demand curve intersects the 45° line. Suppose that full employment calls for an output equal to OY'. To achieve this position planned spending must be increased to the level shown by the $C' + I' + G'$ line. How can fiscal measures bring about this increase in aggregate demand?

(a) Tax changes

By means of fiscal policy the government can influence any or all the components of the aggregate demand function $(C + I + G)$.

The consumption component may be increased by reductions in direct and indirect taxes. A reduction in direct taxes increases disposable income and leaves people more to spend. The multiplier effects will depend upon the size of the marginal propensity to consume. If the tax cuts are biased in favour of the lower income groups the multiplier effect will be greater. A cut in indirect taxes will have a similar effect – a given level of disposable income will now purchase more goods and services. Provided G and I remain unchanged, tax reductions will cause an upward shift of the aggregate demand function.

Tax reductions might also be used to stimulate private investment. Cuts in income tax and indirect taxes will improve business prospects and lead to more induced investment. Cuts in profits tax will improve the profitability of investment. Tax reductions might also take the form of increased tax allowances on investment projects. If these measures are successful, investment will increase and the aggregate demand curve will move upwards.

(b) Change in government spending

The most direct means of increasing aggregate demand is an expansion of public spending. Providing the rates of taxation are not increased, an increase in government spending on goods and services has a direct effect on aggregate demand with the appropriate multiplier effects. This increased spending will raise income initially by the full amount of spending, whereas, as we have already noted, tax reductions of equivalent money value will not increase spending to the same extent since part of the addition to disposable income will be saved.

Alternatively the government may increase its outlays by raising the levels of the various welfare benefits. Higher social security payments will have an immediate effect on demand. Since the bulk of such payments are received by persons with relatively high propensities to consume there would be a substantial effect on consumption spending.

Such measures may be used to raise the $C + I + G$ line in Fig. 22 until full employment income OY^1 is achieved. The increase in expenditure required for this purpose is ab and the multiplier will be

$$\frac{YY^1}{ab}$$

When the problem is one of excess demand at full employment income the measures discussed above can be put into reverse, but there are some serious problems associated with policies to increase taxation and reduce government spending. These are discussed in the next section.

FISCAL POLICY—SOME PROBLEMS

Fiscal policy, in common with other economic policy instruments, has its advantages and disadvantages.

It has the advantage of being a very direct instrument. Changes in G and T will have immediate effects on aggregate demand, although the extent of these effects is rather uncertain because of likely changes in the propensity to consume. Fiscal policy may also be used in a discriminatory manner to alter the allocation of resources both geographically and industrially. Government expenditure may be biased towards projects in development areas or towards certain industries (e.g. coal-fired power stations instead of oil-fired). Tax burdens may be reduced for firms locating themselves in development areas. The government may decide to place heavier tax burdens on service industries than manufacturing industries if it believes, for example, that exports are mainly dependent upon the latter. A major use of fiscal policy is in the pursuit of social and political objectives, especially those which aim to reduce inequalities of wealth and opportunity. The application of progressive taxation to income and wealth, and the redistribution of the revenues in the form of social security benefits, will tend to reduce the extent of these inequalities.

There are disadvantages. Some major part of government expenditure is geared to important social and political programmes which make for a high degree of inflexibility in a downward direction. Where the policy requirement is for a reduction of aggregate demand it will be difficult to make a substantial use of G for this purpose. Any reduction in the expenditures on education, health services, pensions and other social security measures will be very strongly resisted. Unless the situation is very critical, the most that can be hoped for is some slowing down in plans for expansion by postponing the implementation of certain programmes. This lack of flexibility in the short run is particularly applicable to public investment which is largely concerned with long-term projects such as road construction, school building, hospital building and so on. Such projects cannot be 'switched on and off' as a means of varying aggregate demand in the short period. The time interval between the decision to build new roads and the time when large-scale expenditure is actually undertaken may be a matter of years – the planning and organising period will be a long one. Once the work is begun it will be difficult and costly to postpone or reschedule the work.

Major changes in taxation also take a considerable time to implement since they usually involve an immense amount of administrative work. Some degree of flexibility does exist in the form of the 'regulator' whereby the Chancellor of the Exchequer has power to vary the rates of indirect tax either way by up to 10 per cent between Budgets. Fiscal policy is a powerful instrument of control, but it is not very suitable for 'fine tuning' – major changes cannot be carried out more frequently than once a year.

The effectiveness of tax changes has also been seriously questioned in recent years. While tax reductions will certainly increase consumer spending their effectiveness as a stimulant to private investment is more uncertain. Much depends upon the climate of business expectations. Recent British experience has shown that tax reductions on quite a massive scale can fail to produce a major increase in private investment when businessmen are not optimistic about future prospects. Increases in taxes aimed at reducing aggregate demand may also affect aggregate supply if they have unfavourable effects on the incentives to work and invest. In this respect direct taxes such as income tax and profits tax are more likely to have such disincentive effects.

The use of indirect taxation as a means of restricting demand creates problems because such taxes affect prices and an increase in the general price level is almost certain to provoke reaction by organised labour. The proved effectiveness of union action in obtaining compensating wage increases when the cost of living increases now seriously weakens the effectiveness of an increase in indirect taxes as a means of restraining demand.

THE BALANCED BUDGET MULTIPLIER

An increase in government spending on goods and services financed by a corresponding increase in direct taxation will not leave national income unchanged. The fact that G and T will have increased by equal amounts does *not* mean that injections and withdrawals also increase by equal amounts. Even with a balanced budget, the State can still bring about an expansion of aggregate demand. This is possible because the expansionary effects of the government spending are greater than the downward multiplier effects of the increased taxation. If we assume a closed economy in which investment is autonomous and the MPC of the community is less than 1, it can be shown that an increase in government spending on goods and services financed entirely by direct taxation will lead to an increase in national income equal to the increase in G. In other words, in this particular case, the balanced budget multiplier is 1.

Suppose that the MPC is $\frac{3}{5}$, so that $\frac{2}{5}$ of any income received leaks out of the system (savings and taxation). Of each £1 of income received, therefore, 60p will be spent on domestic output and generate a further increase in income. Now if government spending on goods and services is increased by £1m. a sequence of spending rounds will be set in motion as follows.

$$£1\,000\,000 + £600\,000 + £360\,000 + \quad + \quad + $$

Income will eventually increase by £1 000 000 $(\frac{1}{1-\text{MPC}})$

$$= £1\,000\,000 \left(\frac{1}{1-\frac{3}{5}}\right)$$

$$= £2\,500\,000$$

If, at the same time, direct taxes are increased so as to raise revenue by £1 000 000, the immediate effect is to reduce disposable income by £1 000 000. Consumption spending will change initially by $-$ £600 000 and this will set up a downward multiplier sequence as follows.

$$- £600\,000 - £360\,000 - £216\,000 - \quad - \quad - $$

Income will eventually change by $-£600\,000\left(\dfrac{1}{1-\frac{3}{5}}\right)$

$= -£1\,500\,000$

The net change in national income therefore will be
£2 500 000 — £1 500 000 = £1 000 000

Income has increased by an amount equal to the change in government expenditure; i.e.

$$\Delta Y = \Delta G$$

The reason for this, of course, is that the government will be collecting in taxation some income which would otherwise have leaked out of the circular flow of income, but it will be spending all of this income. Some of the income now taken in taxation would have been saved had it remained in the hands of firms and households; now it will be spent.

If the government expenditure had been devoted to increased transfer payments the results would have been quite different. If the recipients of the transfer payments had the same MPCs as the taxpayers there would have been no multiplier effects. The group receiving an increase in disposable income would dispose of it in the same manner as the taxpayers would have disposed of it had they been allowed to do so.

FISCAL POLICY AND THE NATIONAL DEBT

The use of fiscal policy has important implications in respect of the national debt. Where the government is increasing its expenditure but not increasing taxation, or where it is holding its expenditure but reducing taxation, it must be obtaining the necessary funds by borrowing. It will be running a budget deficit, and, in so doing, increasing the national debt. Like any firm or household, a government cannot spend money it does not have. To finance a deficit the government must borrow by selling bonds to households, firms and banks.

Is the National Debt a Burden?

The existence of public debt gives rise to much confusion because many people view it in the same light as a private debt. When a firm or household borrows, it incurs a liability in that interest payments on the debt and its eventual repayment will involve a real loss of resources by that household or firm. When the government borrows internally (i.e. from domestic lenders) *the community as a whole* does not incur any liability. Interest payments to bondholders and the repayment of the debt simply involve transfers of funds from some members of the national community (taxpayers or purchasers of new bonds) to other members of *the same* community (holders of maturing bonds). The internal national debt may be compared to borrowing within a family. If one brother borrows £5 from another brother, the wealth and income of *the family* is in no way affected.

Any part of the national debt which is owed to foreign citizens, however, does constitute a national burden. Interest payments and capital repayments to foreigners represent claims on the resources of the home country – such payments can only be met by exports, thus leaving fewer goods for consumption at home.

Does borrowing transfer the burden?

A common misconception with regard to the national debt is that the burden of current government spending is in some way transferred to future generations. The construction of roadworks which is financed by selling bonds due for repayment, say, in 25 years' time will sometimes be condemned as 'unfair' because the repayment of this debt places the burden of meeting the cost of current road construction on a future generation of citizens. This is not the case at all. The real cost of constructing roads is borne by the community undertaking the work. The true cost of these roads is the desirable foregone alternative uses of the resources. Resources committed to building roads might have been used to build houses, power stations, technical colleges and so on. The opportunity cost of the new roads should be seen in terms of the sacrifice of alternatives incurred at the time the resources were committed. The debt inherited by future generations will not be a 'cost', but merely an instrument for transferring incomes within the community.

Can we have a perpetual public debt?

The government does not have to worry about paying off the existing debt since it makes no call on the nation's resources. When a particular loan is due for repayment the government can make a new issue of bonds and use the proceeds to repay the holders of the maturing bonds. The debt may last forever provided the government raises sufficient revenue to cover the interest payments. In this respect the total interest cost must be judged against the size of the GNP since this is the total tax base. Using this comparison it can be seen that the very large national debt of the UK is a smaller 'burden' than the very much smaller pre-war national debt.

Does a large national debt have any unfavourable effect?

A large national debt presents the government with the task of raising large sums of money to meet the interest charges. These charges have to be met out of tax revenues and they may be a cause of the tax burden reaching levels which have disincentive effects. Large annual interest payments may also lead to an 'undesirable' redistribution of income from the lower income groups to the higher income groups. This would be the case if bonds were held mainly by wealthier groups and taxes paid mainly by lower income groups.

Heavy government borrowing through large sales of securities is likely to drive down the prices of securities and raise the rate of interest. This could have harmful effects on investment.

If we assume that there is some upper limit to the tax burden that a government is prepared to impose, the heavy interest charges of a large national debt may restrict the government's ability to carry out or expand some of its programmes in such fields as education, roads, hospitals, etc.

10
Foreign Trade and National Income

Exports and imports

It is now time to introduce another sector into our model of the economic system. We have proceeded to this present stage of the analysis using a 'closed' system; that is, an economy with no flows of goods and services from within its borders to other nations and from other nations to itself. We are not likely to find such an economy in the real world, and we must now take account of the relationship between a country's international transactions and its national income.

In Chapter 3 it was explained that exports constitute an injection into and imports a leakage from the circular flow of income. We now have to examine the determinants of export and import demands just as, in previous chapters, we have looked at the determinants of consumption and investment demand.

The first point to make is that we are interested in the *creation* of demand and not the *meeting* of a demand. Imports help to meet a home demand, but they do not make any demand on home resources – they do not generate income at home. The demand for imports, therefore, is subtracted from total demand in order to calculate the demand for home resources that makes up the national expenditure. Exports, on the other hand, do contribute to aggregate demand for domestic output.

Export demand, for purposes of analysis, will be treated as autonomous; that is, it will be regarded as being determined independently of the level of income and output. It will be the state of world trade – the level of overall demand in world markets – which will determine the level of a country's exports. Movements in the real incomes of the importing countries and the extent of the barriers to international trade (tariffs, quotas, etc.) are obviously important factors in this respect. Exports will also be affected by the relationship between movements in home prices and movements in world prices and this is a point dealt with later in the chapter on Foreign Exchange.

Import demand by contrast will be related to movements in the national income. As domestic output rises or falls we must expect the imports of raw materials, semi-finished goods, fuels and machinery to rise and fall in the same manner. As incomes increase or decrease imports of finished goods will probably move in the same direction. Imports, too, will be affected by changes in the country's policy with regard to tariffs and other restrictions on international trade. The relationships between home prices and world prices is also an important determinant of the level of imports – again, this is a matter for subsequent discussion.

Equilibrium – an open economy

For an open economy the equilibrium equation, as demonstrated in Chapter 3, is

$$Y = C + I + G + (X - M)$$

The brackets placed round $(X - M)$ draw attention to the fact that the difference between them (which may be positive or negative) is the balance of payments on current account.[1] The equation may be re-arranged as follows,

$$Y - (C + I + G) = X - M$$

This shows that the balance of payments position is directly related to national income and domestic spending. The balance on current account is equal to the national income minus public and private spending on consumption and investment. There is, in fact, a two-way relationship. Changes in exports and imports affect income, and changes in income affect the balance of payments account. This is explained later. The equation above refers to the equilibrium level of income. It tells us the necessary conditions for planned spending to equal planned output at constant prices. The balance of payments introduces the idea of an *external* equilibrium where the expenditure on imports is exactly equal to the revenue from exports at constant prices. There does not appear to be any reason why the conditions necessary for internal equilibrium should produce an equilibrium situation in the current balance of payments. This may be clearer if we look at the equilibrium level of income from the point of view of planned leakages and planned injections.

Planned spending $= C + I + G + X - M$
Planned output ($=$ income) $= C + S + T$

[1]. The current account covers most transactions in goods and services, it does not include capital items. (See pages 200–1).

Equilibrium requires, $\quad C+I+G+X-M = C+S+T$; i.e.
$$I+G+X = S+T+M$$
(Injections)   (Leakages)

It can be seen that there is no need for any pair of injections and leakages to be equal. Savings need not equal investment, government spending need not equal taxation and imports do not have to be equal to exports. The requirement is that total leakages equal total injections. For example, the following values provide an overall equilibrium but there will be deficits on the government account and on the balance of payments.

$$\frac{I}{100} + \frac{G}{100} + \frac{X}{50} = \frac{S}{100} + \frac{T}{75} + \frac{M}{75}$$

In the long run a government must achieve an equilibrium situation in its international transactions and this will entail the use of measures explained in Chapter 18. In the meantime we should note that the task of obtaining equilibrium conditions in the markets for goods and services at home (i.e. stable prices), in the labour market (i.e. full employment) and in the balance of payments (i.e. $X = M$) will obviously present the government with major problems. It is most likely that the pursuit of any one objective, say, full employment, will conflict with the objectives of achieving the other goals.

Foreign trade and the multiplier

Just as we can project a schedule showing the relationship between consumption and income so it is possible to project the relationship between imports and income. If we relate movements in imports to movements in income we obtain the propensity to import or the import function. The *average propensity to import* will give us the level of imports associated with any given level of income and may be represented by

$$\frac{M}{Y}.$$

The marginal propensity to import (MPM or *m*) will tell us what proportion of any increase in income will be spent on foreign goods and services and may be represented by

$$\frac{\Delta M}{\Delta Y}.$$

For example, if, when Y increase by 100, M increases by 10, the marginal propensity to import is 0·1. This MPM is an important concept since it indicates how much of a change in our national income will be transmitted to other countries through variations in our purchases of their goods and services. Similarly exports will be dependent upon the rest of the world's propensity to import.

The marginal propensity to import is a part of the marginal rate of leakage and, as such, will influence the size of the multiplier. Moving from a closed economy to an open economy has introduced a further leakage (imports) and hence reduced the size of the multiplier. The import leakage means that a smaller proportion of any increase in income is now passed on to generate further increases in income. The multiplier expression must now be adjusted to take account of imports.

$$\text{The multiplier} = \frac{1}{s + t + m} = \frac{1}{\text{marginal rate of leakage}}$$

where s = marginal propensity to save
t = marginal rate of taxation
m = marginal propensity to import.

Note that this multiplier applies to any autonomous change in spending. Thus, changes in the levels of exports, investment, government spending or autonomous consumption will all have multiplier effects on income. The introduction of an international sector has given us a *foreign trade multiplier* since changes in exports will have magnified effects on national income.

Planned Injections and Leakages

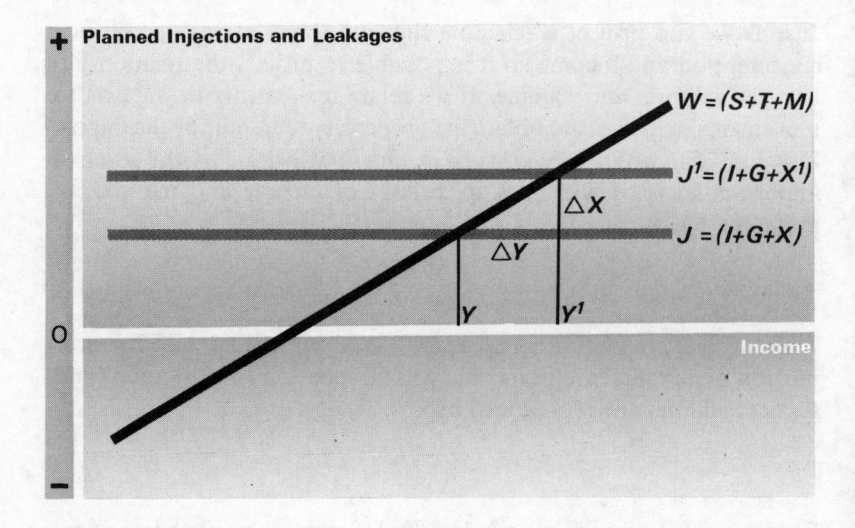

$W = (S+T+M)$
$J^1 = (I+G+X^1)$
$J = (I+G+X)$

Fig. 23

Income changes and foreign trade

Fig. 23 shows the aggregate leakages and aggregate injections for an open economy. W is the total leakage function and is obtained by adding together the schedules of savings, imports and taxation revenues. J is the total injection function obtained by adding together the investment, exports and government spending schedules. Initially equilibrium is at OY, where planned injections equal planned leakages. Now assume that exports increase X to X'. The planned injection line rises to J' and the new equilibrium level of income will be established at OY'. The multiplier, which is the eventual increase in income divided by the originating change in spending, is

$$\frac{\Delta Y}{\Delta X}$$

Several important points emerge from the foregoing analysis.

(*a*) Earlier analysis established that one of the main causes of instability in the level of income and output was the variability of private investment. The introduction of foreign trade has now added another cause of instability–changes in the level of exports. The foreign trade multiplier is a most important relationship for those countries, such as the UK, where exports account for a large percentage of total output (i.e. 20 per cent or more). A rise in exports, through the multiplier effects, can be the cause of a boom, or begin a recovery from a depression, but, equally, a substantial fall in exports can lead a country into a recession.

(*b*) Changes in the level of income will have effects on the balance of payments. The nature of these effects depends on whether the change in income arises from internal or external causes.

If there is a rise in export sales, due, perhaps, to trade liberalisation measures, domestic incomes will rise until the increase in planned injections has been matched by an increase in planned leakages. But only part of this increase in leakages will be due to increased imports; savings and tax revenues will also rise. Hence exports will rise by more than imports and the balance of payments will 'improve'. Conversely the multiplier effects of a fall in exports would reduce income, and imports would fall by a smaller amount than exports. The balance of payments would 'worsen'.

When the change in income arises from causes which have a domestic origin, the effects will be different. An increase in income brought about by a rise in investment would worsen the balance of payments position since imports would increase while exports remain unchanged. The reverse would apply when investment (or government spending) fell.

(*c*) The analysis so far has ignored foreign repercussions of changes in country's exports and imports. If a country is a major exporter and

MACRO-ECONOMICS

The Multiplier Round

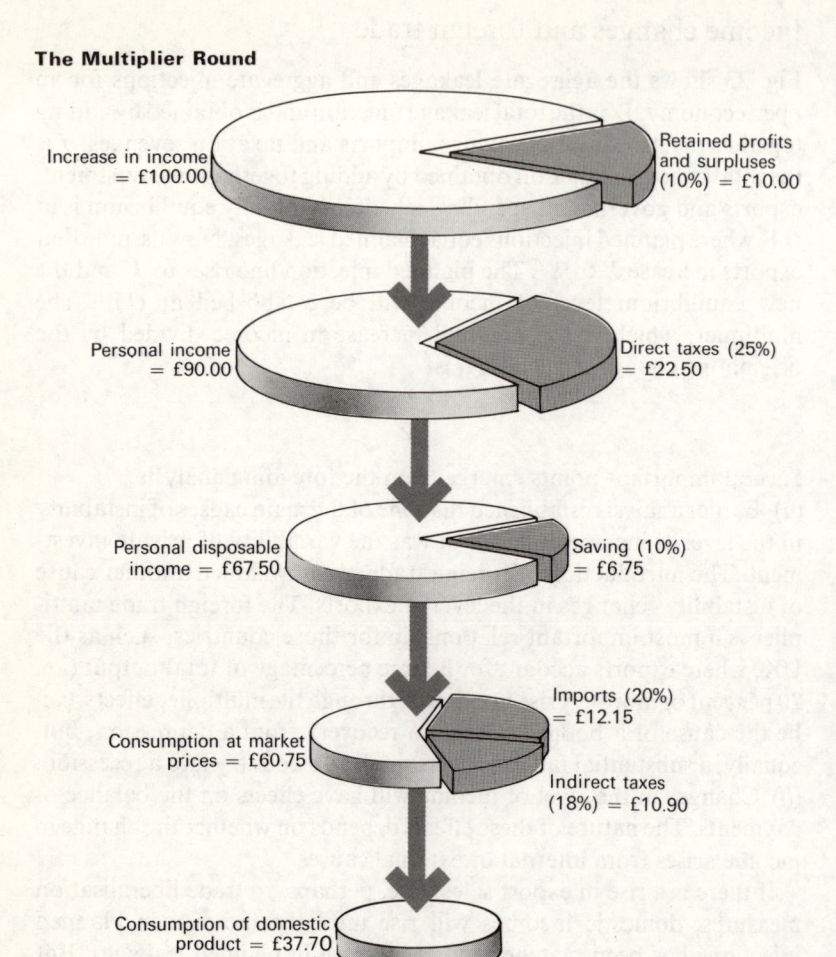

Increase in income = £100.00 — Retained profits and surpluses (10%) = £10.00

Personal income = £90.00 — Direct taxes (25%) = £22.50

Personal disposable income = £67.50 — Saving (10%) = £6.75

Consumption at market prices = £60.75 — Imports (20%) = £12.15; Indirect taxes (18%) = £10.90

Consumption of domestic product = £37.70

Fig. 24

importer (i.e. it accounts for a significant proportion of world trade), there are likely to be 'feedback' effects whenever its exports or imports change substantially. Let us suppose that A stands for the home country and B for the rest of the world (or those countries trading with A).

Now assume that A's income increases due to an increase in G or I or in the propensity to consume. The rise in A's income will bring about an increase in its imports from B, and B's income will rise. This increase in B's income will tend to increase its imports from A. There will be a further rise in A's income and a further rise in its imports from B. And so the process will go on until the multiplier effects have worked themselves out. The dimensions of these effects will depend upon the respective marginal propensities to import and the extent of the savings and taxation leakages. Again we must note that these changes can work in the opposite direction with multiplier effects downwards.

There will also be international feedback effects arising from any autonomous changes in A's exports. Suppose A's exports increase due to an increasing preference for its products in B. Now the rise in B's imports will cause its income to fall and this will tend to reduce its imports from A. But the initial increase in A's exports will have increased its income through the multiplier process and hence its imports from B will tend to increase. This will offset to some extent the fall in B's income. The ultimate effects will again depend upon the marginal propensities to consume and the magnitude of the multiplier effects in each sector.

We have ignored the possibilities of changes in the prices of exports and imports and concentrated on the real income effects. In fact, price changes are an important element in the adjustment processes in the real world. In certain circumstances countries will resort to a deliberate policy of changing the relative prices of exports and imports (devaluation) rather than allow an equilibrium situation to arise through income changes. We discuss these matters in Chapter 18.

Fig. 24 gives very approximate values for the multiplier round in the British economy. What is the value of the multiplier?

Some worked examples

1. In a closed economy, net investment expenditure is at the rate of £1000m. APC = MPC = 0·8 of *disposable* income. There is no government activity.

   (*a*) Calculate the equilibrium level of national income.

   (*b*) What would be the effect of increasing the rate of investment by 50 per cent?

   (*c*) In the original situation, an income tax is introduced which raises £500m. per annum, and this is accompanied by government expenditure of £500m. per annum. What is the new equilibrium level of national income? Assume that APS, MPS and the level of investment remain unchanged.

MACRO-ECONOMICS

ANSWER

(a) In equilibrium, Planned Savings = Planned Investment
and, therefore, Savings = £1 000m.
Now, APS = MPS = $\frac{1}{5}Y$; i.e. $\frac{1}{5}Y$ = £1 000m.
therefore, Y = £5 000m.

(b) The multiplier in this economy, $= \frac{1}{\text{MPS}} = \frac{1}{\frac{1}{5}} = 5$;

therefore, $\Delta Y = 5\Delta I$
$= 5 \times £500\text{m.}$
$= £2 500\text{m.}$

New level of national income = £5 000m. + £2 500m.
= £7 500m.

(c) In equilibrium, Planned injections = Planned leakages;
i.e. $I + G = S + T$,
i.e. £1 000m. + £500m. = S + £500m.
therefore, S = £1 000m.;
but $S = \frac{1}{5}$ disposable Y;
therefore, $S = \frac{1}{5}(Y - T)$
£1 000m. = $\frac{1}{5}(Y - £500\text{m.})$
$\frac{1}{5}Y$ = £1 100m.
Y = £5 500m.

ALTERNATIVE TREATMENT

(a) In equilibrium $Y = C + I$
$= 0.8Y + £1 000\text{m.}$
$0.2Y = £1 000\text{m.}$
$Y = £5 000\text{m.}$

(c) In equilibrium $Y = C + I + G$
$= 0.8(Y - £500\text{m.}) + £1 000\text{m.} + £500\text{m.}$
$= 0.8Y + £1 100\text{m.}$
$0.2Y = £1 100\text{m.}$
$Y = £5 500\text{m.}$

2. In an imaginary economy, there is no foreign trade and no government activity. APC = MPC = $\frac{4}{5}$. In equilibrium, consumption expenditure is £20 000m.

   (a) What is the level of investment expenditure?
   (b) What is the value of the multiplier?
   (c) Suppose investment spending remains unchanged but both APC and MPC fall to $\frac{3}{5}$. What is the new equilibrium level of national income?

FOREIGN TRADE AND NATIONAL INCOME

ANSWER
- (a) Since APC = MPC = $\frac{4}{5}$, then APS = MPS = $\frac{1}{5}$.
  Since this is a closed economy with no government activity,
  $$C = \tfrac{4}{5}Y;$$
  i.e. £20 000m. = $\tfrac{4}{5}Y$
  and Y = £25 000m.,
  therefore S = £5 000m.
  Now in equilibrium $S = I$
  therefore, $\underline{I = £5\,000\text{m.}}$

- (b) The multiplier is the reciprocal of the sum of the leakages (expressed as fractions of income). In this case the only leakage is savings.
  $$\text{The multiplier therefore} = \frac{1}{\text{MPS}} = \frac{1}{\frac{1}{5}} = 5$$

- (c) When APC and MPC fall from $\tfrac{4}{5}$ to $\tfrac{3}{5}$, then APS and MPS increase from $\tfrac{1}{5}$ to $\tfrac{2}{5}$.
  The immediate effect is that
  $$\text{Planned Savings} > \text{Planned Investment.}$$
  But adjustments of income will take place until
  $$\text{Planned injections} = \text{Planned leakages; i.e.}$$
  $$\text{Investment} = \text{Savings}$$
  Since investment does not change,
  $$£5\,000\text{m.} = S.$$
  But $S = \tfrac{2}{5}Y$;
  therefore, $\underline{Y = £12\,500\text{m.}}$

3. In a closed economy in equilibrium, consumption spending is at the rate of £75m. per annum and investment spending is £25m. per annum. Consumption is a constant proportion of *disposable* income whatever the level of income. There is no government activity.

   (i) (a) What is the level of national income?
   (b) What is the value of the multiplier?

   (ii) Assume now that government activity is undertaken. Taxation is levied at the rate of $\tfrac{1}{5}$ of all incomes and government spending on goods and services is held at £25m. per annum.
   (a) What is the new level of national income?
   (b) What is the budget surplus or deficit?

(iii) Assume now that international trade is introduced into the situation (ii). Exports are constant at £25m. per annum, and imports are always $\frac{1}{6}$ of consumption spending.
   (a) What is the new level of national income?
   (b) What is the surplus or deficit on the balance of payments?

ANSWER

(i) (a) In a closed economy in equilibrium (no government activity),
$$Y = C + I$$
$$Y = £75m. + £25m.$$
$$\underline{Y = £100m.}$$

(b) Since C is a constant proportion of disposable Y,
$$APS = MPS = \tfrac{1}{4};$$
therefore, Multiplier $= \dfrac{1}{MPS} = 4$.

(ii) (a) In equilibrium, Injections = Leakages;
i.e. $\qquad I + G = S + T \qquad$ (1)
Now $S = \tfrac{1}{4}$ of disposable income, and disposable income $= \tfrac{4}{5}Y$, therefore $S = \tfrac{1}{4} \times \tfrac{4}{5}Y = \tfrac{1}{5}Y$.
Substituting in 1 we have
$$£25m. + £25m. = \tfrac{1}{5}Y + \tfrac{1}{5}Y$$
$$\tfrac{2}{5}Y = £50m.$$
$$\underline{Y = £125m.}$$

(b) Taxation $= \tfrac{1}{5}Y = £25m.$
Government spending $= £25m.$
Budget is balanced.

(iii) (a) This could be tackled in the same way as (ii) (a) by equating injections and leakages. For purposes of illustration we use a slightly different approach.
In equilibrium $Y = C + I + G + (X - M) - - -$ (1)
Now $C = \tfrac{3}{4}$ disposable income
$$= \tfrac{3}{4} \times \tfrac{4}{5}Y \quad = \tfrac{3}{5}Y$$
and $M = \tfrac{1}{6}C = \tfrac{1}{6} \times \tfrac{3}{5}Y = \tfrac{1}{10}Y.$
Substituting in (1) we have
$$Y = \tfrac{3}{5}Y + 25 + 25 + 25 - \tfrac{1}{10}Y$$
$$\tfrac{1}{2}Y = £75m.$$
$$\underline{Y = £150m.}$$

(b) Exports $= £25m.$
Imports $= \tfrac{1}{10}Y = £15m.$
Balance of Payments surplus $= £10m.$

Questions on Chapters 3–10

ESSAY QUESTIONS

1. Define the terms 'average propensity to consume' and 'marginal propensity to consume'. In what ways and for what reasons would you expect the APC and MPC of an advanced economy to differ from those of an underdeveloped economy? **(JMB)**

2. What are the factors which encourage or reduce private investment? **(AEB)**

3. What effect do variations in interest rates have on industrial investment? **(O & C)**

4. The following data describe the consumption function for a particular economy.

Income £m.	Consumer expenditure
2 000	750
2 500	1 125
3 000	1 500
3 500	1 875
4 000	2 250

    (*a*) Calculate the value of the APC when income is £3 500m. and the MPC at levels of income from £2 500 to £4 000m.

    (*b*) If net investment increases by £40m., by how much would you expect the level of national income to increase?

    (*c*) Explain the assumptions involved in using the consumption function above and outline what additional factors are relevant in determining the effects of new investment on the level of income. **(JMB)**

5. How are savings and investment made equal to each other in an economy which is almost always fully employed? **(O & C)**

6. Is the level of investment the sole determinant of national income in the UK? **(C)**

7. Explain the concept of 'an equilibrium level of income' and demonstrate why decisions to save must be matched by decisions to invest. **(C)**

8. 'The Keynesian theory of employment rests wholly on the relations between Saving and Investment'. Discuss. **(S)**

9. What is the Multiplier? How is it related to the marginal propensity to consume? **(L)**

MACRO-ECONOMICS

10. How important to the economy are the concepts of the accelerator and the multiplier? **(AEB)**

11. Describe and assess the acceleration principle as an explanation of the behaviour of private investment. **(L)**

MULTIPLE CHOICE QUESTIONS

1. National Product is at its equilibrium level when,
    (a) It is identical with National Income.
    (b) It is equal to aggregate demand.
    (c) It is at that level which requires full employment of resources.
    (d) Realised saving is equal to realised investment.

2. As used by economists the word 'Saving' means
    (a) The same thing as investment, since $S = I$ when the economy is in equilibrium.
    (b) The amount of money people do not spend in the course of some given time period.
    (c) That part of income not spent on consumption during some given time period.
    (d) The total amounts of money which people have accumulated in the past.

3. Only one of the following counts as investment in the macro-economic sense. Which is it?
    (a) A company's purchase of land on which to build a new factory.
    (b) An individual's purchase of newly issued shares in a company.
    (c) A business firm's purchase of a new car for use by its salesmen.
    (d) An individual's purchase of government securities.

Questions 4, 5 and 6 are based on the following data which refers to a two-sector economy

National income	Planned consumption	Planned investment
1 000	1 100	200
1 200	1 200	200
1 400	1 300	200
1 600	1 400	200
1 800	1 500	200

4. What is the value of the MPS as income changes from 1 400 to 1 600?
    (a) 0·125
    (b) 0·14
    (c) 0·875
    (d) 0·5

5. What is the equilibrium level of income?
   (a) 1 200
   (b) 1 400
   (c) 1 600
   (d) 1 800

6. If, at the equilibrium level of income, investment were to increase by 100, what would be the eventual increase in National Income?
   (a) 100
   (b) 200
   (c) 300
   (d) 400

7. The downward slope of the marginal efficiency of capital schedule means that
   (a) The lower the rate of interest, the less will be the inducement to invest.
   (b) As investment increases, it will cause the rate of interest to fall.
   (c) Firms are being prevented from investing as much as they would like because of the limited availability of credit.
   (d) At higher rates of interest, there are fewer investment projects on which the expected profitability exceeds the cost of financing them.

Questions 8 and 9 are based on the following information. In a two-sector economy, $Y = 1 000$, I is constant, $C = 900$ and the economy is in equilibrium. The community's propensity to save now increases to 0·2.

8. The effect of this change will be to cause income to
   (a) Remain unchanged.
   (b) Fall by 200.
   (c) Fall by 100.
   (d) Fall by 500.

9. The effect of the change will be to cause realised saving to
   (a) Remain unchanged.
   (b) Fall by 100.
   (c) Increase by 100.
   (d) Increase by 200.

10. A consumption function is such that APC = MPC at all levels of income. Which of the following statements will apply to a graphical representation of such a function?

(i) The consumption function must be a straight line.
(ii) The consumption function must pass through the origin.
(iii) The consumption function must be straight line at 45° to the horizontal axis.
   (a) (i) only.
   (b) (ii) only.
   (c) (iii) only.
   (d) (i) and (ii) only.

11. When the market rate of interest is 10 per cent, the present value of £121 due in two years' time will be,
   (a) £96·8
   (b) £100
   (c) £100·5
   (d) £101

12. Of each extra £1 of income received, the community plans to spend 50p on consumption, save 25p, and 25p will be taken in taxation. Imports account for one-fifth of consumption spending. What is the value of the multiplier?
   (a) 2
   (b) 1·66
   (c) 1·43
   (d) 4

13. In a two-sector economy the saving and investment functions are as follows,

$$S = -10 + 0·2Y$$
$$I = -3 + 0·1Y$$

What will be the equilibrium level of income?
   (a) 70
   (b) 80
   (c) 90
   (d) 100

14. A change in the rate of spending on exports causes a change in income as follows

$$100 + 70 + 49 + 34·3 + + + + +$$

The value of the multiplier is
   (a) 0·3
   (b) 0·7
   (c) 1·43
   (d) 3·33

PROBLEMS

1. In the UK personal disposable income is roughly four-fifths of GNP. The MPC out of personal disposable income is about three-quarters. Imports are usually about 30 per cent of GNP. What is the approximate value of the multiplier?

2. In Country X, consumption spending is always equal to one half of personal disposable income. The government is currently spending £150m. on goods and services; its revenue is derived from a tax of 20 per cent on factor incomes. Investment is £250m., Exports are £100m. and Imports are one-fifth of Gross National Product. There are no indirect taxes, undistributed profits or transfer payments. Calculate,
    (i) The equilibrium level of Gross National Product.
    (ii) The current level of consumption.
    (iii) The budget surplus or deficit.
    (iv) The balance of payments position.

11
Money

Money is a subject which has received little or no attention in the preceding sections of this book. This is, perhaps, rather surprising since the earning and spending of money are essential, and most obvious features of economic activity in the modern world. A study of the monetary aspects of the economy has been postponed until now, not because they are of minor importance, but because it is the production and distribution of goods and services which determine the material welfare of the community. Similarly it is the stock of real assets—houses, factories, machines, stocks of materials and the like—which comprise the real wealth of the nation. We have concentrated on *output*, because it is the flow of *real* income per unit of time which determines the standard of living.

Nevertheless we know that income and wealth are given monetary values, and it is this which gives rise to the common confusion between money and wealth. Money gives people a command over goods and services, and its possession represents wealth to the extent of the goods and services for which it can be exchanged. It is not money itself but the things it will buy which represent wealth. A nation cannot grow richer by creating more money since money is merely *a claim* to things and, if there are not more things to claim, more money cannot make people as a whole better off.

Money is one of man's greatest inventions—it is impossible to imagine the operation of an advanced industrial society without money. The fact that all but the most primitive societies make use of money indicates that it is an essential tool of civilisation. Money has been described as a kind of lubricant which greatly increases the efficiency of the economic mechanism. If this were its only role we would not have to spend long on the subject; it would only be necessary to describe its effectiveness as a device for facilitating exchange transactions. Unfortunately money is not a passive or neutral element in the economic system. It exerts a powerful independent influence on the real macroeconomic variables we have been discussing—consumption, investment, exports, imports, national income and employment. The importance of money's role has led to the development of a large specialised branch of economics—monetary theory—which attempts to explain how changes in the demand for and supply of money can affect the economy. In this and succeeding chapters we shall look at the role of money in a modern economy. It is a subject which is currently the basis of a major controversy among economists.

The nature of money

In spite of the fact that everyone uses money there is still some disagreement on the meaning of the word. Most people would define money in terms of coins and banknotes. Yet this definition would not include the most important form of money in advanced societies, namely, bank deposits. The problem of definition has two aspects. First we must try to define the functions of money and then decide which things are, in fact, carrying out these functions. There is broad general agreement on the functions of money.

Money may be functionally defined as anything which is generally acceptable in exchange for goods and services. To serve efficiently as money an object does not have to have any distinguishing characteristics, neither does it have to possess intrinsic value. At one time or another all sorts of things have served as money—shells, beads, salt, precious metals, and even cigarettes. The most advanced form of money—bank deposits—are no more than a series of marks on a computer tape. 'Money is as money does'—anything can be called money if people *accept it* as money. Money has four important functions.

(*a*) A MEDIUM OF EXCHANGE

Money is unique since it is the only asset which will be taken in exchange by every transactor at all times. In a 'money economy', money serves as a medium of exchange and one side of almost every transaction takes the form of a money payment.

Where there is no money, goods have to be exchanged under a system of *barter*. This is a cumbersome system in which exchange transactions are dependent upon a double coincidence of wants. It is necessary to find someone who not only wants what you have to offer, but also happens to be offering what you are seeking. This is not very likely to occur where there are many traders and many commodities in the market. To satisfy one's wants, it may be necessary to go through a whole series of intermediate transactions. As specialisation developed and more and more commodities had to be bartered the more complicated and inconvenient the barter system became. The introduction of money eliminated the restrictions of the barter system. Goods and services are exchanged for money and the money can then be exchanged for whatever things are required. The system works as long as everyone will accept the means of payment, whether it be scraps of paper, precious metals or entries in bank ledgers. For anything to serve as a medium of exchange it must possess *general acceptability*.

(*b*) A UNIT OF ACCOUNT

Even when goods were exchanged under barter it is likely that man was using some common standard of value so that exchange values could be determined. This is probably the oldest function of money. When the values of economic goods are expressed in terms of some common measure we have what is known as a unit of account. In our own society all goods have money prices and we can easily determine the value of one good in terms of another by comparing prices.

(*c*) A STORE OF VALUE

For many reasons people may not wish to consume the whole of their current output. They may wish to save some of the fruits of their labours for future consumption or for other purposes. Money has advantages as a store of value. It does not suffer any physical deterioration, it costs nothing to store and it can easily and quickly be turned into other forms of wealth. Furthermore its *money value* is certain. When a person decides to hold his wealth in the form of goods or property he has assets of uncertain money value. In periods of inflation, however, money is a poor store of value since its exchange value is falling.

(*d*) A STANDARD OF DEFERRED PAYMENTS

Modern economies make great use of credit. Payments for goods and services are not made when the things are acquired, but at some later date. Many articles are bought on hire purchase terms where the purchaser enjoys the use of the article while paying for it by instalments. Such contracts involving future payments are made in terms of money, because, whatever his future needs, the creditor will be able to satisfy them with money. Since no one can foresee, with certainty, his future needs, a promise to make future payments in terms of any other commodity is not likely to be so acceptable.

Liquidity and near money

The general acceptability which is an essential characteristic of money also makes it the most *liquid* of assets. Liquid assets may be defined as those assets which can quickly and easily be exchanged for money without loss. Money, therefore, by definition is 100 per cent liquid. It is common practice to classify assets according to their degree of liquidity. Some assets such as houses, factories and specialised machinery are illiquid. When the holders of such assets wish to exchange them for money, they will have to meet marketing costs, they may have to wait for a considerable time before a buyer appears and they cannot be certain of the value such assets will realise. Assets can be arranged in descending order of liquidity from whatever is serving as a medium of exchange, through time deposits in various financial institutions, highly marketable securities, and so on, right down to physical properties of various kinds. This brings us to the question of what assets should be counted as money.

On the basis of our original definition, that money is whatever is generally acceptable in exchange for goods and services, we must include notes and coin (currency) and bank deposits held on current account.[1] Although time deposits cannot be transferred by cheque, banks will often transfer funds from deposit to current accounts without insisting on the seven days' notice. Some authorities will only accept the first group of assets as money whereas others include all bank deposits as money.

There is, however, a group of assets identified as *near-money* or *quasi-money* because they are extremely liquid. Building society deposits, National Savings deposits and similar holdings can be exchanged easily and quickly for money without loss. This is an important group of assets because a person's ability to spend depends not only on his holdings of money but also on the extent of his holdings of near-money assets.

The U.K. money supply

The problems of defining *the content* of the money supply is illustrated by the fact that the official statistics for the UK contain two different series (there were three until very recently). These two definitions are,

M_1 = notes and coin in circulation plus sterling current account bank deposits held by the private sector.

M_3 = notes and coin in circulation plus all deposits (current and time deposits) held by UK residents in both the public and private sectors, whether denominated in sterling or other currencies.

1. Bank deposits are of two kinds, current accounts and deposit accounts. Money held in current accounts can be withdrawn on demand and is transferable by cheque. Money in time deposits can only be withdrawn after 7 days' notice and cannot be transferred by cheque.

Table 6. *UK Money Supply   October 1977*

	£m	
Notes and coin in circulation	6 939	
Sterling current accounts	14 564	
		21 503 = M^1
Sterling deposit accounts		
Private sector		20 072
Public sector		1 253
UK residents' deposits in other currencies		3 988
		46 816 = M^3

Source: Bank of England Quarterly Bulletin, December 1977

Which definition of the money supply should be used depends upon the purpose of the enquiry. If the question relates to the relationship between the supply of money and aggregate demand, M_3 would seem to be the appropriate definition. If we are concerned with the liquidity aspects of money then M_1 seems the more relevant definition.

Table 6 brings out the fact that notes and coin are the 'small change' of the system. Bank deposits are by far the most important constituent of the money supply. The table probably understates the importance of bank deposits since virtually all large transactions are made by transferring bank deposits (i.e. payments are made by cheques).

The evolution of money

COMMODITIES AND COINS

Although a wide variety of things have served as money, almost everywhere man has eventually adopted metallic money by making use of the precious metals, gold and silver. Gold and silver are generally acceptable in all parts of the world no matter what stage of economic development has been reached. Their general acceptability as money derives from the fact that they have an intrinsic value – they are wanted for their own sake. The precious metals are a convenient monetary medium since they are portable – a small quantity commands a high value in exchange for goods. They are not subject to deterioration – an essential requirement if money is to serve as a store of value. They are divisible – the subdivision of a quantity of gold or silver into a number of smaller quantities does not diminish the total value.[1] They are easily recognisable and can fairly easily be produced to some uniform standard of fineness. Gold and silver are limited in supply – there is little or no danger of sudden massive increases in supply destroying their value.

Originally used by weight (the British pound derives its name from a pound of sterling silver), the metals were eventually used in the form of coins. It is a great convenience when each piece of metal carries some identification which can be accepted as a guarantee of its weight and fineness.

PAPER MONEY

The next important step in the development of money was the use of paper money. The banknote developed from the practice of depositing gold for safekeeping in the goldsmith's strongrooms – a practice which was common in the days when these were virtually the only places available for the safe storage of valuables. Since gold was the main form of money, payments for value received involved the withdrawal of gold from the goldsmith and the transfer of this gold to the creditor who would no doubt proceed to return it to the goldsmith's vault. It was much more convenient to use a goldsmith's receipt as a form of payment. The buyer would simply endorse such a receipt, making it payable to the seller. Claims to gold, therefore, came to be used in lieu of gold itself. As this practice became more widespread, depositors would ask the goldsmiths for a number of receipts of convenient denominations. Twenty £5 receipts would be more useful than a single receipt for £100. When these receipts, or claims to gold, came to be made payable to bearer, we have the first fully fledged banknote. Banknotes at this stage of development were *fully backed by gold* and convertible on demand into gold.

The next stage in the evolution of money came when paper money was only *fractionally backed by gold*. As confidence in paper money increased and people made greater use of it in settling their debts, it became unnecessary to maintain 100 per cent gold backing for the note issues. Every day some depositors would be converting their notes into gold, but, equally, others would be depositing gold. The goldsmith-bankers discovered that any given stock of gold would support an issue of banknotes greatly in excess of the monetary value of the gold. Convertibility could still be maintained so long as only part of the note issue was presented at any one time for conversion into gold. When bankers began to issue banknotes of greater value than the gold held in their strongrooms, we have the origin of bank lending – the unbacked

---

1. This is not the case with some other things which have served as money, such as cattle and hides.

part of the note issue was used to make interest-yielding loans. The value of that part of the note issue not supported by an equivalent value of gold is known as a *fiduciary issue*. The bankers who had originally made a charge for holding deposits could now start to attract deposits by offering depositors an interest payment. The two stages may be illustrated by using a simplified picture of the banker's balance sheet:

Stage 1. A fully backed note issue.

Liabilities		*Assets*	
Notes issued	£1 000	Gold	£1 000

Stage 2. A fractionally backed note issue.

Liabilities		*Assets*	
Notes issued	£2 000	Gold	£1 000
		Loans	£1 000

In the early 19th century, paper money was issued by most banks; the commercial banks issued their own notes backed by their own reserves and the Bank of England issued notes backed by the nation's gold reserves. All these notes were freely convertible into gold and the nation was said to be on a gold standard. The adoption of a fractionally backed note issue presented the bankers with a great temptation to 'over-issue' banknotes, and the history of banking contains many examples of banks which were imprudent, over-issued, and then found themselves unable to meet unexpectedly large demands for gold. Such bank failures meant that depositors were holding worthless bits of paper and confidence in the banking system was seriously weakened. During the second half of the 19th century, as a result of the Bank Charter Act of 1844, the function of note-issuing was gradually removed from the commercial banks and vested in the central bank – the Bank of England.

FIAT OR TOKEN MONEY

After the First World War, most nations abandoned the gold standard and nowadays paper money is not convertible into gold (although the wording on our banknotes has not changed!). Paper money is valuable today simply because it is generally acceptable and the loss of convertibility has not damaged its efficiency as a medium of exchange. Our paper money is fiat or token money. The note issue is entirely fiduciary (i.e. backed by government securities and not by gold), and our coins no longer contain a commodity value of precious metal equal to their monetary value. The important feature of fiat money is that the supply of such money is directly under the control of the government which can create as much or as little money as it wishes. When a currency is convertible its supply is linked to the nation's stock of gold, and this governments cannot fully control.

BANK DEPOSITS

Although the note-issuing function was gradually restricted to the central bank, the commercial banks retained the power to create money. In all advanced societies the major part of the money supply consists of bank deposits. Notes and coin are issued by the central bank and are known as currency, but bank deposits are a creation of the commercial bank sector. Earlier banks issued notes which were claims to gold, modern banks issue (create) bank deposits which are claims to currency. Bank customers do not usually use the cumbersome system of withdrawing currency when paying their bills; they prefer to use the more convenient system of transferring bank deposits by means of written instructions to their bankers. These written instructions which circulate so freely are the familiar cheques. A cheque is not money, but an order to a banker to transfer money from one account to another – the money consists of the bank deposit. The same problem regarding over-issue remains. Since bank customers have the right to convert their deposits into currency, banks must keep some safe proportion of currency to deposits.

The creation of bank deposits

THE CONVERTIBILITY OF BANK DEPOSITS

Deposit banking is based upon the principle that all depositors will not simultaneously exercise their right to withdraw their funds. It is an obligation of a bank to encash its deposits, if asked to do so, by providing notes and coin to the holders of bank deposits. On any day some of the customers will be withdrawing cash from the banks, but, at the same time, other customers will be paying it in. Since such receipts and payments of cash are not likely to balance each other exactly, banks will need to keep some reserves of cash.

These reserve holdings of cash comprise notes and coin held in the branches of the various banks together with the banks' current account balances at the Bank of England. These latter balances are included in the banks' cash reserves since they can be exchanged for notes and coin on demand. The cash reserves of the banks will be kept to some agreed minimum since holdings of cash earn no income. The cash balances expressed as a percentage of deposits is known as the *cash ratio*. The size of this ratio is determined by experience. If there is a large measure of public confidence in the banking system, the bank deposit will be the most important form of money, most payments will be made by cheque and quite small cash reserves will be adequate to meet demands for cash.

This is the situation in most developed countries. One further reason why banks are able to operate with such relatively small reserves of cash is the availability of extremely liquid assets which the banks hold as secondary reserves.

Securities such as Treasury Bills (see page 138) are earning assets which are secure and readily convertible into cash with little risk of capital loss. In addition the banks arrange things so that a proportion of their loans are repayable on demand or at very short notice.

This fractional reserve system may be seen in the balance sheets of the commercial banks. A combined balance sheet appears as Table 7 on page 143. This balance sheet shows the banks' total assets and liabilities on a particular date. The liabilities of a bank are its debts to its customers in the form of bank deposits. These deposits are claims on the bank since it can be called upon to convert such deposits into currency. The bank's assets consist of its claims on other parties. Bank assets consist of notes and coin (claims on the Bank of England), various interest-bearing securities, and its loans to firms and households (who have a legal obligation to repay).

The current situation is that all banks in the UK have to maintain a *reserve assets ratio* whereby they must hold certain specified liquid assets to a value of not less than $12\frac{1}{2}$ per cent of their sterling liabilities. This ratio is described in some detail on pages 141–3.

A CASH BASE THEORY

Bank deposits come into being in a variety of ways:

1. When someone makes a deposit of currency he will acquire a bank deposit equal in value to the cash received by the bank. No money has been created at this stage – a member of the public has merely changed the form in which he holds money. Both sides of the bank's balance sheet have increased – assets by the amount of notes and coin received, and liabilities by the amount of the deposit.
2. When a bank makes a loan, the amount is credited to the borrower's account. A deposit is created and the money supply increases by the amount of the loan. Again there are balancing entries on both sides of the bank's balance sheet. The new account (i.e. the deposit) increases the liabilities' side, while the borrower's promise to repay increases the figure for advances on the assets' side.
3. When a bank buys securities and pays for them with cheques drawn on itself, its assets increase by the value of the securities and, when the cheques are paid in, the sellers of the securities acquire bank deposits.

It is principally through activities described in (2) and (3) above that bank deposits are created – both are examples of bank lending. It is important to grasp the point that a deposit is created when a bank makes a loan, because measures to control the money supply will be designed to act on the banks' ability to lend. Since the interest charged on loans is the major source of the banks' income they have every incentive to maximise their lending.

We can now turn to the banking mechanism itself and, with the help of simplified models, try to understand how the process of deposit creation takes place, and the limitations on the banking system's ability to create deposits. Later we shall see how the monetary authorities are able to control the lending activities of the commercial banks.

In the examples which follow we are assuming,
(a) the public's demand for cash is constant,
(b) the supply of cash is determined by the government,
(c) the banks have only two kinds of assets; cash which earns no income, and loans which do,
(d) the banks maintain a minimum cash ratio of 10 per cent.

A single bank system

A bank system which consists of a single monopoly bank with many branches could carry out an immediate expansion of its loans on the basis of any additional cash it might receive. Thus, if such a bank acquired an addition to its cash reserve of, say, £100 000, it could proceed to expand its lending activities until its deposits had increased by £1 000 000. We are assuming that the public do not wish to hold any more notes and coin so that none of the additional cash would leave the bank and the addition to the money supply is entirely in the form of bank deposits. The development may be shown by noting the changes in the bank's balance sheet.

1. The situation immediately following the new deposit of cash.

Liabilities		Assets	
Deposits	£100 000	Cash	£100 000

The bank has acquired an asset in the form of additional cash, and a liability in the form of a deposit.

2. The situation after the bank has extended its lending activities.

Liabilities		Assets	
Deposits	£100 000	Cash	£100 000
	£900 000	Loans	£900 000
	£1 000 000		£1 000 000

The bank has now acquired additional assets in the form of claims against borrowers (i.e. loans) and new liabilities in the form of additional deposits. Note that a cash ratio of 10 per cent has permitted the monopoly bank to carry out an expansion of deposits equal to

$$\frac{100}{10}$$

times the amount of the addition to its cash reserve. This model is too simple, however, because, in the UK and many other countries, the banking system is made up of a number of separate banking firms.

A multi-bank system

When there are several banks in the banking system, the process of deposit creation is more complex. The first problem is that when cheques are drawn on Bank A, payable to a person with an account in Bank B, it is not possible to settle this transaction by means of internal book entries as is the case with a single bank. Bank A now owes money to Bank B. These difficulties are overcome by making use of *a clearing house* such as the London Clearing House. Every day there are thousands of cheques drawn on one bank, payable to persons with accounts in other banks, but most of these payments will offset each other, Example: Mr X, with an account in Lloyds, pays £500 to Mr Y with an account in Barclays. Mr A, with an account in Barclays, pays £400 to Mr B with an account in Lloyds. All such cheques will be sent to the clearing house where the daily totals of inter-bank indebtedness are arrived at by offsetting mutual claims. It is a simple matter for the banks to make a single payment, using their accounts at the Bank of England to cover the final amounts outstanding. In the example given above there will be a net transfer of £100 from Lloyds to Barclays. What is important is that any payment from one bank to another involves a transfer of bankers' deposits at the Bank of England. These deposits form part of the commercial banks' cash reserves so that any movement in these deposits changes the levels of the individual bank's cash balances, and hence its cash ratio.

When a single bank in a multi-bank system expands its lending, some of the deposits will be paid to households and firms holding accounts at other banks. Now if these other banks are not expanding their lending, the bank making the new loans will be losing some of its cash reserves to these other banks at the daily clearings. It is this possibility of losing cash to other banks (or to the public if they decide to hold more cash) which determines the individual bank's lending policy. Using very simplified balance sheets we can trace out the process of deposit creation in a multi-bank system. We assume that an individual bank (A) has received a deposit of notes and coin amounting to £100 000.

1. The immediate effect on the balance sheet of Bank A.

Liabilities		Assets	
Deposit	£100000	Cash	£100000

Bank A will not wish to remain in this very liquid but unprofitable position. It has excess cash reserves of £90000 and it will proceed to put these reserves to work – if creditworthy borrowers are forthcoming. Let us assume that it lends £90000 to White and Co.

2. The situation after Bank A has loaned £90000 to White and Co.

Liabilities		Assets	
Deposits	£100000	Cash	£100000
	£90000	Loans	£90000
	£190000		£190000

The bank has not made the loan in cash, but simply credited the sum of £90000 to the account of White and Co. Bank deposits have increased by £90000, but so have the bank's assets in the form of a claim against White and Co. Note that the cash reserves are still well in excess of the required 10 per cent. It appears that the bank would be perfectly justified in making many more loans, but it knows that White and Co. have asked for a loan because they intend to spend the money. The next step reveals why the bank did not proceed to grant more loans. White and Co. purchase goods from Brown and Co. to the value of £90000 and pay for them by cheque. Brown and Co. have an account in a different bank (Bank B), and duly pay this cheque into their account. The balance sheet of Bank A now looks like this:

3. Balance sheet of Bank A after White and Co. have spent the money

Liabilities		Assets	
Deposits	£100000	Cash	£10000
		Loans	£90000
	£100000		£100000

The transfer of bankers' deposits (at the central bank) from Bank A to Bank B (Brown and Co.'s bank) has reduced Bank A's cash reserve to £10000, while the spending of £90000 has removed the deposit formerly held by White and Co. Bank A is now in equilibrium – its cash reserves are equal to 10 per cent of its deposits. But the banking system as a whole is not in equilibrium. As a result of the payment to Brown and Co., and the subsequent transfer of funds from Bank A, Bank B has excess cash reserves.

4. Bank B's balance sheet following the transfer of funds from White and Co. to Brown and Co.

Liabilities		Assets	
Deposits	£90 000	Cash	£90 000

Bank B now has excess cash reserves and will feel free to expand its loans by £81 000. Suppose it makes a loan of this amount to Black and Co.

5. Bank B's balance sheet following the loan to Black and Co.

Liabilities		Assets	
Deposits	£90 000	Cash	£90 000
	£81 000	Loans	£81 000
	£171 000		£171 000

If Black and Co. now spend the money they have borrowed by making payment to a firm with an account in a third bank (Bank C), Bank B will be in equilibrium.

6. Bank B's balance sheet following expenditure of loan by Black and Co.

Liabilities		Assets	
Deposits	£90 000	Cash	£9 000
		Loans	£81 000
	£90 000		£90 000

It should be apparent that this process will continue, and, as a result of the initial deposit of cash, there will be an expansion of bank lending in the form of a diminishing series,

$$£100\,000 + £90\,000 + £81\,000 + £72\,900 + + + +$$

The sum of this series is £1 000 000, which means that the ultimate effect on total deposits is exactly the same as that for the single bank system. A cash ratio of 10 per cent implies a multiplier of 10.

We must note that the multiplier effect works both ways. Any reduction in the banks' holdings of cash will lead to a fall in the level of bank deposits much greater than the fall in the cash balances.

If banks always maintain cash reserves equal to some given proportion of their deposits, then their ability to create money in the form of bank deposits is determined by the amount of cash they can acquire. If we express the cash ratio as r, the level of bank deposits as D and the amount of cash held by the banks as C then,

$$D = \frac{1}{r} \times C$$

Thus with a cash ratio of 8 per cent and cash reserves of £1m.,

$$D = \frac{1}{\frac{8}{100}} \times £1\text{m.} = £12\cdot5\text{m.}$$

The effect of any change in the cash reserves may be expressed in the form,

$$\Delta D = \frac{1}{r} \times \Delta C$$

Some qualifications

The process outlined above is obviously a very simplified picture and in practice it does not work out quite like this. It is true that when a single bank makes a loan it is likely to lose cash to other banks, but a rise in the cash reserves is likely to affect all banks at the same time. They will all be making loans so that inter-bank indebtedness will tend to cancel itself out. The individual bank is not likely to lose cash to other banks unless it pursues a lending policy very much out of line with these other banks.

The explanation given above assumed that bank customers tended to hold a constant amount of cash. Again, this is not very realistic since both cash and bank deposits are used as a means of payment. It is much more likely that an increase in the money supply, especially if it is associated with an increase in income, will lead to an increase in the public's demand for cash. A cash leakage at each round of lending and spending will substantially reduce the size of the multiplier.

Our explanation also assumed that banks stick fairly close to the given cash ratio, but if banks choose to maintain cash reserves above the conventional (or, in some countries, legal) cash ratios, an increase in cash reserves may have little or no effect on the level of bank deposits

A RESERVE ASSETS RATIO

The theory outlined above presupposes a systematic link between the cash base and the supply of bank credit. The theory simply states that if an economy has certain characteristics and the banking system works to certain rules, then bank deposits will bear a definite relationship to the banks' cash reserves.

The mechanism outlined is not necessarily confined to a cash base. A fractional reserve system could operate whenever banks keep to a fixed ratio between deposits and some group of specified assets. If this is so then any change in the banks' holdings of these assets would lead to a multiple change in the level of bank deposits. If D represents total deposits, R represents bank's holding of reserve assets and r represents required ratio of reserves to deposits then

$$D = \frac{R}{r} \quad \text{and} \quad \Delta D = \frac{1}{r} \times \Delta R$$

Thus, if banks are obliged to maintain reserve assets equal in value to 10 per cent of their deposits, then total deposits are limited to a maximum equal to ten times the value of the reserve assets.

Holdings of reserve assets equal to £100m. would enable them to maintain deposits of £1 000m.

$$D = \frac{£100m.}{\frac{10}{100}} = £1\,000m.$$

The British banking system is now subject to a restriction of this kind. It is obliged to maintain a minimum reserve assets ratio of $12\frac{1}{2}$ per cent. This is fully explained on pages 141–3.

12
The Structure of Banking

The central bank

The Bank of England is the central bank for the United Kingdom and is publicly owned. It is responsible for the supervision of the entire banking system and for the implementation of the government's monetary policy. For this purpose it is under the control of the Treasury, but the Governor often displays an independence of mind on economic policy. The main functions of the central bank are summarised below.

(a) It is the sole note-issuing authority for England and Wales. Some banks in Scotland and Northern Ireland still retain the right to issue their own notes. The note issue is a liability of the central bank.

(b) It is the bankers' bank. The clearing banks (i.e. the 'Big Four', Lloyds, National Westminster, Barclays and the Midland plus two smaller banks) keep accounts at the central bank. These accounts are used for settling inter-bank indebtedness and, since they are current accounts, the deposits are counted as part of the banks' cash reserves.

(c) It is the government's bank and holds the government's two main accounts, the Exchequer Account and the National Loans Fund. Government borrowing and lending pass through the National Loans Fund, while tax revenues and current spending pass through the Exchequer Account.

(d) It carries out various international monetary duties on behalf of the government. It manages the Exchange Equalisation Account and operates in the foreign exchange market to influence the external value of the pound. These functions are discussed in Chapter 18.

(e) It is the lender of last resort. This function is also discussed later, but it means that the Bank of England will always ensure that the banking system can meet its obligations to pay cash to its customers.

(f) It manages the National Debt. The Bank is responsible for floating new loans, the repayment of maturing loans and the payments of interest to current holders of government securities. It is concerned with the problem of managing the money and capital markets so

that it is not inconvenient or too costly for the Exchequer to borrow money.
(g) It carries out the government's monetary policy.

The Bank of England is divided into two departments, the Issue Department and the Banking Department, each of which produces a weekly return. A specimen is reproduced below.

The Issue Department weekly return Nov. 16 1977 £ million

Liabilities		Assets	
Notes issued:			
In circulation	7 338	Government securities	6 490
In Banking Dept.	12	Other assets	860
	7 350		7 350

The liabilities of this department consist of the note issue. The notes in circulation are those held outside the Issue Department, by households, firms and banks. Some notes are held in the Banking Department in order to meet the demands of the clearing banks. The assets consist almost entirely of government securities so that the note issue is wholly fiduciary. Any increase in the note issue is accompanied by an increase in the Issue Department's holdings of securities.

The Banking Department weekly return Nov. 16 1977 £ million

Liabilities		Assets	
Deposits:			
Public	20	Government securities	1 709
Bankers'	292	Discounts, Advances	236
Other Accounts	613	Other Securities	154
Special Deposits*	1 171	Notes and Coin	12
	2 096		2 111

(Note: The two sides do not balance because certain small items have been omitted.)
* See page 144

LIABILITIES

Public deposits represent the balance in the government's accounts. The amount shown is misleadingly small since there is a very large daily turnover amounting to perhaps several hundred million pounds in these official accounts. Large balances are not allowed to accumulate – any surplus is used to reduce the government's borrowing requirements.

Bankers' deposits are those of the clearing banks, and other banks.

As already explained, these balances are treated as cash by the banking system.

Other accounts comprise the accounts of overseas central banks, international monetary institutions and the current accounts of a small number of private customers.

ASSETS

Government securities comprise longer dated securities, Treasury Bills and temporary loans to the government known as 'Ways and Means' advances. The central bank buys and sells securities in the open market in order to influence the liquidity position of the banking system (see page 160).

Discounts and advances are loans to the London Money Market and are discussed in the next section.

Other securities are any other securities of whatever sort and include market purchases of commercial bills (explained in next section).

Notes and coin are held as stock in trade to meet the demands of the Bank's customers. The notes shown here are a counterpart of the item shown as a liability in the return from the Issue Department.

The London money market

This is the market for short and very short term loans and centres around the activities of a small number of discount houses which are members of the London Discount Market Association. A number of institutions play a part in the operations of the London Money Market including the Bank of England, the head offices of the clearing banks, the merchant banks, the discount houses and the London branches of overseas banks. Their work principally involves dealings in certain important instruments of credit, namely, Treasury Bills, bills of exchange (commercial bills) and short-dated government bonds.

THE BILL OF EXCHANGE

This is a kind of IOU – a promise by one person to pay a fixed sum of money to another person on a given date. It is used to finance all forms of trade and has a very important history in the finance of international trade. The buyer of goods will sign such a bill acknowledging his indebtedness to the seller and promising to make payment in, say, three months time. The seller may now hold the bill for three months and then present it to the buyer for payment. More likely he will require funds immediately. In this case he may get the bill *accepted* by a London Acceptance House (usually one of the well-known merchant banks) which, by endorsing the bill, guarantees payment should the buyer of the goods default. Once accepted by a house of high repute, the bill becomes a marketable asset and may be *discounted* by a London Discount House. Discounting is simply the procedure of buying a security for less than its face value (the value of the bond on maturity). The difference between the price paid by the Discount House and the face value of the bill may be seen as a payment of interest for a loan. The seller of the goods by discounting his bill has now received payment for his goods, while the buyer has three months in which to meet his obligations. An alternative system enables certain traders to obtain acceptance credits with a bank so that bills of exchange covering their purchases can be drawn directly on this bank which accepts the bills in its own name. Bills drawn on and accepted by London banks of high standing are known as 'fine trade bills'.

THE TREASURY BILL

These are short-term government securities which normally run for 91 days and are the regular method of providing short-term government finance. They are gilt-edged securities and hence immediately marketable – no acceptance procedure is required. The Bank of England conducts a weekly sale of Treasury Bills on an auction basis. Each week it asks for tenders from prospective buyers of the bills to be offered in the following week. These bills are then allotted to the highest bidders. By attracting the highest possible bids for these bills, the government is, in effect, borrowing at the lowest possible rate of interest. Bids are submitted by the Discount Houses, by bill brokers outside the Association, by accepting houses and overseas banks. The clearing banks do not submit tenders on their own account.

SHORT-DATED BONDS

In practice the Discount Houses deal in bonds which have less than two years to run.

The work of the discount houses

The London Discount Houses borrow money from the commercial banks and other financial institutions (e.g. branches of overseas banks) and then use this money to discount commercial bills and Treasury Bills. By promising to repay their loans 'at call' or very short notice, they obtain their funds at very low rates of interest. Discount houses earn their income from the difference between the rates of interest they pay on their loans from the banks and the rates they charge for discounting bills. If a discount house buys (discounts) a three-month bill face value £100 at £98·50 and holds it until it matures, it has charged a rate of interest of approximately 6 per cent per annum for a three-month loan. The bill will be redeemed at its face value. Discount houses do not usually hold all the bills until they mature. Some they sell to the commercial banks in order to meet the banks' demands for liquid assets. The commercial banks buy (rediscount) these bills and, by holding them until they mature, earn an income from the difference between the prices they pay for them and their values on maturity. In buying these bills the banks obtain parcels of bills having a spread of maturities which will match the banks' foreseeable commitments in regard to future outflows of cash. Since some bills fall due for repayment each day, banks can replenish any loss of cash by purchasing bills of a smaller total value than those maturing.

Discount houses are at risk in the sense that a large proportion of the money they use for discounting bills is subject to immediate recall or to repayment at very short notice. When the banks' cash reserves are under pressure they will react by calling some of their money market loans. The discount houses may then find themselves in a position where they are obliged to make immediate repayment of funds which they have 'locked up' in bills. When only one or a few banks are making such calls, the discount houses may be able to make repayment by new borrowings from other banks. When all banks are 'calling', however, the discount houses must approach the lender of last resort – the Bank of England. The Bank will always meet the discount houses' demands for money, but it will set its own price for such a loan. This price is known as the *minimum lending rate*[1] and is the rate of interest which the central bank charges for rediscounting first class bills or for making loans against the security of such bills. First class bills are either Treasury Bills, or commercial bills carrying two signatures acceptable to the Bank.

When the market is 'forced into the Bank', that is, the discount houses are obliged to borrow from the lender of last resort, they are probably losing money, because the minimum lending rate is normally higher than current rates of interest. For this reason it is often known as the penal rate. If they are borrowing at the minimum lending rate the institutions will be paying a higher rate of interest for these loans than they are earning on their own lending. Since they know that they can, at any time, be forced into the Bank of England, discount houses will always relate their own lending rates to the minimum lending rate in such a way that potential losses will be minimised. There is, in other words, a market link between the rate charged by the central bank and other money market rates. If the Bank of England does not wish to exert any upward pressure on market rates of interest it can provide

1. Minimum lending rate was originally fixed at $\frac{1}{2}$ per cent above the market rate on Treasury Bills. In May 1978 this formula was abandoned and MLR is now directly administered by the authorities.

loans to the money market 'through the back door'. This means that the Bank is prepared to supply funds at current market rates of interest. Loans at minimum lending rate are said to be provided 'through the front door'.

The loans to the money market provide the commercial banks with an extremely liquid asset which enables them to maintain a much smaller cash ratio than would otherwise be the case. The discount houses also provide the banks with a very useful service by allowing them to purchase bills of varying maturities to suit their particular liquidity requirements. They also provide a service to the monetary authorities since they guarantee to take up the whole of the weekly Treasury Bill issue. Normally the rate offered by the discount houses is lower than bids from other sources so that they only obtain a proportion of each week's issue.

Under the new banking regulations which came into effect in September 1971 the discount houses have agreed to keep at least 50 per cent of their funds in public sector securities.

The commercial banks

The major commercial banks are the London Clearing Banks–those banks which are members of the London Clearing House. Their number has been reduced by the mergers of 1968 and 1969, from eleven to six and the business is dominated by the 'Big Four', Barclays, Lloyds, the Midland and the National Westminster. The commercial banks are privately-owned profit-seeking enterprises and have three main sources of income:

(*a*) the interest they charge on their loans,
(*b*) the charges they make for operating current accounts, and
(*c*) the commissions they earn on a variety of services such as the provision of foreign exchange, acting as trustees for investment funds, and acting as executors for the disposal of the estates of deceased persons.

The special importance of the commercial banks lies in their ability to create bank deposits. This main activity of the banks may be seen as a process of providing an extremely liquid asset (money) in exchange for illiquid assets. When the bank makes a loan it provides the borrower with a claim against the bank–the borrower has the right to withdraw money from the bank. The deposit created by the loan is a liability to the bank but an asset to the borrower. The loan, however, provides the bank with a claim against the borrower–a claim which is usually supported by some kind of collateral security or charge on the borrower's property. The loan is an asset to the bank but a liability to the borrower. The main

THE STRUCTURE OF BANKING

assets of a bank are its loans (claims on others) while its liabilities consist of deposits (claims on the bank)

It is the assets of the bank which generate its profits and since banks are private-enterprise institutions, they will attempt to maximise these profits. In addition to this obligation to their shareholders, however, banks have obligations to their depositors. They must be able to meet all depositors' demands for cash. Bankers, therefore, are presented with a dilemma; they have to reconcile two conflicting objectives, *liquidity and profitability*. The obligation to meet all demands for cash means that they must maintain an adequate supply of cash and other very liquid assets. But liquid assets are not so profitable as illiquid assets since the longer term and more risky loans carry higher rates of interest than short-term and more secure loans. The profitability of an asset tends to vary inversely as its liquidity. Cash, the most liquid asset, earns no income so that banks will try to maintain cash reserves at some absolute minimum.

RESERVE ASSETS

In order to ensure that commercial banks could always meet depositors demands for notes and coins they were, until 1971, obliged to maintain cash reserves equal to at least 8 per cent of their deposits and liquid assets (including cash) equal to a minimum of 28 per cent of their deposits. These liquid assets consist of very short-term loans which can be easily and quickly converted into cash. In 1971 the Bank of England introduced its 'Competition and Credit Control' measures for controlling the activities of the banking sector. The 8 per cent and 28 per cent ratios were abandoned. The current situation is that all banks must hold certain specified reserve assets (liquid assets) whose aggregate value must not fall below $12\frac{1}{2}$ per cent of their eligible liabilities.

Eligible liabilities consist of the short-term sterling deposits of the banking system including the ordinary person's current and deposit account balances. They also include the large deposits placed with the banks for fixed periods of up to two years and all deposits of whatever periods from UK banks as well as deposits against which banks have issued certificates of deposit (see page 148). Just as banks can raise funds by the issue of certificates and borrowing from other banks, so they can buy certificates of deposit and lend to other banks. These latter sums are deducted from their liabilities and inter-bank transactions and certificates of deposit are counted on a *net* basis.

Reserve assets (see Table 7) have been defined by the authorities to include:

i. Balances with the Bank of England (other than Special Deposits)
These are the current account balances held at the central bank by the

commercial banks. These balances together with the notes and coins held in the banks' tills make up the banks' cash reserves, but note that the notes and coins do *not* count as reserve assets.

ii. Money at call

This item comprises all sterling funds loaned to the discount houses and other borrowers such as jobbers and Stock Exchange brokers. These loans are repayable on demand.

iii. Treasury Bills

These are bought (i.e. re-discounted) from the discount houses when they have about half or less of their life to run.

iv. Local Authority Bills

These are short-term securities (similar to Treasury Bills) issued by UK local authorities.

v. Commercial bills

These are bills of exchange eligible for re-discount at the Bank of England. Such bills can be counted as reserve assets up to a maximum value of 2 per cent of eligible liabilities. The banks buy these bills from the money market (see page 139).

vi. Government securities with less than one year to run to maturity.

The $12\frac{1}{2}$ per cent reserve assets ratio applies to all banks in the UK other than the National Giro and the Discount Houses. Finance Houses must maintain a reserve assets ratio of 10 per cent. Apart from the limitation on the value of commercial bills counting as reserve assets, there are no restrictions on the distribution of funds among the different types of reserve assets. The London Clearing Banks, however, have agreed to maintain balances at the Bank of England equal to $1\frac{1}{2}$ per cent of their eligible liabilities.

The importance of the reserve assets ratio lies in the fact that it provides the Bank of England with the ability to control bank lending and hence the money supply. The assets classified as reserve assets are those whose supply can be regulated by the central bank. They are mainly public-sector assets and where private-sector assets have been included (e.g. commercial bills) steps have been taken to limit the amounts which can be counted as reserve assets.

Although banks can always replenish any loss of cash by converting some of their liquid assets (e.g. calling back some of the money market loans), the point is that this would still leave the total of such assets less than it was before the depletion of the cash reserves. If the banks were operating at or near the $12\frac{1}{2}$ per cent limit before the loss of cash occurred, they will be obliged to reduce the level of total deposits in order to restore the $12\frac{1}{2}$ per cent reserve assets ratio. The credit base of the banking system is now $12\frac{1}{2}$ per cent of sterling deposits and, in theory, this implies a multiplier of 8. If the banks stick rigidly to the $12\frac{1}{2}$

per cent ratio then any changes in their holdings of reserve assets will lead to changes in total deposits eight times as great. If, however, the banks choose to maintain holdings of reserve assets substantially greater than the required minimum, a loss of reserve assets may not cause them to contract bank lending. On the other hand, they may not be able to expand deposits to the legal maximum when they obtain additional reserve assets if the supply of willing and credit-worthy borrowers is inadequate.

THE COMMERCIAL BANKS' ASSETS AND LIABILITIES

Table 7. *The London Clearing Banks–combined balance sheet* 19 October 1977 £m

Liabilities		Assets	
Sterling deposits		Notes and coin	727
Demand and time deposits	25 339		
Certificates of deposit	1 275	*Reserve Assets*	
		Balances at	
Other Currency Deposits		Bank of England	356
Demand and time deposits	5 165	Money at call	1 107
Certificates of deposits	285	Treasury bills	460
		Other bills	489
Capital and other		Gov. securities	
liabilities	6 554	(0 to 1 year)	526
		Total reserve assets	2 938
		Other Sterling Assets	
		Market loans (other than reserve assets)	
		Discount market and UK banks	2 833
		Local authorities	388
		Certificates of deposit	652
		Bills and other loans	487
		Investments	2 365
		Advances	16 778
		Special deposits	649
		Miscellaneous assets	5097
		Other Currency Assets	5 704
	38 618		38618

Source: *Bank of England Quarterly Bulletin,* December 1977.

Table 7 shows us how the banks reconcile their various objectives (liquidity, profitability and security).

Liabilities

The liabilities of the commercial banks comprise their deposits in sterling and other currencies together with the certificates of deposit issued by the banks in acknowledgement of the longer-term deposits made with them.

Assets

The notes and coin held in the banks' tills and the reserve assets have been explained earlier.

Liquid Assets:

Cash, money market loans and bills are the traditional liquid assets of the banking system. Loans to the discount houses, brokers in the money market and dealers in the Stock Exchange can be recalled immediately (money at call) or are due at short notice. The banks also hold Treasury Bills, commercial bills and government securities nearing maturity which can be sold in the money market or to the Bank of England at any time with little risk of capital loss. The certificates of deposit shown on the assets side of the balance sheet are those which the banks have purchased (i.e. discounted).

Illiquid Assets:

The most profitable but least liquid assets are investments and advances. *Investments* consist almost entirely of gilt-edged securities. They will be arranged so that some of them mature every year and the greater part of them will have less than five years to run to maturity. These investments give banks a degree of flexibility in their asset structure since the securities can be sold at any time on the Stock Exchange. Heavy sales of such securities, however, might drive down their prices and involve the banks in capital losses.

Advances are the most profitable of the banks' assets and provide a most important source of short-term capital to industry and commerce. Interest is charged at varying rates according to the credit standing of the borrower and the size and duration of the loan. Until recently the banks operated a cartel agreement whereby they all charged the same base rate to the most credit-worthy borrowers and paid the same rate of interest on time deposits. This agreement was abandoned in 1971 and banks are now free to set their own base rates. The traditional bank loan is of a fairly short duration but is subject to renewal. In recent years banks have been much more willing to negotiate medium- and longer-term loans.

Special deposits consist of funds held in a special account at the Bank of

THE STRUCTURE OF BANKING

England and are a kind of 'frozen asset'. These deposits are called from the banks when the monetary authorities wish to reduce the reserve assets held by the banking sector. The function of special deposits is more fully explained on page 162.

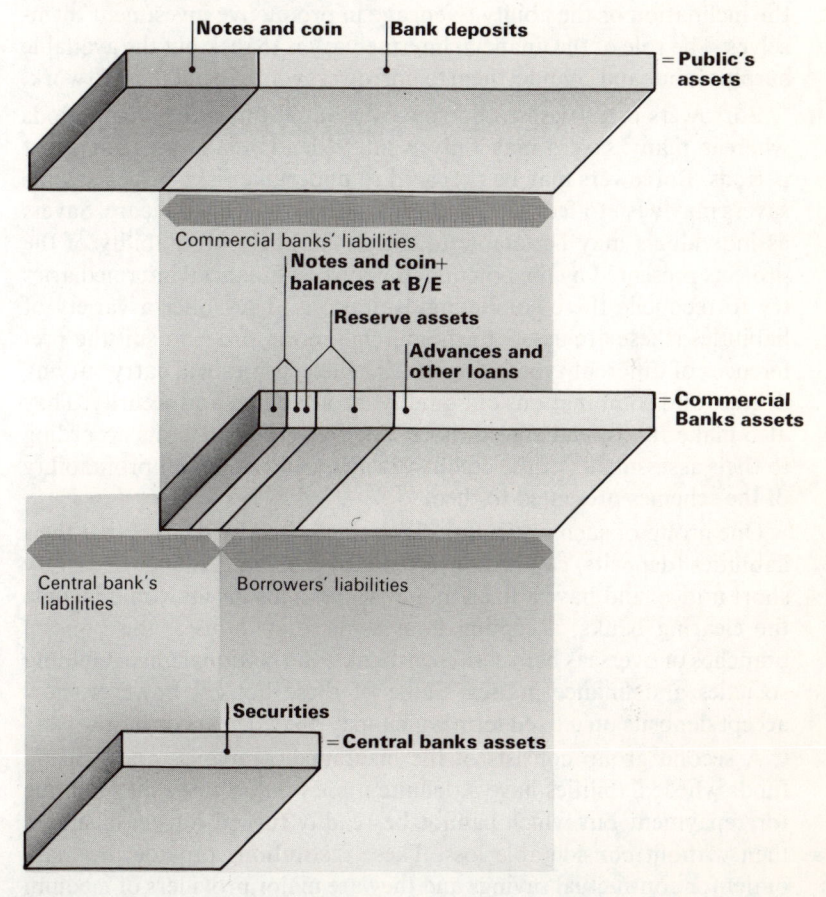

The Structure of the Money Supply

Fig. 24A

Other financial intermediaries

Financial intermediaries is a term generally applied to those institutions whose business consists mainly of accepting deposits from people with funds to spare and making loans to those in need of funds. Banks are the most important type of financial intermediary, but they are only one type and it is important to see the banks in the context of financial institutions as a whole rather than in isolation.

Were it not for the activities of financial institutions, potential borrowers wishing to spend more than their income would not find it easy to borrow and potential savers wishing to spend less than they receive would find difficulty in lending. Savers probably do not have the inclination or the ability to engage in productive investment themselves. The role of the financial intermediary is to seek out the available surplus funds and channel them to borrowers who can put them to work.

Borrowers often wish to borrow substantial funds for long periods whereas many savers may only want to lend small sums for short periods. Borrowers may be prepared to undertake risky projects while savers may wish to feel confident that their loans will be secure. Savers as individuals may be unable to assess the likely profitability of the projects presented by the potential borrowers. Financial intermediaries try to reconcile these conflicting aspirations. They offer a variety of liabilities (these are assets to the purchasers) in order to suit the preferences of different types of lender. Their securities will carry varying degrees and combinations of liquidity, profitability, and security. They also make funds available to borrowers on different terms according to their assessments of the creditworthiness and potential profitability of the schemes presented to them.

One group of such institutions is characterised by the fact that their liabilities (deposits) can be converted into cash on demand, or at very short notice, and have a fixed money value. This group would include the clearing banks, accepting houses, discount houses, the London branches of overseas banks, savings banks, the National Giro, building societies and finance houses. Some of these houses, however, now accept deposits on a fixed term which may be two years or more.

A second group consists of life insurance companies and pension funds whose liabilities have a definite money value when they fall due for repayment but which cannot be readily turned into cash before then without considerable loss. These institutions provide the main outlet for contractual savings and they are major providers of medium and long term loans for industry, commerce, the government and property development.

The third group of financial intermediaries are those whose liabilities may change in value from day to day. They are the investment and unit trusts.

SECONDARY OR PARALLEL MONEY MARKETS

Most of the financial institutions mentioned above have been established for many years carrying out activities which were, in the main, ancillary to the work of the clearing banks. They competed with the banks to the extent that they were all bidding for the savings of households and firms, and, in the provision of short-term loans, several of them (accepting houses, finance houses and overseas banks) were directly competitive with the commercial banks. Nevertheless up to the early 1950s clearing bank deposits accounted for about 80 per cent of total bank deposits[1] in Britain. By the mid-1970s this proportion had fallen to about 20 per cent.

One explanation for this development is the fact that, traditionally, the clearing banks have abstained from price competition between themselves and with other financial institutions. A cartel agreement on interest rates was in operation until September 1971. In the rapid development of important new credit markets during the 1960s, the clearing banks' reluctance to compete on the basis of price (i.e. the rate of interest) restricted their growth as financial intermediaries relative to that of other financial institutions.

A series of developments contributed to the growth of the 'secondary' or 'parallel' markets in credit. In 1958 both hire purchase undertakings and the banks themselves were set free from restrictions on lending and rapid expansion followed. In the same year a widespread movement towards convertibility made possible an expansion of deposits of foreign currency. A few years earlier government restrictions had forced local authorities to borrow in the open market. These changes led to a greater awareness of alternative sources of finance and of the comparative yields available to lenders. The trend towards larger business units was also making managements more conscious of the possibilities of more profitable uses for the company's liquid resources.

Another important reason for the rapid growth of secondary markets was the series of credit squeezes imposed during the 1960s. The effects of these, as we shall see later, were felt mainly by the clearing banks and their restricted ability to lend caused borrowers to seek alternative sources of funds. Finance houses, accepting houses, and overseas banks were able to meet this demand at interest rates significantly higher than those charged by the commercial banks. In times of boom and inflation it is the availability of credit rather than its price which is important.

The secondary banks were not subject to the constraints of the 8 per cent cash and 28 per cent liquidity ratios required of the clearing banks. By working to comparatively low liquidity ratios, the secondary banks have been able to lend a higher proportion of their deposits than was possible for the clearing banks. This is one of the reasons why these banks could afford to attract deposits by offering higher rates of interest than those offered by the clearing banks. Another reason for this ability to offer depositors a higher rate of interest arises from the economies of

---

1. Including foreign currency deposits.

scale achieved by 'wholesale' banking. For many banks in the secondary system, the minimum amount they will accept is £50 000 and they attract large deposits from industrial and commercial companies by offering particularly attractive rates of interest for fixed-term deposits. Sterling certificates of deposit, one of the newer instruments of credit in these markets, have a minimum denomination of £50 000 with a maturity in the range 3 months to 5 years. Dealings in Eurodollars, another important activity of secondary banks, are limited to large amounts, usually $1m. or more.

Local authorities now raise large sums in the money market, much of it on a seven-day basis. They also borrow by issuing short-term securities (similar to the Treasury Bill). The merchant and overseas banks are particularly active in the market for local authority borrowing and the local authority bills are attractive to the discount houses since, under certain conditions, they are eligible for rediscount at the Bank of England. Finance houses provide funds mainly for hire purchase and instalment credit schemes.

The market in *Eurodollars* has grown rapidly in recent years. The merchant banks (or accepting houses) and the London offices of overseas banks (particularly American banks) are the main dealers in this market. Eurodollars are dollars deposited with commercial banks outside the USA. The large market in borrowing and lending these dollars resulted from the continuing deficits in the US balance of payments which increased the supply of foreign-held dollar balances (see page 216), and from monetary restrictions in the USA which made it more profitable to hold dollars abroad. Eurodollars are used mainly to finance international trade.

The most recent of the new money markets deals in *sterling (and dollar) certificates of deposit*. These take the form of fixed deposits for which a certificate is issued. The certificate is negotiable so that holders, if they wish, can redeem these deposits by selling them to third parties. The discount houses are particularly active in providing a market for certificate holders who wish to sell (i.e. discount) their certificates before maturity.

The direct participation of the clearing banks in these secondary markets has been very small, but, by taking over finance houses and establishing subsidiaries, they have acquired a large indirect stake in the markets.

In direct competition with the clearing banks as a payments system are the National Giro and the current account facilities of the Trustees Savings Bank. Deposits with these institutions possess qualities hitherto confined to deposits in the joint stock banks – they serve as money rather than as claims to money. Clearing bank deposits transferred to these banks will be invested in government securities with a consequent decline in clearing bank deposits and liquid assets.

It has been necessary to mention these financial intermediaries because, as subsequent discussion will show, their existence has important implications for monetary policy.

13
The Demand for Money – Liquidity Preference

This chapter is concerned with the demand for money 'to hold'; that is, the demand for money as an asset. As a means of holding wealth, money has certain advantages. Its money value is certain and it is the most liquid of assets. It has a serious disadvantage, however, in that it earns no income. In this sense it is a sterile asset. Keynes said that the demand for money, which he defined as *liquidity preference,* was made up of three elements: the transactions demand, the precautionary demand, and the speculative demand.

The transactions demand

This demand for money arises because it is not possible to obtain a perfect synchronisation between the receipt of income and the spending of that income. A person receives income weekly or monthly, but he is spending that income every day. If, for example, he receives £28 each week and spends that money evenly over time, his average holding of money would be £14. If it could be arranged that he be paid daily at a rate of £4 per day, his average money holdings would be only £2, but his real income would be unchanged.

The transactions demand for money, therefore, is determined by such factors as the level of income, the frequency of income payments and the spending habits of the community. Methods of remuneration and spending habits are not likely to change in the short run and the transactions demand will depend mainly on the level of income and the general price level. The larger a person's income, the more money he will tend to hold for transaction purposes. Similarly, the higher the level of prices, the more money he will hold in order to maintain the same real income.

The precautionary demand

In addition to the money held to meet day-to-day expenses, households and firms tend to hold additional sums as a means of insurance against unforeseen contingencies. No other asset possesses the same degree of liquidity as money and for this reason it is held to deal with sudden misfortunes, to take advantage of unexpected bargains, or in case expenses prove to be higher than budgeted for. To some extent this demand will depend upon the state of people's expectations. If they are pessimistic the precautionary motive will be strong. The money demanded for this purpose probably depends mainly on the level of income, as does the transactions demand.

The speculative demand

There are substantial holdings of money over and above what is required to meet the transactions and precautionary demands. But why should households and firms hold these *idle balances* rather than income-earning assets? The answer lies in the uncertainty associated with the possession of non-money assets whose money values vary from day to day. The possession of such assets involves a sacrifice of liquidity and a risk of capital losses.

Money balances held in excess of those required for transactions and precautionary purposes are known as speculative balances. Households and firms hold such balances when they fear the risk of capital losses on other assets. There are of course many types of income-yielding assets which provide alternatives to holding money. But since we are dealing with the speculative demand for money, the alternatives which present themselves are those which can be quickly acquired or disposed of; that is, liquid financial assets. Typical of such assets are fixed-interest government securities which have a ready market on the Stock Exchange. There is a high degree of substitution between such assets and money. The fixed rate of interest on these securities is known as *the nominal rate* and is expressed as a percentage of the face value of the bond. For example, a 4 per cent bond, face value £100, yields an annual income of £4.

It is, however, the *yield* or *market rate of interest* which is important in this analysis. The market rate of interest is the annual money income expressed as a percentage of the market price of the bond. The market prices of securities will fluctuate from day to day according to supply and demand conditions. There are many types of fixed interest securities, both long term and short term. For purposes of illustration we shall use an irredeemable (i.e. bearing no fixed date for repayment) government bond, nominal value £100, carrying a fixed rate of interest of 4 per cent. If the market price of such a bond is £80, the yield will be

$$\frac{4}{80} \times 100 = 5 \text{ per cent.}$$

This yield is the current market rate of interest on this type of loan.

Now suppose the holder of such a bond believes that the market rate of interest is about to rise (i.e. bond prices are expected to fall). He may decide to sell now at a price of £80 and hold a money balance. Let us imagine he sells his bond, his expectations prove correct, and, in the course of the year, the price of these securities falls to £60. Our speculator now believes that this price represents a floor–the next movement in prices will be upwards–and he repurchases one of these same securities. By holding money rather than securities, he has avoided a net loss of £16. If he had retained the bond, its capital value would have fallen by £20, but he would have received £4 in the form of interest–a *net* loss of £16. Speculators will prefer to hold money rather than financial assets if they expect security prices to fall (i.e. interest rates to rise).

Note that it is the movements in the prices of securities which cause changes in the market rates of interest. It is the price which people are prepared to pay for a fixed annual income which indicates their willingness to lend. If people in general are only prepared to pay £60 for a return of £4 per annum, this is an indication that a market rate of interest of at least $6\frac{2}{3}$ per cent is necessary to persuade them to surrender liquidity. At a market price of £60, an annual income of £4 would represent a return of

$$\frac{4}{60} \times 100 = 6\frac{2}{3} \text{ per cent.}$$

The liquidity preference theory

The rate of interest may be seen as the price which has to be paid to persuade people to forgo the advantages of holding money. It is the price which must be paid in order to overcome people's liquidity preference. People will distribute their wealth between money balances and bonds according to their attitudes towards risk and income. Money balances provide zero income with no risk of capital loss (but inflation reduces their purchasing power); bonds provide income but carry a risk of capital loss. The speculative demand for money will vary with the rate of interest, or, more accurately, with expectations of future changes in the rate of interest. If interest rates are expected to rise (i.e. bond prices expected to fall), people will prefer to hold money balances rather than bonds. When interest rates are relatively low, speculators will anticipate a future upward movement which would, if it materialised, involve capital losses on any bonds held. The speculative demand for money will tend to be high as speculators try to convert their bonds into money balances. When interest rates are high relative to past rates, expectations will be that future movements in interest rates will be downwards (bond prices will rise), so that holders of bonds will have an opportunity to make capital gains. The speculative demand for money will be low as people try to buy bonds in anticipation of a rise in their prices. Relatively high interest rates mean that the cost of holding money balances in terms of income forgone is also high. This is a further disincentive to holding money balances when interest rates are high.

The essential ideas of the theory are illustrated in Fig. 25. The rate of interest is set out on the vertical axis and the quantity of money along the horizontal axis. The supply of money (M and M^1) is determined by the monetary authorities and may be taken as fixed in the short run. The diagram is drawn on the assumption that prices and income are constant so that the transactions and precautionary demands will also be constant. These two demands which together make up the demand for *active balances* are aggregated in L^1. Since this demand is not affected by changes in the rate of interest it is represented by a vertical demand curve. The speculative demand for money tends to vary inversely with the rate of interest and is represented by L^2. The total demand for money, therefore, is $(L^1 + L^2) = L^3$. Thus when the supply of money

Rate of interest

Note: $L^3 = L^1 + L^2$

Quantity of money

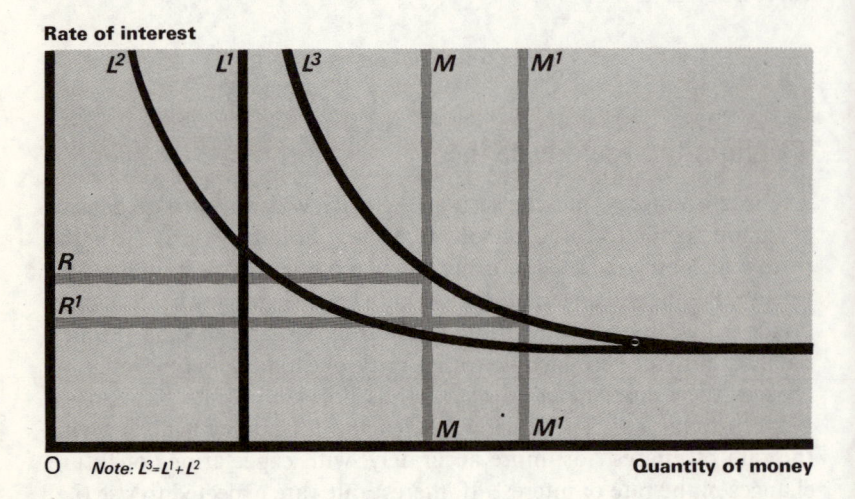

Fig. 25

THE DEMAND FOR MONEY—LIQUIDITY PREFERENCE

is OM, the rate of interest is OR. This is the price which equates the demand for money to hold and the supply of money.

Note that the total demand curve, or liquidity preference curve (L^3) becomes horizontal at a positive rate of interest. We can say that it becomes perfectly elastic with respect to the rate of interest. The liquidity preference theory assumes that there is some positive minimum rate of interest which must be paid to compensate lenders for the costs, trouble and risks of exchanging money for other assets. This minimum rate is believed to be about 2 per cent.

CHANGES IN THE SUPPLY OF MONEY

Fig. 25 shows that an increase in the supply of money from OM to OM' would lower the rate of interest from OR to OR'. What happens is that, given the state of liquidity preference, the increased supply of money will leave households and firms with excess money balances. They will try to shed this excess liquidity by buying bonds. The increased demand for securities will raise their prices and bring down the rate of interest. The lowering of the interest rate will increase the quantity of money demanded for speculative purposes until an equilibrium is achieved where the larger supply of money will be willingly held. Fig. 25 could also be used to demonstrate the effects of a reduction in the money supply. Households and firms would then find that their money balances had fallen below the desired levels, and they would try to restore the position by selling bonds. An increased willingness to sell bonds does not create any additional money; all it does is to increase the rate of interest. As interest rates rise the public is content to hold a smaller supply of money. A new interest rate will now emerge at which the public is willing to hold the reduced supply of money.

CHANGES IN LIQUIDITY PREFERENCE

The liquidity preference curve (L^3) in Fig. 25 is drawn on the assumption that influences on the demand for money, other than the rate of interest, remain unchanged. These other influences can, and do, change, and the effect of such changes is to shift the position of the liquidity preference curve.

Changes in output and income

The demand for money will vary positively with the level of real income. As the level of real income rises so does the transactions demand, and the liquidity preference curve moves to the right. We need a different liquidity preference curve for each level of income.

Changes in prices

The demand for money will vary positively with the general price level.

The higher the general price level the greater the amount of money needed to facilitate the exchange of a given quantity of goods.

Expectations

Liquidity preference will vary inversely with the expectation of future price increases. If everyone believes that prices are going to rise they have an incentive to reduce money balances and purchase commodities or assets whose money value might be expected to rise in line with the price level.

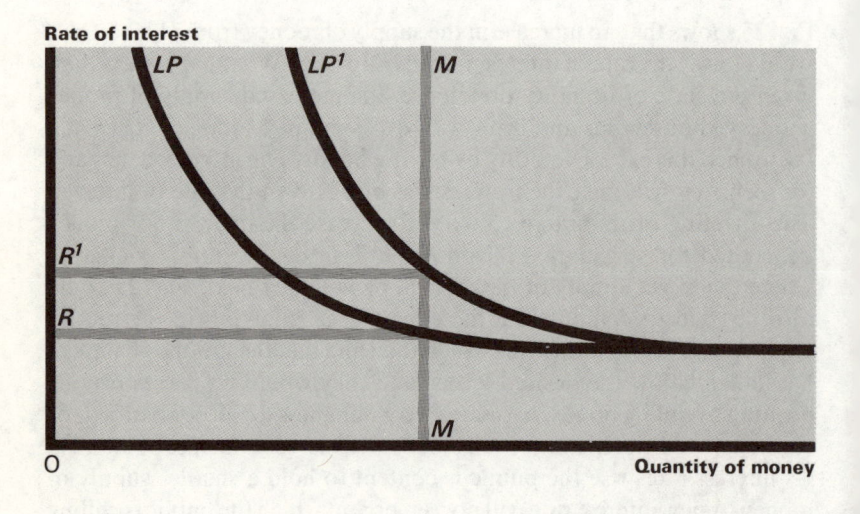

Fig. 26

Fig. 26 shows the effect of a change in liquidity preference. LP is the total demand for money and MM the supply of money. Initially there is equilibrium at a rate of interest of OR. An increase in liquidity preference, LP to LP^1 due, say, to an increase in income, causes the rate of interest to rise to OR^1. The increase in liquidity preference reveals itself in an increased willingness to sell bonds as people attempt to increase their money balances. But people in general cannot hold greater amounts of money since the supply is fixed. Their desire to do so merely drives down the price of securities and increases the rate of interest.

We can now see how this theory of the rate of interest might be fitted into our model of the economy. In this chapter we have noted how the demand for money and the supply of money interact to determine the rate of interest. The demand for money, given constant prices, has two components: a demand for active balances which depends on the level of income; a demand for idle balances which depends on the rate of interest. If we assume the supply of money and the price level to be constant, any movement in Y will affect the rate of interest. Thus, *at each level of income, there will be some determinate rate of interest which will equate the demand for money to hold and the supply of money.*

Chapter 6 explained investment in terms of the marginal efficiency of capital and the market rate of interest. Thus, *for any given rate of interest there will be a determined rate of planned investment.*

In Chapter 7 it was shown that, with a given propensity to consume

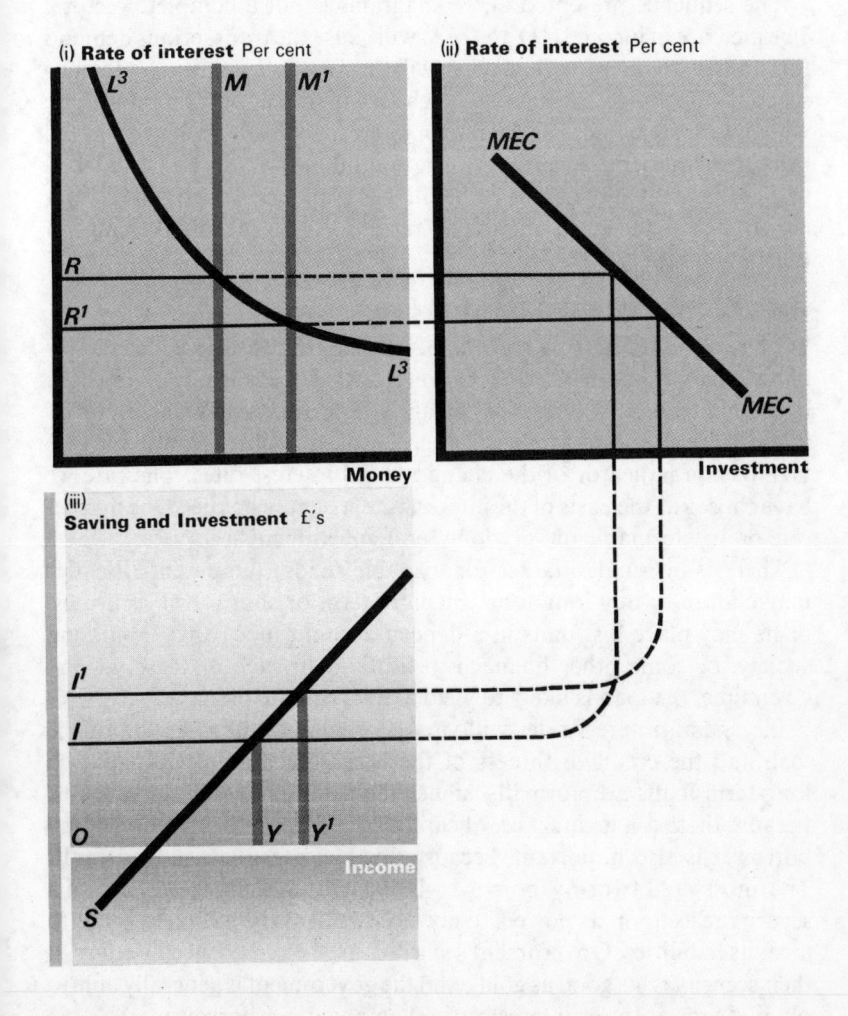

Fig. 27

(i.e. a given propensity to save), the level of planned investment will decide the equilibrium level of output. *Thus, the level of planned investment, given the propensity to consume, will determine the equilibrium level of output.* Fig. 27 illustrates these linkages.

In Fig. 27(i) there has been an increase in the supply of money M to M^1, and the rate of interest has fallen from OR to OR^1. This fall in the rate of interest has led to an increase in investment, as shown in Fig. 27(ii). The effect of this increase in investment is shown in Fig. 27(iii) where the multiplier effect has led to an increase in income from OY to OY^1.

The sequence presented in the diagrams is not a complete picture. The increase in income (OY to OY^1) will cause the transactions demand for money to increase and this will move the liquidity preference schedule to the right. Assuming no change in the supply of money there will now be an increase in the rate of interest and some falling off in the rate of investment. Eventually a new equilibrium will be established with investment and income rather higher than they were originally but not so high as the levels apparently resulting from the initial change in the money supply.

THE STRUCTURE OF INTEREST RATES

We have been talking of *the* rate of interest, but the most elementary knowledge of the financial world reveals that there is not one rate of interest but many. This does not invalidate our analysis if we assume that interest rates tend to move together so that one interest rate may be taken as an indicator of the changes in all interest rates. The rate we have chosen as the basis of the interest rate structure has been the market rate on irredeemable or very long term government securities.

There is no single market for loanable funds; the potential lender may choose to buy long-term, medium-term or short-term securities, or he may place his funds in a deposit account in a bank, a building society, or some other financial institution. In each of these, at any given time, the loan is likely to yield a different rate of interest.

In general, interest rates will vary according to the duration of the loan and the creditworthiness of the borrower. Rates of interest on long-term loans are normally higher than those on short-term loans, because there is a greater risk of capital loss. The credit standing of the borrower is also important, because this indicates the risk of default. The most creditworthy borrower is the government itself, since its security rests upon its powers to tax the wealth of the nation in order to meet its liabilities. Government securities are described as 'gilt-edged' – their security is 'as good as gold', and the government is generally able to obtain loans at lower interest rates than any other borrower.

14
The Control of the Money Supply

This chapter deals with the techniques by which the authorities (the Treasury acting through the Bank of England) aim to control the supply of money. These techniques are the instruments of monetary policy. Since the supply of money consists predominantly of bank deposits, policies designed to control the money supply must be concentrated on the activities of the commercial banks. Although the supply of notes and coin is under the control of the Bank of England, the authorities do not attempt to use the supply of currency as a direct means of controlling the banking sector. Notes and coin are always available to the banks as and when required.

The previous chapter dealt with the important relationship between the supply of money and the rate of interest, and this relationship presents the monetary authorities with a dilemma. In attempting to control the supply of money they cannot avoid affecting the rate of interest. This is clearly demonstrated by Fig. 26. The rate of interest is also a policy objective of the monetary authorities since it has important effects on the costs of servicing the national debt, the level of investment and other important macro-economic variables. If the authorities wish to maintain some given level of interest rates then they must supply whatever quantity of money is required to maintain that rate of interest. They will have to respond in a passive manner to any shift in the demand for money. If they choose to control the quantity of money then they cannot also control the rate of interest – it will vary as the demand for money varies. We return to this important point later.

Since banks operate on the basis of some conventional (or legal) ratio of reserve assets to total deposits, monetary instruments of control may be directed at influencing the banks' holdings of reserve assets. If the central bank can effectively control the supply of these reserve assets it has a powerful weapon for acting on the level of bank deposits since any change in the reserve assets ratio will have multiplier effects on the level of deposits (assuming the banks stick strictly to the specified ratios). For example, if the banks maintain a reserve assets ratio of

10 per cent, a loss of reserve assets of £100 would force a contraction of deposits equal to £1 000. Under the present British system, where banks are obliged to hold reserve assets equal in value to $12\frac{1}{2}$ per cent of their total deposits, the theoretical multiplier is 8.

Open market operations

The reserves of the banks are affected by the central bank's open market operations. This is the term applied to the central bank's own sales and purchases of bonds in the money and capital markets.

Suppose the central bank sells securities to households and firms in the private sector. The latter will pay with cheques drawn on their accounts at the commercial banks. The central bank now has a claim on the commercial banks which will be settled by deducting the amount from the bankers' balances at the Bank of England. A reduction of these balances means that the banks' reserves of cash have fallen and, assuming this brings the reserve ratio below the required minimum, they will be obliged to reduce their deposits by some multiple of the loss of reserves.

In the opposite case, where the central bank buys securities in the open market, it will pay for them with cheques drawn on itself. When the sellers pay these cheques into their bank accounts, the commercial banks will have outstanding claims on the central bank which will settle them by adding the amount to the bankers' balances. This increases the banks' reserves and hence their ability to lend.

Open market operations may be used on a day-to-day basis to smooth out any large random changes in the banks' supply of cash, or as a deliberate attempt to alter the reserves of the banking system with a view to changing the level of bank deposits. In other words, open market operations can be used to bring about a required change in the money supply.

The problem, as already indicated, is that the buying and selling of securities in the open market will affect their prices and hence the rate of interest. If the authorities wish to maintain some given level of interest rates they will still use open market operations, but in a passive rather than an active manner. Instead of buying and selling securities with the aim of changing the level of bank deposits, the authorities would now have to conduct these operations on the initiative of the private sector. If the private sector shows an increased willingness to sell securities the central bank will be obliged to buy in order to maintain security prices. When the private sector increases its demand for securities the authorities will be obliged to sell. In order to hold the rate of interest, the central bank must maintain the current prices of securities.

Interest rate policy

If the authorities wish to act mainly on the price of credit (i.e. the rate of interest) they can use the position of the Bank of England as a lender of last resort. It is normally the policy of the central bank to use the weekly issue of Treasury Bills to create a shortage of cash in the money market. Sales of Treasury Bills will reduce the bankers' balances at the central bank. Now if it does not wish to see any change in the present structure of interest rates, the Bank will relieve this cash shortage by buying Treasury Bills or other first class bills from the Discount Houses, or from the banks themselves, at current market rates. If, however, the Bank wishes to see interest rates rising, it will not take the initiative just described. The commercial banks will react to the cash shortage by drawing back their call loans to the Discount Houses. The Discount Houses will be forced 'into the Bank' in order to obtain the funds needed to repay their bank loans. By charging the minimum lending rate for these loans the Bank of England can force up the market rate of interest. If they are persistently forced to borrow from the central bank the Discount Houses will be obliged to increase their own lending rates and this will raise other short-term rates of interest. By their actions in the money market, the Bank of England can indicate whether it expects interest rates to rise or not and, since it has the power to enforce its requirements, the market will usually respond.

Funding

Although open market operations may be successful in altering the level of the banks' cash reserves, they will not be an effective instrument for restraining bank lending when the banks have large supplies of very liquid assets. The banks may readily make good any loss of cash by re-discounting Treasury Bills. If the central bank wishes to maintain the Treasury Bill rate it will be obliged to purchase these Treasury Bills at the current rate of interest. If the banks have more than adequate supplies of such liquid assets, open market operations may have to be carried out on a massive scale in order to reduce the banks' reserve assets to proportions which make the banks susceptible to this policy. But very large scale operations of this kind will have undesirable effects on security prices and interest rates. In circumstances such as these it is necessary to reduce the availability of liquid assets to the banking system. Since Treasury Bills are an important liquid asset, this objective may be achieved by *funding* whereby the central bank issues more long term securities and reduces the issue of Treasury Bills. In so doing, it will be lengthening the average maturity of the national debt.

Special deposits

As an alternative and more direct method of reducing the reserves of liquid assets held by the banking system, the Bank of England, in 1960, introduced a new device—*special deposits*. The Bank of England has power to call upon the commercial banks (and finance houses) to place deposits in a special account at the central bank. The amounts deposited will carry interest at the current Treasury Bill rate, but they do not count as part of the banks' cash reserves. They are, in effect, a 'frozen' asset. A call for special deposits is a deliberate and direct reduction of the banks' reserve assets. Initially the banks managed to evade the intended squeeze on their advances because they reduced their investments (i.e. sold securities) in order to provide the funds for the special deposits. The Bank of England later made it clear that it expected the banks to allow the impact of special deposits to fall on their advances (see also page 168).

Quantitative and qualitative controls

In recent years the Bank of England has supplemented its controls over the money supply by making increasing use of direct requests to the banking institutions. Each bank has been asked to limit the amount of its deposits to some specified figure. These *ceilings* have not been confined to the clearing banks but have applied to all banks and a wide range of financial institutions. Quantitative restrictions have usually been accompanied by qualitative guidance as when banks have been asked not to restrict loans to assist exports, or to firms in development areas, but to restrict loans for speculation, imports or personal consumption. Ceilings applied to advances became the most important direct control in the 1960s, but its consequence was a serious limitation on the banks' ability to compete among themselves and with other financial intermediaries. Depositors are attracted by a bank's willingness to make loans. If banks are not permitted to make loans for consumption purposes some depositors will be attracted by the higher interest rates offered by other institutions.

Another type of direct control which has been used extensively by the authorities is the power to vary the terms of hire purchase contracts. The government can at any time specify the size of the minimum deposit and the maximum repayment period. If the size of the minimum deposit is increased and the period allowed for repayment reduced, demand will fall since the consumer is now called upon to save a greater proportion of the purchase price before he can acquire the good and then make greater weekly or monthly payments. In 1971, the UK government removed all such restrictions on hire purchase. It will now use its monetary controls over the finance houses to influence the availability of credit for hire purchase sales.

Monetary policy

Monetary policy refers to any deliberate action by the monetary authorities which is designed to change the availability or cost of money. The previous section outlined the instruments of monetary policy and we now look at some of the problems of making effective use of monetary policy.

THE DECLINE OF TRADITIONAL MONETARY POLICY

Traditional monetary policy was based upon the assumption that the demand for investment goods was particularly sensitive to changes in the rate of interest and it was on this point that the theory was attacked in the 1930s and 1940s. Keynesian theory had shown that there were situations where changes in the money supply would have little effect on interest rates (where liquidity preference becomes perfectly elastic: Fig. 28)[1]. More important, the theory had emphasised the role of expectations as a major determinant of investment behaviour. A serious loss of confidence on the part of entrepreneurs would completely override any changes in interest rates. In support of these views empirical evidence from the UK and the USA had revealed that businessmen, when questioned on this matter, indicated that they were not seriously influenced by changes in the rate of interest when formulating their investment plans.

The role of monetary policy was seriously diminished by the effects of the Second World War. The massive increases in government spending greatly increased the scale and effectiveness of the fiscal weapons. There had also been large-scale borrowing through sales of long-term government securities. The government after the war felt honour bound to protect the market values of these securities, so that effective monetary policy was ruled out. Effective use of monetary policy requires variations in the rate of interest and this would have meant variable security prices. The government believed that this would be grossly unfair to those who had purchased the large volume of securities during the war. A further argument advanced in favour of fiscal policy was that it could be used more selectively and hence was more equitable than monetary policy.

THE REVIVAL OF MONETARY POLICY

Monetary policy was revived in the 1950s in economic conditions very different to those which applied before the war. The enormous increase

[1] Page 176.

in the national debt meant that a major part of the total supply of marketable securities consisted of government debt. Much of this public debt had been acquired by financial institutions (banks, insurance companies, pensions funds, etc.). These institutions, therefore, were particularly vulnerable to changes in the market values of government bonds. If the rate of interest rose (i.e. security prices fell), institutions would be extremely reluctant to sell securities in order to provide funds for investment, because such sales would involve them in capital losses.

If this analysis is correct, it follows that, under these circumstances, monetary policy might be used to restrict the availability of investment funds. A rise in interest rates would 'lock in' the financial institutions. They would not be prepared to suffer capital losses in order to provide funds for borrowers. The important aspect of this policy lay in its emphasis on the *availability* of investment funds whereas earlier exponents of monetary policy had emphasised the *price* of loans as the controlling factor. These views received support from the Radcliffe Committee[1] which regarded this particular use of interest rate policy as more effective than measures to restrict the lending capacity of the clearing banks. Note, however, that this revival of monetary policy was seen as appropriate only as a restrictive measure during boom conditions. It was recognised that in a depression easing the availability of credit might not be a sufficient stimulant for reviving investment spending.

LIMITATIONS ON EFFECTIVENESS OF MONETARY POLICY

Liquidity

The effectiveness of monetary policy as a means of limiting the lending activities of the financial institutions depends upon the liquidity positions of these institutions. As we have already noted, they will not be susceptible to changes in the rate of interest if they are holding a large supply of very liquid assets. Such changes have little effect on the capital values of securities which are very near to maturity. For example, a change in the rate of interest from 3 per cent to 4 per cent would reduce the market value of a security with three months to run by only 0·25 per cent, whereas if this security had 15 years to run its capital value would fall by about 16 per cent.

Velocity of circulation

The effectiveness of a restrictive monetary policy (a credit squeeze) may be severely impaired if there is an offsetting increase in the velocity of circulation of money (V). How can such an increase in V come about?

1. Committee on the Working of the Monetary System (1958) Cmnd. 857

At any moment of time part of the money supply will be held in active balances (i.e. financing transactions) and a part will be lying in idle balances. V is simply an average rate of movement of each unit of money in the total stock. For example, suppose the money stock were made up of £500 000 in idle balances, and £500 000 in active balances. If each unit of money in the active balances changed hands, on average, 5 times in a year, total spending would be £2 500 000 and the value of V would be 2·5. It should be apparent, therefore, that V will increase if there is a movement of funds from the idle balances to active balances.

An increase in the rate of interest could lead to just such a movement. Higher interest rates increase the opportunity cost of holding money balances (in terms of the income forgone) so that households and firms will be more willing to lend. The speculative demand for money will also fall as bond prices fall, because expectations of a further decline in prices will diminish. This again will reduce the level of idle balances. Another factor which has tended to increase the efficiency with which any given stock of money may be utilised has been the rapid expansion of non-bank financial intermediaries (see page 146–8).

Limitations on the use of interest rate policies

While accepting the fact that an increase in the velocity of circulation would limit the effectiveness of monetary policy, many economists believe that the main explanation for any lack of success lies in the restrictive framework within which the monetary authorities have to work. There are several factors which determine the official policy on interest rates, and these factors limit the freedom of the authorities to make full use of the interest rate regulator for controlling the money supply:

(*a*) With a large national debt higher interest rates necessitate a higher tax burden in order to service the debt.
(*b*) Where there is a substantial amount of overseas debt, higher interest rates will have unfavourable effects on the balance of payments.
(*c*) Since high interest charges have a disproportionate effect on the cost of longer-term projects, restrictive measures may prejudice those developments which are favourable to a faster rate of economic growth.
(*d*) The cost of residential construction and house purchase through mortgage schemes are severely affected by increases in the rate of interest. Such effects will be very unpopular.

On the other hand there is no doubt that what is regarded as a 'normal' rate of interest has risen over the past two decades. This is partly due to the widespread acceptance of continuous inflation which has led creditors to demand, and debtors to accept, higher 'normal' rates of interest. This has meant that interest charges have become an increasingly important element in the cost structure. If this development continues, the demand for investment could become more and more sensitive to higher interest rates. But a good deal depends upon the relative flexibilities of interest rates and the prices of final goods and services. If the pace of inflation quickens and the rate of interest increases at a more sluggish rate, the *real* rate of interest will be declining. If the prices of goods and services are rising at an annual rate of 8 per cent, a nominal rate of interest of 10 per cent represents a real interest rate of about 2 per cent. In such circumstances relatively high nominal rates of interest will not provide much of a deterrent to borrowers.

THE CENTRAL BANK AND MONETARY POLICY

In pursuing its economic objectives the government has usually given fiscal policy the leading role. Major changes in fiscal policy, however, cannot take place more frequently than once a year because of the great administrative problems in giving effect to such changes. Monetary policy enters the picture because the estimates and forecasts on which fiscale plans are based are very uncertain. An open economy is particularly vulnerable to influences from outside which cannot be foreseen or predicted. Monetary policy provides instruments of control which can be applied very quickly and in large or small degrees. It offers a much more flexible collection of economic controls which can be used for maintaining equilibrium between changes in fiscal policy. But efforts to operate an effective monetary policy present many problems for the monetary authorities. The central bank's responsibility for the management of the national debt often restricts its freedom of action in the use of monetary policy.

For much of the post-war period the government has had a large borrowing requirement which has presented the central bank with the task of ensuring a receptive market for new issues of government securities and a continuing responsibility for the repayment of maturing securities. Some idea of the magnitude of this task is provided by the fact that between 1978 and 1982 about £15,000 million worth of government securities will mature. Since maturing loans will generally be repaid from the proceeds of new issues, the central bank must manage the securities market so that the market prices of securities (and hence the market rate of interest) are favourable to prospective purchasers and existing holders.

This obligation to maintain security prices (i.e. interest rates) at desired levels for purposes of debt management obviously restricts the central bank's freedom to use interest rate manipulation for purely monetary purposes (i.e. controlling the supply of money).

NEW DEVELOPMENTS IN MONETARY POLICY

In general the restraints imposed by the need to manage the national debt led the central bank to concentrate on interest rates rather than the supply of money. In the 1960s, however, the view gained ground that control over the quantity of money is a more effective means of influencing aggregate demand. Evidence has been produced which purports to show an association between changes in the supply of money and changes in the level of economic activity (see page 177). Whilst a debtor to the International Monetary Fund in the late 1960s and mid-1970s Britain was placed under some pressure to pay more attention to the money supply.

Another feature of the British monetary system which came in for increasing criticism was the use of restrictive practices in the banking sector. The cartel agreement between the clearing banks which restricted competition on interest rates, and the convention whereby the discount houses made a collective bid at an agreed common price at the weekly Treasury Bill auction were held to cause rigidities and to operate against change and innovation.

These and other factors led the authorities to seek a more flexible and effective monetary policy. Important new measures came into effect in September 1971. Many features of this new policy have already been discussed.

One important aim of the new policy was to set interest rates free to be determined by market forces. To this end the clearing banks' cartel agreement was abandoned; banks now compete with each other by setting their own rates of interest on an independent basis. The discount houses' syndicated bid for the weekly issue of Treasury Bills was also brought to an end. In addition the central bank made it clear it was no longer prepared to support the market in government securities to anything like the extent it had done so in the past. It would no longer operate as an automatic buyer or seller in order to stabilise security prices (i.e. interest rates) at some desired level. This increased competition was expected to speed up the rate of innovation and generally increase efficiency in the banking world.

The quantitative controls on bank lending were also removed, as were the cash and liquidity ratio requirements for the clearing banks. Instead the new reserve assets ratio has been applied to all banks in the UK banking sector, and a similar ratio of 10 per cent applies to finance houses. The instrument of special deposits has been retained and made uniform across the whole banking sector including the finance houses.

Monetary policy will aim to influence the liquidity position of the institutions in the banking sector by acting upon the availability of reserve assets and upon the capital values and yields of the assets held by these institutions. The main instruments of control will be open market operations and special deposits. Open market operations can be used to influence the availability of reserve assets and the market rate of interest, and their impact can be powerfully reinforced by means of calls for special deposits. By extending the controls to the whole banking sector the authorities hope to exercise a more effective control over the total money supply (i.e. M_3).

Supplementary Special Deposits

A type of quantitative control on the level of bank deposits was introduced by the Bank of England in December 1973. This scheme acts rather like a progressive 'tax' on the growth of bank deposits and takes the form of an automatic levy known as Supplementary Special Deposits.

The Bank of England specifies a maximum figure for the growth of bank deposits over some given time period (say, three months). If bank deposits are allowed to exceed this target figure, the banks become liable for calls for special deposits according to the extent to which their deposits exceed the specified maximum. For example, an excess of 1 per cent might lead to a call for a special deposit equal to 5 per cent of the excess; for an excess of between 1 per cent and 3 per cent the call might be for 25 per cent, and for excesses greater than 3 per cent the call might be for a payment of special deposits equal to 50 per cent of the excess.

Unlike normal special deposits, these supplementary deposits do not earn interest.

This scheme may be activated at any time.

Questions on Chapters 11–14

ESSAY QUESTIONS

1. Explain the connection between the quantity of money and the rate of interest. **(L)**

2. 'The rate of interest is determined entirely by the demand for and supply of investible funds'. Discuss. **(S)**

3. What are the main motives for holding money instead of interest earning assets? How may an increase in the money supply affect the rate of interest? **(C)**

4. What would you include in a definition of money? How might this definition change over time? **(O & C)**

5. 'A commercial bank will always arrange its liabilities and its assets in such a way as to maximise its profits'. Explain and discuss. **(S)**

6. What function do the Discount Houses fulfil in the British monetary system? **(JMB)**

7. How effectively can the Bank of England control the supply of money in Britain? **(O & C)**

8. 'It is possible to control either the money supply or the rate of interest, but not both.' Explain and discuss. **(O & C)**

9. Do banks create money? **(O & C)**

10. What have been the principal methods used by the monetary authorities to regulate the British economy in recent years? **(C)**

MULTIPLE CHOICE QUESTIONS

1. The essential characteristic of whatever serves as money is that it must
(*a*) Be issued by the state.
(*b*) Not be wholly fiduciary.
(*c*) Be generally acceptable.
(*d*) Have some intrinsic value.

2. Which of the following is *not* a function of the commercial banks?
(*a*) The provision of safe deposit facilities.
(*b*) The provision of a cheque system for settling debts.
(*c*) Lending to the private and public sectors.
(*d*) Acting as a lender of last resort.

MACRO-ECONOMICS

3. The note issue is a liability of:
1. The commercial banks.
2. The Issue Department of the Bank of England.
3. The Banking Department of the Bank of England.

(*a*) 2 only.
(*b*) 3 only.
(*c*) 1 and 2.
(*d*) 1 and 3.

4. Which of the following are instruments of monetary policy?
1. Investment grants.
2. Capital gains tax.
3. Open market operations.
4. Special deposits.

(*a*) 3 only.
(*b*) 2 and 3.
(*c*) 3 and 4.
(*d*) 1, 2, 3 and 4.

Questions 5, 6, and 7 refer to the following transactions:
(*a*) Large tax payments by bank customers.
(*b*) The Bank of England buys securities in the open market.
(*c*) The banks buy Treasury Bills from the Discount Houses.
(*d*) The Bank of England makes a call for Special Deposits.

5. Which transaction has the immediate effect of reducing bank deposits and bank cash by equal amounts?

6. Which transaction has the immediate effect of increasing bank deposits and bank cash by equal amounts?

7. Which transaction is most likely to cause the Bank of England to provide assistance to the money market 'through the back door'?

8. Suppose a long-term bond pays a fixed rate of interest of 4 per cent on its nominal value of £100. What is the current market price of the bond when the market rate of interest is 6 per cent?

(*a*) £60.
(*b*) £150.
(*c*) £66·6.
(*d*) £100.

9. A large speculative demand for money is likely to exist when,
(*a*) People wish to borrow money in order to speculate on the Stock Exchange.
(*b*) The current rate of interest is high.

(c) The current rate of interest is lower than people expect it to be in the near future.
(d) People expect the prices of goods and services to rise.

10. Which of the following is *not* a determinant of the demand for money?
(a) The general level of prices.
(b) The current volume of output.
(c) The pattern of relative prices of goods and services.
(d) The current level of interest rates.
(e) The payments conventions of the community.

PROBLEMS

1. The question is based on the following simplified balance sheets of the central bank and the commercial banks.

Central Bank £m.

Liabilities		Assets	
Commercial banks' deposits	400	Securities	800
Government deposits	400		

Commercial Banks

Liabilities		Assets	
Deposits	4 000	Reserve assets	400
		Investments	1 600
		Advances	2 000

The required reserve assets ratio is 10 per cent.

Now suppose the central bank sells £50m. of securities to the public. What will be the effect on
(a) The commercial banks' reserves?
(b) The commercial banks' deposits?

2. In Country X the payments conventions are such that the transactions demand for money is always equal to one-fifth of annual money income. The demand for money for other purposes is £500m. when the current rate of interest is 2 per cent but it falls by £50m. for each percentage point by which the rate of interest exceeds 2 per cent. If the current money income is £5 000m., and the money supply is £1 350m., what is the equilibrium rate of interest?

15
The Quantity of Money and the Price Level

In the simplified economic models used earlier we assumed that the prices of goods and services remained unchanged. This was convenient because it meant that any changes in the components of aggregate demand brought about corresponding changes in *real* income. Since we also assumed that techniques of production were unchanged these same changes in demand could be related directly to employment.

As everyone is well aware, prices do not remain unchanged over time. It has been estimated that in the UK there are something like one million price changes in any one year. In this book we are not concerned with movements in individual prices, but with movements in the general price level – the average level of prices. We have now to develop our analysis to take account of the fact that changes in aggregate demand are likely to affect prices as well as output and income, and these changes in prices will also lead to economic changes which in turn react on output and employment.

Table 8. *Movements of consumer prices*
1970 = 100

Year	USA	Japan	France	West Germany	Italy	United Kingdom
1970	100·0	100·0	100·0	100·0	100·0	100·0
1971	104·3	106·3	105·5	105·3	105·0	109·5
1972	107·7	111·5	111·7	111·1	110·9	117·0
1973	114·4	124·5	119·9	118·8	122·4	126·7
1974	127·0	153·4	136·3	127·1	146·2	147·0
1975	138·6	171·4	152·2	134·7	171·3	182·5
1976	146·6	187·5	166·8	140·8	199·6	211·4
1977[1]	158·0	204·5	185·3	146·9	241·8	249·7

[1] 3rd quarter

Source: *National Institute Economic Review*.

In discussing movements in the general price level we are, of course, discussing changes in the value of money, since money can only be valued in terms of what it will buy. The value of money varies inversely with the price level, but the change in one is not a mirror image of the other. For example, if you have £5 you can buy 5 articles costing £1 each. If the price of these articles rises to £1·25 your £5 will now only purchase 4 of them. Prices have risen by 25 per cent, but the value of money has fallen by 20 per cent.

Table 8 is included to give some idea of the extent of recent price changes in some major industrial countries.

The quantity theory

One of the oldest and best-known theories dealing with the determination of the general price level is the Quantity Theory of Money. It has been refined over the years and is now stated with varying degrees of sophistication. The earlier versions concentrated on the role of money as a medium of exchange. It was assumed that money was demanded purely for transactions purposes. The general price level is then determined by the relationship between the quantity of money and the supply of goods and services. It was also assumed that the rate at which money changed hands was constant so that there was a direct proportionate relationship between the quantity of money and the price level. In other words $M \propto P$, where M is the stock of money and P the general price level. The traditional quantity theory was based on the proposition that the value of money varies inversely as its quantity and the causal agent is the variation in the quantity of money.

THE EQUATION OF EXCHANGE

Later version of the theory paid more attention to the rate at which money changes hands and introduced the variable V to represent the *velocity of circulation* of money. V is simply the number of times, on average, which each unit of money changes hands in a given period of time. A £1 note which changes hands 10 times represents the same purchasing power as a £10 note which changes hands once. The quantity of money is now seen, more realistically, as a flow and not a stock. It may be expressed as MV, the product of the stock of money and the average velocity of circulation. MV is the value of total expenditure in any given time period. The value of the flow of goods and services which satisfies this demand may also be expressed as the product of two variables, P and T. P stands for the average price of the goods and services, and T for the number of transactions. The relationships are normally formulated in the equation of exchange

$$MV = PT$$

THE QUANTITY OF MONEY AND THE PRICE LEVEL

This is, in fact, an identity for it is quite obvious that total spending (MV) must be equal to total receipts (PT). Note that the V in this equation is the *transactions* velocity of circulation and includes expenditures on intermediate and second-hand goods. The equation of exchange is not a theory, because it does not indicate any causal relationships. It tells us what will happen if any or all of the variables change, but not what might cause the variables to change. Nevertheless the formulation is useful, because it does highlight the assumptions necessary for the strict Quantity Theory to be effective, namely, V and T must be constant. It also, therefore, points to conditions under which this theory could be disproved.

In fact, it is not very likely that V and T are constants. If there are unemployed resources, and V remains unchanged, an increase in M is likely to lead to an increase in output so that T will increase and P may well be unchanged. It is possible for the supply of goods and services to change independently of any changes in M. For example, an increase in productivity or a lowering of tariffs would increase aggregate supply and this would cause a change in P not related to any change in M.

V might change because of a change in expectations. If people anticipate a rise in prices, spending will increase because V increases and prices will rise although no change in M has taken place. Indeed, an increase in V is one of the major features in a runaway inflation. An increase in M might well be offset by a fall in V. During periods of economic depression an increase in the stock of money might simply find its way into idle balances (i.e. V falls) so that there is little or no increase in spending.

THE CAMBRIDGE VERSION

The equation of exchange was put forward by an American economist Irving Fisher. An alternative formulation of the theory was developed by a number of economists working in Cambridge. Their version of the theory relates the quantity of money to the level of income. Whereas in the Fisher version V and P refer to all transactions, the Cambridge version is only concerned with transactions affecting final goods. Instead of PT, we now have $P'0$, where 0 is the physical output of final goods and services, and P' is the average of their prices. The substitution of 0 for T means that the velocity of circulation appropriate to this treatment is the *income velocity of circulation* (V'). V' is the rate of turnover of money in the purchase of final goods and services. More simply

$$V' = \frac{\text{National income}}{M}$$

The equation is now written, $MV' = P'0$, and since $P'0$ must be equal to national income,

MACRO-ECONOMICS

$$MV' = Y$$

More usefully, however, the relationships are expressed in the form, $M = kY$ where k is the average fraction of income which people wish to hold in the form of money. It may be more helpful to see k in the form

$$k = \frac{1}{V'}.$$

If money 'turns over' say four times each year, then each unit of money must be held, on average, for a quarter of that time. If V' is 4, therefore, people must wish to hold, on average, $\frac{1}{4}$ of their real income in the form of money.

The equation $M = kY$ brings together the supply of money (M) and the demand for money to hold (kY) and shows that equilibrium obtains when they are equal. The Cambridge equation emphasises the importance of income and indicates that changes in money national income may come about through changes in prices, or changes in output or both. It is also important for the fact that it draws attention to the demand for money to hold rather than the supply of money as a factor in the determination of money national income.

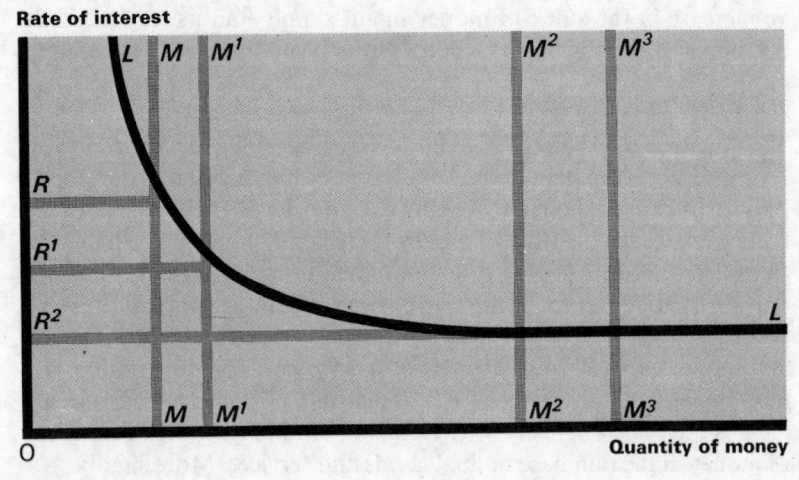

Fig. 28

THE ATTACK ON THE QUANTITY THEORY

The attack on the traditional quantity theory developed mainly on the basis of the Keynesian view that the rate of interest could exert a decisive influence upon the general price level. It was admitted that changes in the stock of money might lead to changes in the general price level, but the effects would be felt indirectly rather than directly. An increase in the quantity of money would lead to a fall in the rate of interest (M to M^1 in Fig. 28).

The fall in the rate of interest would now stimulate investment and, via the multiplier effects, cause an increase in aggregate demand. Under the conventional assumptions of full employment conditions the increase in demand would raise prices. If the assumption of full employment is dispensed with, the change in quantity of money would affect output rather than prices. Critics of the traditional quantity theory also pointed out that changes in the quantity of money would have no effect on prices when the rate of interest was 'on the floor'. The liquidity preference theory assumes that there is some minimum level to the market rate of interest. When the rate of interest is down at this level any further increase in the quantity of money will be absorbed in idle balances and, since the velocity of an idle balance is zero, it means that an increase in M reduces V. The situation is illustrated in Fig. 28, where an increase in the quantity of money from OM^2 to OM^3 has no effect on the rate of interest and hence no influence on the level of investment. We should also note that Keynes emphasised the importance of the effects of changing expectations in the markets for securities. These changes would cause changes in the rate of interest quite independently of any changes in the quantity of money.

THE REVIVAL OF THE QUANTITY THEORY

In recent years there has been a great revival of interest in the whole subject of the quantity of money. The traditional theory was designed to explain the causes of changes in the general price level. The modern quantity theory attempts to demonstrate causal relationships between changes in the quantity of money and changes in the money national income. The modern Keynesian approach also accepts that the impact of a change in the money stock will reveal itself either in output or price changes depending upon the extent of unemployment, but the modern quantity theory sees the link between M and P as being much more direct and predictable than it is in the Keynesian theory.

The revival of the quantity theory is largely the work of Milton Friedman and a group of economists known as the Chicago School. According to Friedman the determinants of the demand for money are fairly stable and subject to only slow change over time, whereas the money stock may rise or fall fairly rapidly. Thus, changes in money national income are largely determined by changes in the supply of money. This implies that the monetary authorities should pay more attention to the quantity of money and less to the level of interest rates.

THE CURRENT CONTROVERSY

The major areas of conflict lie in the question of what constitutes an effective substitute for money balances. The Keynesian view is that the only really close substitute for money is a range of paper financial assets (securities). If the monetary authorities increase the supply of money excessively, the public will try to shed its excess liquidity by purchasing securities. The prices of these financial assets will rise and interest rates will fall. A fall in the rate of interest reduces the 'cost' of holding money and money becomes *relatively* more attractive than other assets. The rate of interest will continue to fall until an equilibrium is reached when the increased volume of money is willingly held at the current price (the rate of interest). The effect of these changes on the levels of consumption and investment spending may be very limited. Investment demand is assumed to be rather insensitive with respect to the rate of interest (expectations playing the major role) and the effects of the changes in the value of financial assets would, it is assumed, not be very great as far as the propensity to consume is concerned[1].

The modern quantity theory regards money as a substitute for all assets whether real or financial. Anyone finding himself short of money might well forgo some planned spending on goods and services rather than sell securities. The monetarists believe that an increase in the supply of money will lead people to acquire a wide range of assets. Goods which are not immediately consumed may be thought of as yielding future services; like financial assets, they yield an income, but it cannot be measured by an explicit rate of interest. In other words, the monetary school believe that an increase in the supply of money will lead to spending on a wide range of income yielding assets, some of these assets will be securities which yield an explicit rate of interest, others such as durable goods will yield an income which cannot be measured, but is nevertheless real.

The modern quantity theory holds that the impact of changes in the quantity of money will be widely spread rather than working through changes in interest rates. It predicts that the money supply is the most important determinant of the level of economic activity and that changes in the money supply provide the best indicators of future changes in aggregate expenditure.

---

[1] An increase in the value of a person's financial assets makes him wealthier, but it is not likely to cause him to consume a lot more goods and services.

16
Output, Demand and the Price Level

The earlier analysis of income determination was based on an assumption of constant prices so that we could concentrate on the way in which the volume of national output was determined. The 45° diagram used in that analysis enabled us to relate changes in aggregate demand directly to changes in real income. In this chapter we have to take account of price changes. A change in the general price level alters the value of money national income and hence will affect money expenditures. But the quantities of goods and services demanded depends upon real income so that when money incomes change it is necessary to know what has happened to real incomes if we wish to know the likely effects on national output.

Changes in wages rates will affect both the level of money incomes and the cost conditions of firms. The level of money incomes and the price level will both change. The problem then is to distinguish between changes in volume, and changes in the value of output. For this analysis we need to make use of aggregate demand and supply curves which relate total output to the general price level.

An aggregate supply curve

A total supply schedule will indicate the various total real outputs of final goods and services which profit-maximising entrepreneurs are prepared to supply at each price level. We confine the concept to final goods and services since we are interested in that output which comprises the national income. The analysis is restricted to the short period since we assume that each industry has a fixed capacity (land, machines, buildings, etc.) and firms can only change their outputs by varying their inputs of labour and materials (the variable factors).

The aggregate supply curve will then be based on the costs of production and pricing policies of firms with given capacities and given prices of the variable factors of production (i.e. wages and raw material prices are constant).

Total costs may be subdivided into fixed costs and variable (or, direct) costs. Fixed costs, by definition, do not vary as output varies. They comprise depreciation, interest on loans, rent, insurance, rates and so on. Variable or direct costs are directly related to output and include wages and costs of raw materials. If these costs are divided by total output we obtain average total costs per unit of output, average fixed costs and average direct costs.

It appears from empirical evidence that average direct costs are reasonably constant over a fairly wide range of output. When the firm's output has expanded to near full-capacity operation, however, costs turn sharply upwards. At this point the organisation is under much greater pressure; less efficient workers may be engaged; less efficient stand-by machines may be pressed into use; make-shift methods may have to be adopted; more overtime is worked, and so on. In other words, there are diminishing returns to the variable factors. It is common industrial and commercial practice to add some conventional gross profit margin (often referred to as 'the mark-up') to average direct costs in order to establish the selling price. Given the constancy of average direct costs this means that firms will supply a wide range of output at fairly constant prices. In manufacturing industry especially, frequent price changes have a very unsettling effect on orders and make production planning extremely difficult. This further reinforces the relative 'stickiness' of prices. Once full capacity working is achieved there will be a movement to raise prices to cover the sharp upward movement of variable costs. In view of the experience of inflation in the post-war period it must be emphasised that here we are dealing with short-run price effects.

Economists use the term *supply price* to indicate the minimum price which is necessary to persuade firms to supply a given output. This supply price, we are assuming, is equal to average direct costs plus some 'mark-up' to cover average fixed costs and the profit margin. Since a large part of total output is produced in anticipation of demand, it might be more realistic to talk in terms of *expected prices* and *expected revenues* since it is these anticipated returns which give rise to production decisions.

An aggregate supply curve can now be projected which relates real output to anticipated revenue. In Fig. 29 the vertical axis represents expected aggregate receipts and the horizontal axis represents the volume of output. The Z curve is the aggregate supply function. Points on this curve show the different amounts of total expenditure which would be just sufficient to persuade firms to supply the corresponding outputs.

The supply prices for any given output can be obtained very easily

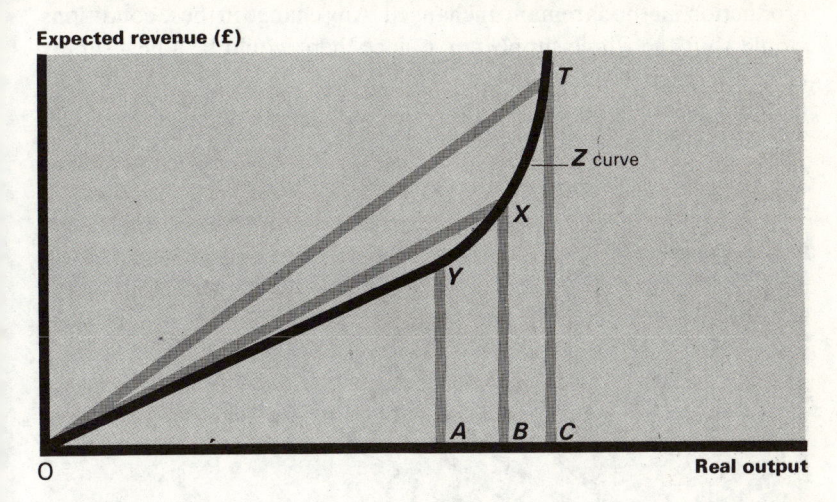

Fig. 29

from this diagram. The output OA would be forthcoming when total expected revenue was YA.

$$\text{Therefore } \frac{YA}{OA} = \text{supply price.}$$

$$\text{But } \frac{YA}{OA} = \text{gradient of the line } YO$$

It is fairly obvious, therefore, that the gradients of lines such as YO, XO and TO, give the required supply prices for the respective outputs, OA, OB and OC. Notice that over a considerable range of output (up to OA) the supply price will be constant – this is in line with the assumption of constant average direct costs over a wide range of output.

OC represents a full employment output so that the Z curve terminates at this point. It should be noted that the supply price starts to rise before full employment output is achieved. It is realistic to expect shortages and bottlenecks to appear in some sectors of the economy before full employment generally is achieved. Rising aggregate demand does not mean that all sectors of the economy experience the same proportionate increases in demand. The demands for some goods will rise more rapidly than for others. Occupational and geographical immobilities of resources will mean that the rapid growth sectors may reach full capacity working while there is still excess demand in others. We should expect some prices to start rising even when some industries are not fully employed.

The Z curve is drawn on the assumption that factor prices and production methods remain unchanged. Any change in these conditions would shift the whole supply curve since there would be a new supply price for each level of output. An increase in wage costs or raw material prices would move the curve upwards as from Z to Z^1 in Fig. 30. A fall in factor prices would move the curve downwards as

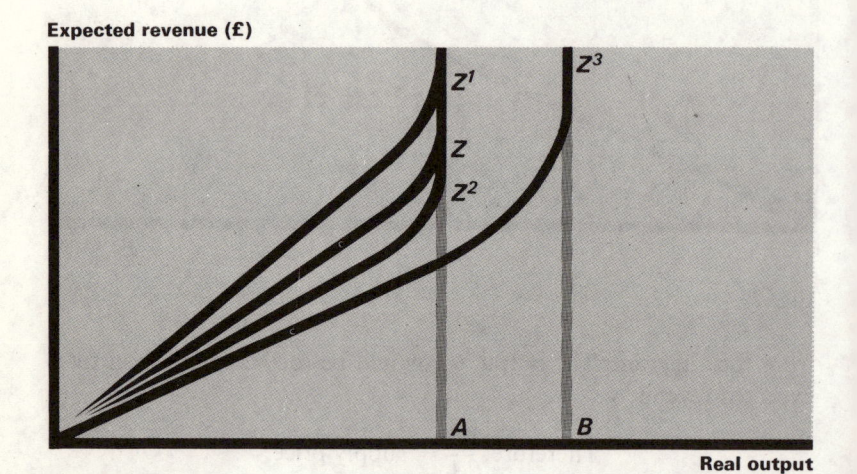

Fig. 30

shown by the change from Z to Z^2. In both cases the Z curve will terminate at the same output OA since productive capacity has not changed. On the other hand a change in the basic conditions of production will move the curve to the right or left. An increase in labour productivity giving a greater output per unit of input would shift the curve to the right (Z to Z^3). It now terminates at a greater output (OB) since productive capacity has increased.

An aggregate money demand curve

The aggregate demand curves used in the earlier chapters were developed with an underlying assumption that prices remain constant. Any movement of these demand curves, upwards or downwards, meant that more or less goods and services were being demanded at each level of national income. In other words, such changes in demand were changes in real terms – they represented changes in *the volume of demand*.

OUTPUT, DEMAND AND THE PRICE LEVEL

The present analysis aims to take account of the fact that prices do not remain constant. Movements in aggregate demand will affect prices as well as output and changes in prices will affect demand. We have already seen how changes in factor prices affect the aggregate supply curve.

To deal with changes in prices *and* output we need to use an aggregate *money* demand function which relates money expenditures to real output. It will represent planned money expenditures on goods and services at different levels of real output. Now, movements of such a demand curve do not necessarily indicate changes in the volume of demand. An increase in prices (and hence in incomes) could mean that the aggregate money demand curve moves upwards but leaves the volume of demand at each level of real income unchanged. There would be a greater total expenditure at each level of real output, but the increase in prices would leave real demand unchanged. In other words, price changes might move the aggregate money demand curve, but not alter spending plans in real terms.

Our earlier analysis of the components of aggregate demand indicate that the shape of the aggregate money demand curve will be similar to that of the D curve in Fig. 31 where the aggregate demand and supply curves are brought together.

Planned spending and expected revenue (£)

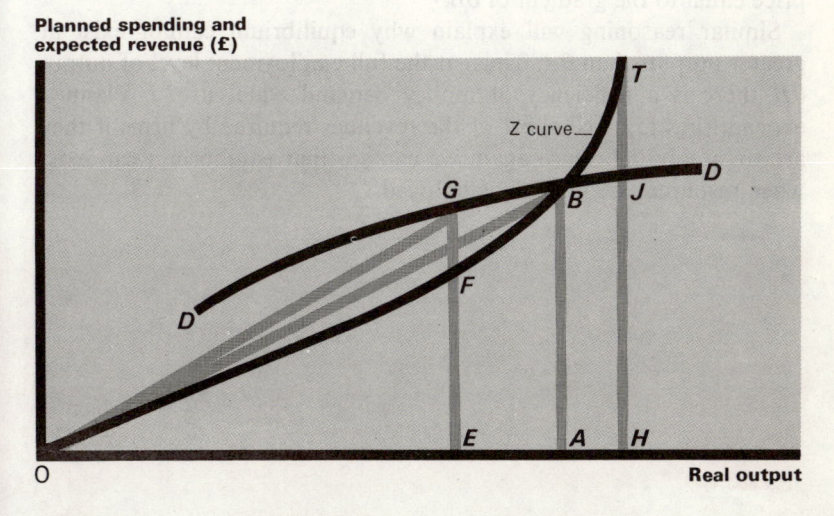

Fig. 31

OUTPUT AND THE PRICE LEVEL

The Z curve shows the total outputs which firms will supply at different levels of expected total revenue. The D curve shows the planned expenditures on domestic output at different levels of real income. The curves intersect at the output level OA. Firms will produce this output when their anticipated total receipts are equal to AB. When output is OA, planned spending is equal to AB. OA, therefore, is the equilibrium level of output, since aggregate money demand is equal to the total revenue which firms require in order to supply this output. Aggregate output OA will be offered at a supply price per unit (the general price level) of

$$\frac{AB}{OA}$$

and this is equal to the gradient of the line OB.

At lower levels of output there will be some excess money demand. At output OE, for example, anticipated revenue is EF, but planned expenditure will be EG. Excess money demand at this level of output will be GF. This excess money demand will provide firms with an incentive to expand output to the equilibrium position OA. The required supply price for output OE is the gradient of the line OF, but this output could be sold at a price equal to the gradient of the line OG. If firms raise their prices, the increased profits will stimulate increased production, output will expand to OA, which will be disposed of at a price equal to the gradient of OB.

Similar reasoning will explain why equilibrium cannot exist at greater outputs than OA. Thus, at the full employment level of output OH there is a deficiency of money demand equal to TJ. Planned expenditures fall well short of the revenues required by firms if they are to supply OH. Once again we can see that equilibrium can exist when resources are not fully employed.

17
Inflation

The analysis of the previous section will help us to understand one of the most serious and universal economic problems – inflation. This is a term which has acquired several meanings. It may be used to describe a situation where aggregate demand increases and exceeds aggregate supply at the current price level. In this case rising prices are not, necessarily, a feature of inflation since unemployed resources may be available to satisfy the increased demand.

The term may also mean an excess of aggregate demand under conditions of full employment. In this case prices will probably rise, but where prices are 'sticky' the excess demand may show itself in the form of waiting lists, long order books and queues. This definition tends to concentrate on the employment aspect, but, as we have seen, prices tend to rise before national capacity is fully employed.

The most common feature of inflation is the persistent upward movement of prices and it seems reasonable to accept the general view that inflation means rising prices. It is now customary to classify inflation as being either *demand-pull* or *cost-push*. Although the distinction is still subject to some dispute, it is a useful classification.

Demand inflation

Demand inflation may be defined as a situation where demand persistently exceeds supply at current prices so that prices are being 'pulled upwards' by the continuous upward shift of the demand function. Micro-economic theory demonstrates that an increase in price will lead to a choking off of the excess demand and a new equilibrium at the higher price. This would indeed be the case if prices were rising and money incomes were constant, but we are now dealing with the economy as a whole and any rise in the general price level means a corresponding rise in money incomes. Higher prices generate increased purchasing power and it is this which makes inflation a continuing process. We can use our aggregate demand and supply curves to illustrate the demand-pull process.

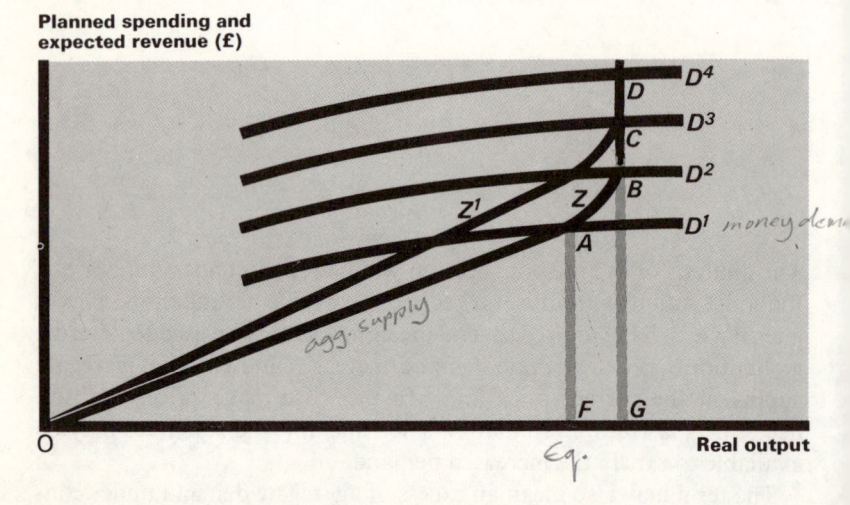

Fig. 32

In Fig. 32 aggregate money demand (D^1) and aggregate supply (Z) are in equilibrium when real output is OF, and the supply price is equal to the gradient OA. Now suppose there is a steady upward movement of demand, due, perhaps, to an increase in autonomous investment or an increase in the propensity to consume. Over some range of output, prices will be stable since we are moving along that part of the Z curve which is a straight line through the origin. As full employment is approached, costs increase and the Z curve turns upwards. Increasing money demand will cause prices to increase. When demand reaches the position D^2 we have an equilibrium situation at full employment output (OG). Planned money expenditure (BG) is exactly equal to the revenue required to persuade firms to produce output OG. The price level is represented by the gradient of BO.

Now suppose there is a further increase in aggregate money demand to D^3. There will now be excess money demand at full employment output. Planned expenditure is CG and the excess money demand is CB. Firms and households are trying to buy a greater volume of goods and services than can be supplied at current prices. In the short period output cannot be increased so that the whole effect of the excess money demand falls on prices. But this excess demand will also affect factor prices. Firms trying to meet the additional demand will bid up the prices of scarce labour and materials. Unions will also use their increased bargaining powers to raise wages. Direct costs will increase and the Z curve will move upwards from Z to Z^1. The supply price of the national output will increase from gradient OB to gradient OC.

We have not reached an equilibrium position, however, since the increase in wages and other factor prices which raised the Z curve will give a further upward impetus to the demand curve which now rises to D^4. Once again there is excess demand (CD) at the current price level (gradient OC). And so the process will go on. Here we have the inflationary process, increasing demand——increasing prices——increasing costs——increasing incomes——increasing demand——and so on.

Two questions now present themselves:
1. What causes the aggregate money demand to increase and generate inflationary pressures?
2. Will the inflationary process gradually peter out or will it be perpetual?

EXCESS DEMAND

Demand-pull inflation is usually associated with conditions of full employment where increases in aggregate demand cannot be matched by corresponding increases in supply. There are several ways in which excess demand may arise under full employment conditions.

There may be an increase in government expenditure not matched by a corresponding increase in taxation. If the deficit is financed by borrowing from the banks it means that the additional expenditure is being financed by an increase in the money supply.

Autonomous investment might increase when there is no corresponding increase in current savings. The additional funds may be obtained from past savings. If there is no corresponding increase in taxation there will be excess demand and an upward pressure on prices.

Excess demand may also arise from an increasing surplus on the balance of payments. Exports, remember, are inflationary since they generate income at home, but remove a corresponding value of output from the home market. If an export surplus is not balanced by increased taxation or savings, domestic expenditure will be greater than the value of domestic supplies at current prices.

A diversion of resources to the production of military equipment, or increased capital formation (possibly due to attempts to increase the rate of growth) may also result in inflationary pressures. Incomes will not fall, but the supply of consumer goods and services is reduced. There will need to be increased savings or taxation in order to remove the excess money demand.

Major inflations have often occurred during immediate post-war periods. During a war people are encouraged to save in order to reduce inflationary pressures and to help finance the war. Once hostilities cease there is a strong desire to return to 'normal' patterns of consumption. There will be a strong desire to spend, backed up by a massive ability to spend, since current incomes will be supplemented by a large accumulation of past savings. But supply will be inadequate to meet this demand at current prices since a major part of post-war output will be required for reconstruction and capital replacement.

Once the inflationary pressures have begun, they set up expectations of further price increases. Money will become less attractive as an asset and people will prefer to hold commodities, property, and company shares. Prices will tend to rise even faster as the velocity of circulation increases[1].

WILL INFLATION PETER OUT?

Inflation could, theoretically, continue indefinitely if, every time factor incomes increase, aggregate money demand increased in the same proportion. This would mean that real demand remains unchanged but the excess money demand would not be eliminated. If, however, the D curve in Fig. 32 moves upwards by less than the upward shift in the Z curve the process would be a converging one. Monetary demand would be increasing at a slower rate than prices and an equilibrium position will be reached eventually. There are some reasons why this latter development is a possibility.

(a) The propensity to consume may fall as money incomes increase so that C increases at a slower rate than Y. A progressive system of income tax would be another reason for a slowing down in the rate of growth of money demand.

(b) Some groups may not receive increases in money income which fully compensate for the rise in prices. Although money incomes rise by the full extent of the price increases, income is redistributed and the overall propensity to spend may fall. If this is so, aggregate money demand will not rise by the same amount as the Z curve.

(c) Rising prices at home will tend to reduce the volume of exports and increase the volume of imports. A fall in X and an increase in M will tend to reduce the growth of aggregate demand.

(d) As prices rise and money incomes increase, so will the transactions demand for money. This will shift the liquidity preference curve to the right and, assuming no change in the money supply, the rate of interest will increase. If it is sensitive to changes in the rate of interest, investment will fall and so will aggregate demand, or the rate of increase will diminish.

---

[1] When inflation accelerates to the point where a price explosion develops, money loses its value and we have a situation of *hyper-inflation*.

Although it is possible for the inflationary process to work itself out to a new equilibrium, recent experience demonstrates that this will only be achieved after very large, and politically unacceptable, increases in prices. It seems inevitable that official action will be required to deal with the inflationary problem.

Cost-push inflation

The demand-pull theory of inflation indicates that prices will go on rising as long as there is excess demand to pull them upwards. Rising prices may be sustained, however, by pressures which push them upwards rather than pull them upwards.

Cost inflation is due to autonomous increases in firms' costs, and it is usually regarded as being primarily a wage-inflation process. This is due to the fact that wages make up by far the greater part of total costs (about 70 per cent). Nevertheless cost inflation can originate in any other item of costs such as a rise in import prices or an increase in indirect taxation. Focusing attention on wages may be justified not only because wages are the most important cost item, but because, if other components of total costs increase, there seems no reason why an upward *trend* of prices should be set in motion. A rise in import prices or an increase in indirect taxation could lead to a once and for all increase in the general price level. A rise in wages which leads to an increase in prices is likely to generate an inflationary spiral because the increase in prices is one of the main causes of further wage demands.

In times of full employment, or near full employment, trade union bargaining powers are very strong. They will certainly be strong enough to maintain the 'real' incomes of their members by raising money incomes to match any increases in prices. In fact, they have proved that they can achieve more than this and claims for higher wages are usually based on adjustments designed to increase the real income of union members.

In industries where productivity has been increasing at a favourable rate, such wage claims will not be strongly resisted since labour costs will not be seriously affected. A major basis of union wage claims, however, is the 'comparability argument'. Unions are concerned to maintain the same relative differentials between the rates of pay of different groups of workers. A major settlement in a key industry will be followed by a chain reaction of wage claims designed to restore the previous differentials. Such claims, if pressed successfully, will almost inevitably exceed the general increase in productivity and raise labour costs. Employers will attempt to protect their profit margins by raising prices. This increase in prices will lead to further wage claims and a

MACRO-ECONOMICS

further settlement which increases costs, and prices rise once again. This is the familiar pattern of the wage-price spiral. In this sequence factor costs are pushing up prices.

A cost-push inflation may be a logical outcome of a rise in prices due initially to a rise in aggregate demand. This is not always the case and cost inflation may begin and continue even when aggregate demand is insufficient to maintain full employment. Provided unemployment is not so serious as to severely reduce union membership and bargaining power, organised labour is quite capable of pushing up wages and prices even when the supply of labour is in excess of the demand for it at current wage rates. Recent British experience has shown that union bargaining strength is now much less susceptible to unemployment than it was some years ago.

Any autonomous increase in costs can initiate a cost-push inflation, but it seems that it is wage-push pressures which keep the process going. We can use the aggregate demand and supply curves developed earlier to illustrate the cost-push process.

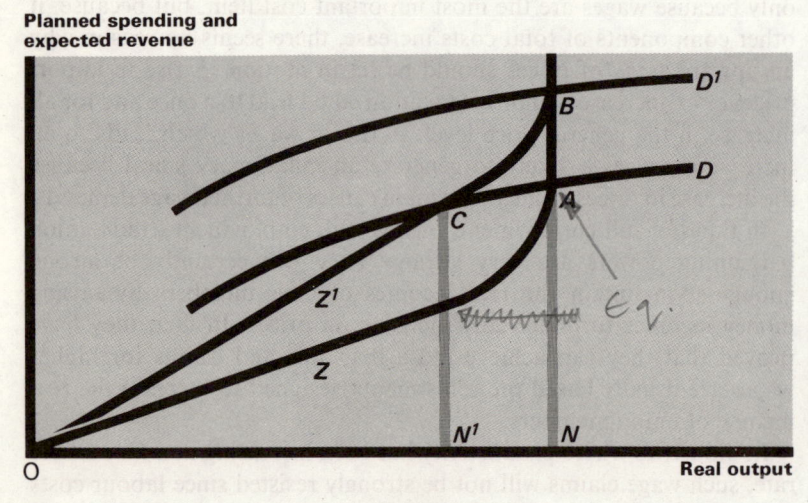

Fig. 33

Initially output is at an equilibrium level ON, where aggregate demand (D) is equated with aggregate supply (Z). The general price level is

$$\frac{AN}{ON}$$

An increase in wages which exceeds any increase in productivity will

190

raise labour costs and hence the expected revenues required to call forth any given supply. The aggregate supply curve will move upwards from Z to Z^1 and the supply price increases from slope OA to slope OC. If demand does not change this movement in supply would cause the level of output to fall to ON^1. This will not be the case, however, since the increase in wages will increase demand. If the aggregate demand curve moves to D^1 and fully compensates for the shift in supply we have a new equilibrium at the same level of output (ON), but at a higher price level

$$\frac{BN}{ON}$$

This rise in prices will probably provoke a further round of wage demands and the process will continue. This is the wage-price spiral. If, because of reasons discussed earlier, D does not increase sufficiently to fully balance the movement in Z, the process will not continue indefinitely – the rise in prices will gradually come to an end.

The distinction between demand and cost inflation is crucial for policy purposes. Demand inflation can be dealt with by measures to reduce total demand, but, where the inflation is due to an autonomous increase in costs, there is no reason to believe that it can be dealt with by reducing aggregate demand. (See also page 254.)

Unemployment and inflation

The preceding discussions have brought out the important distinction between an increase in spending in a fully employed economy and in an under-employed economy. The relationship between unemployment and inflation has been generalised in the well-known curve named after the economist A. W. Phillips, who first plotted it. The original version of the *Phillips curve* plotted the relationship between the rate of increase of wages and the unemployment percentage for the period 1861–1957. Phillips found a remarkably stable inverse relationship between changes in wages and the rate of unemployment. Since there is a fairly close connection between the rate of increase of money wages and the rate of increase of prices, it is now usual to present the Phillips curve as showing the relationship between the level of unemployment and the rate of change of prices. Fig. 34 gives the general picture revealed by Phillips' investigation.

The diagram shows that low levels of unemployment are more conducive to increases in prices than are high levels. Phillips concluded that if productivity is rising at about 2 per cent per annum, an unemployment rate of about $2\frac{1}{2}$ per cent would be consistent with

Annual percentage change in prices

↑ Increase

Low　　　　　　　　　　　　　　　　　　　High
　　　　　　　　　　　　　　　　　　　Unemployment

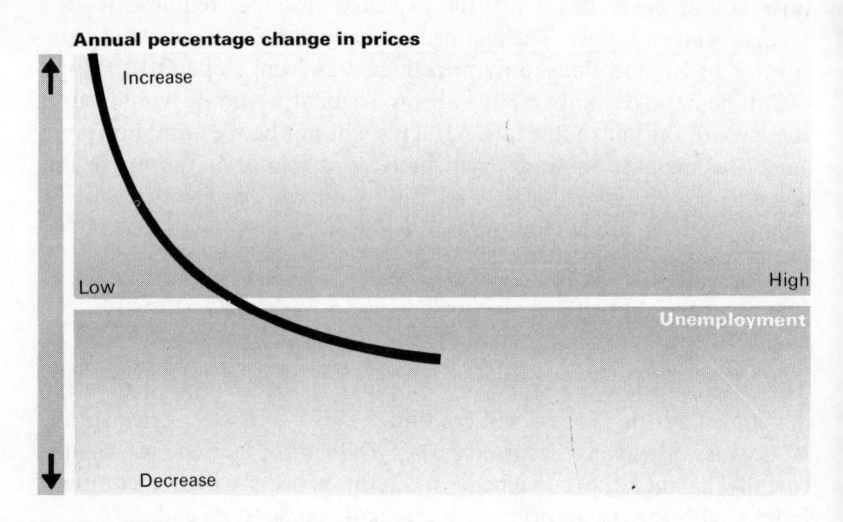

↓ Decrease

Fig. 34

stable prices. To maintain stable wage rates he estimated that unemployment would have to be as high as $5\frac{1}{2}$ per cent.

The Phillips curve seems to present a convincing statistical relationship between the rate of unemployment and price movements, but it does not, in itself, imply any causal relationship. Many economists, however, assume that the main thread of causation runs from labour scarcity to increases in wages and so to increases in prices. It is recognised, however, as Phillips himself acknowledged, that changes in money wages are also influenced by recent changes in prices, especially in retail prices.

The connection between the level of unemployment and inflation revealed by the Phillips curve would seem to have serious implications, because both stable prices and full employment are major objectives of economic policy. If these implications are accepted, the policy makers appear to have a choice between inflation and unemployment. Economists usually refer to this problem as the 'trade off' between rising prices and unemployment. It is interesting to note that in the USA, where the percentage of unemployment since the Second World War has been about twice that of Western European countries, the rate of inflation has been roughly half the European rate.

Fig. 35 shows that in the UK from 1951 to 1966 there was some inverse relationship between the level of unemployment and the annual percentage rise in prices. Since 1967, however, a new pattern has developed. Prices (and wages) have been rising quite sharply although

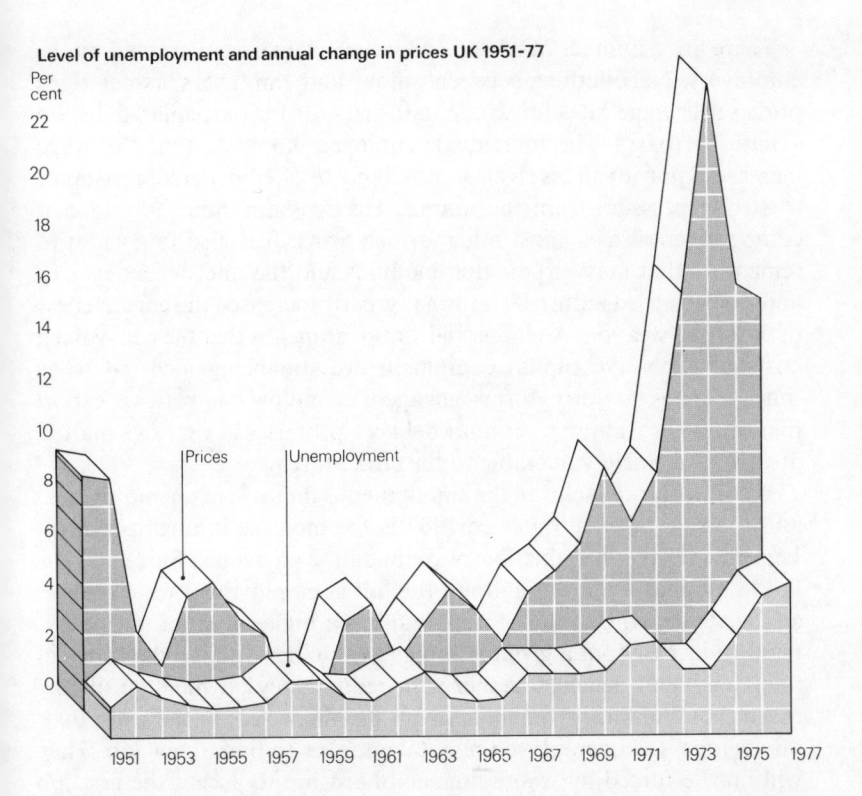

INFLATION

Level of unemployment and annual change in prices UK 1951-77

Source: Economic Trends HMSO.

Fig. 35

unemployment has been at relatively high levels. These recent developments in the UK provide a fairly striking example of cost-push inflation. A full analysis of the causes would be a very difficult exercise, but we can identify some of the major elements.

The higher import costs brought about by the 1967 devaluation began to affect domestic price levels in 1968 and 1969. There were also substantial increases in indirect taxes in 1968 and 1969 which led to further price increases. In 1969 and 1970 the restraints of the incomes policy which had been in operation since 1965 were substantially relaxed and this tended to raise the expectations of union negotiators. In spite of rising unemployment, substantial wage rises greatly exceeding any increases in productivity were granted during the period 1969–1971. Escalating wage claims, and high rates of inflation continued to be features of the UK economy until more effective incomes policies were introduced in the later 1970s (See Appendix).

There are a number of reasons why such claims were granted by the employers. Negotiations between unions and employers' associations often settle wage rates for whole industries, or for particular skills, on a national basis. The individual employer, knowing that the wage increases apply to all his rivals, is not likely to offer any great resistance to strong pressure from the unions. He does not suffer any loss of competitiveness as against other British firms. It is also important to remember that mass production methods and the interdependence of highly specialised industrial units has greatly increased the effectiveness of the strike weapon. An industrial stoppage means that the heavy fixed costs of expensive capital equipment are still being incurred when output drops to zero. Firms engaged in highly competitive export markets where failure to honour delivery promises is a serious matter, are also extremely vulnerable to the strike threat.

A contributory factor in the simultaneous increase in unemployment and the rate of inflation since 1967 is the increase in unemployment benefits and the introduction of redundancy payments. Since it is the fall in purchasing power and not the fall in employment which causes aggregate demand to fall, it now requires a higher level of unemployment to bring about a given fall in aggregate demand. Higher rates of unemployment benefit together with redundancy payments probably mean that 'voluntary' unemployment has increased, in the sense that, on average, the unemployed may take longer to find a new job. They will not be forced by severe financial hardship to accept the first job which comes along. Another factor has undoubtedly been the gradual adjustment of expectations. Experience of inflation creates a general feeling of insecurity—everyone tries 'to get in first' with their wage claim. There is an acceleration of the bargaining cycle and a swelling of the demands for higher incomes.

Rising prices and rising unemployment would seem to imply that the general shape of the Phillips curve no longer applies to current events. Some economists have suggested that these recent developments may be explained by a movement of the curve to the right. In other words, a given reduction of demand may bring about the same increase in unemployment as before, but it does not bring about the same reduction in the rate of inflation. It now requires a much greater increase in unemployment to achieve any given reduction in inflation. Hence, although the Phillips curve may have the correct shape, its position has moved to the right.

The effects of inflation

Inflation is generally regarded as undesirable because it produces some serious social and economic problems. It leads to an arbitrary redistribution of real income. Although a rise in the price level produces a corresponding increase in money incomes, all prices do not rise to the same degree, and different income groups will be affected in different ways. There will be losers and gainers.

The 'losers' are those whose incomes are fixed, or relatively fixed in money terms. This group includes those incomes derived from fixed interest securities, controlled rents and some private pensions schemes. In a similar category are those people receiving salaries or pensions which are adjusted only after long time intervals. All income recipients in this group will suffer a fall in their real incomes.

Where money income is linked to price movements, real incomes will remain relatively unchanged. The incomes of salesmen and professional groups (architects, surveyors, estate agents), where fees and commissions are expressed as a percentage of the value of the work undertaken, fall into this category.

A substantial group of wage earners also come into this class since many workers have their wages linked to the Retail Price Index.

The effects on incomes derived from profits depends upon the type of inflation. During a demand-pull inflation profits will tend to rise. The prices of final goods and services are often more flexible in an upward direction than factor prices (costs) and the margin between the two price levels tends to widen, because of the time lag. When cost-push inflation is being experienced, profits tend to be squeezed. Since there is no excess demand it will be much more difficult for entrepreneurs to pass on the full effects of the rising costs in the form of higher prices.

Wage earners generally more than hold their own when the price level is rising. In the UK, and most other industrial countries, wages have tended to rise faster than prices. But there is some redistribution effect. What has tended to happen is that certain groups with superior bargaining power have gained at the expense of other groups.

Inflation has important effects on the debtor–creditor relationship. Debtors tend to gain since the purchasing power of the money repaid at the end of a loan is less than the purchasing power of the money borrowed. This may encourage 'spending' rather than 'lending' and hence reduce the funds available for investment. It may lead also to higher interest rates as creditors demand some additional return as a compensation for the falling value of money.

Demand-pull inflation is associated with buoyant trading conditions. Excess demand is associated with a sellers' market where the risks of trading are greatly reduced and firms can sell almost anything. These easy market conditions might well give rise to complacency and inefficiency since the competitive pressures to improve the products and production techniques are seriously weakened. But this is certainly not the case in a cost-push inflation. These conditions place a premium on efficiency and firms which cannot absorb some of the increased factor prices by improving efficiency will find it difficult to survive.

Demand inflation, it has been argued, is favourable to economic growth since the excess demand and easy marketing conditions will stimulate investment and expansion. On the other hand, as noted above, it may also lead to inefficiency which is not conducive to growth.

In economies such as the UK, which are dependent upon a high level of exports and imports, inflation usually leads to balance of payments difficulties. If other countries are not inflating to the same extent, the rise in the domestic price level will make exports less competitive and imports more competitive. If this process is not checked it must lead to a deficit on the current account of the balance of payments. This problem is particularly acute during a demand-pull type of inflation when, in addition to the unfavourable price movements, the excess demand in the home market will 'draw in' an increased volume of imports. These balance of payments effects, of course, apply where a country is operating on a system of fixed exchange rates. Otherwise, as the next chapter explains, a flexible exchange rate can prevent the rise in home prices having unfavourable effects in the international sector.

We have already discussed some of the fiscal and monetary instruments which might be used to combat a demand-pull type of inflation. The cost-push type creates more difficult problems. Policies to deal with inflation are examined in Chapter 20 and the Appendix.

Questions on Chapters 15–17

ESSAY QUESTIONS

1. What is the connection between the quantity of money and the price level? **(L)**

2. Is credit expansion really inflationary? **(L)**

3. What do you understand by the terms 'inflation' and 'productivity'? Would the rate of inflation be slower if productivity rose faster? **(O & C)**

4. 'Demand-pull and cost-push are merely different names for the same type of inflation'. Discuss this statement. **(L)**

5. To what extent is the general level of prices influenced by government budgetary policy? **(O & C)**

6. Explain why some major groups stand to lose and some to gain from inflation. **(AEB)**

7. What measures can a government take to deal with inflation? **(JMB)**

8. How is Aggregate Money Demand (AMD) usually subdivided? Explain the effects of an increase in AMD on output, employment and prices. **(L)**

9. Is full employment compatible with stable prices? **(L)**

10. If the quantity theory of money has validity why are fiscal measures necessary to stabilise the price level? **(C)**

MULTIPLE CHOICE QUESTIONS

Questions 1, 2 and 3, are based on the following identity, $MV \equiv PT$. Which of these variables is most likely to be the first affected by:

1. An increase in the cash reserves of the commercial banks.

2. A large proportion of the working population change from weekly wage rates to monthly salaries.

3. An increase in total output.

Questions 4 and 5 are based on the following data: On average, people choose to keep one-tenth of their annual expenditure in the form of money balances. The stock of money is £1m. The total number of transactions in one year is 5m.

4. What is the transactions velocity of circulation of money?

(a) 6.
(b) 10.
(c) 5.
(d) 50.

5. What is the average price of the transactions?
(a) £2.
(b) £0·5.
(c) £0·2.
(d) £0·02.

6. For the main effect of an increase in the money supply to be an increase in the general price level, which of the following conditions must be satisfied?
1. The physical volume of output must be fixed for the time being.
2. The economy must be operating well below full employment capacity.
3. The payments conventions of the community must be fairly inflexible.
4. The demand for money must be insensitive to change in the rate of interest.
(a) 1 and 3.
(b) 1, 3 and 4.
(c) 2, 3 and 4.
(d) 2 and 4.

7. The Phillips curve shows that:
(a) Inflation is caused by low levels of unemployment.
(b) Prices will be low when there is a high level of unemployment.
(c) At high levels of unemployment wages will be falling.
(d) The annual percentage rise in prices tends to be inversely related to the percentage of unemployment.

8. Cost-push inflation,
(a) Requires some degree of excess demand to initiate the process.
(b) Is caused by wages rising faster than prices.
(c) Can occur even when the economy is operating with idle resources.
(d) Means that there is a shortage of labour which is causing wages to rise faster than productivity.

18
The Balance of Payments and The Rate of Exchange

We have already encountered the concept of the balance of payments when we discussed the relationship between internal and external equilibrium. The equilibrium equation may be written in the form, $Y - (C + I + G) = X - M$. This formulation demonstrates that any excess of national product (Y) over home demand ($C + I + G$) must be equal to the export surplus. Conversely, an excess of home demand over national output implies an import surplus. Changes in the balance of payments are related directly to national income and the level of home demand.

But the balance of payments is more commonly used to refer to the system of accounts which show, in summary form, the country's financial transactions with the rest of the world. It is an annual statement of the foreign currency received by residents of the home country and the foreign currency paid out by those residents. By 'residents' we mean households, firms and public authorities.

The first point to note is that the word 'balance' implies some kind of equality and, indeed, in an accounting sense the balance of payments always balances. This is because, for the balance of payments as a whole, every receipt of foreign currency must be matched by a corresponding payment. If the residents of a country spend and lend more abroad than they receive from abroad, the deficit must be met by running down reserves, borrowing or the sale of overseas assets. Similarly if residents receive more foreign currency than they spend abroad there will be some additions to reserves, an increase in overseas lending or additions to overseas assets. When all current and capital items are recorded the net balance will be zero.

Although the balance of payments must necessarily balance since it is a book-keeping exercise, it does not mean that it is always in equilibrium. We shall discuss this point when we have examined the presentation of the accounts.

MACRO-ECONOMICS

The structure of the balance of payments

It is normal practice to classify the various types of transaction and set them out under specific headings. The actual form in which they are presented varies slightly from country to country. We shall use the UK tables for purposes of explanation. The values are recorded in pounds sterling although, in fact, they refer to transactions in foreign currency.

Table 9. *UK balance of payments summary 1975–1977*   £m.

	1975	1976	1977
Current Account			
Visible trade	−3 205	−3 510	−1 612
Invisible trade	+1 591	+2 403	+1 577
1. *Current balance*	−1 614	−1 107	−35
2. *Investment and other capital flows*	+203	−2 806	+4 802
3. *Balancing Item*	−54	+285	+2 596
Total Currency Flow (1 + 2 + 3)	−1 465	−3 628	+7 363
4. *Official Financing*			
Official borrowings drawn (+) repaid (−)	+810	+2 775	+2 225
Official reserves drawings on (+) additions to (−)	+655	+853	−9 588
	+1 465	+3 628	−7 363

Source: The Times 9 March 1978.

THE CURRENT ACCOUNT

The current account reflects the day-to-day dealings between UK residents and residents of overseas countries in those things most familiar in international trade – goods and services. It is divided into two parts. The first deals with *visible trade* and shows the difference between the values of exports and imports of goods. This difference is known as the Balance of Trade and these figures are published monthly. The second part contains the earnings from and payments for such services as shipping and aviation and insurance banking and tourism; it also includes interest and profits earned by British investments abroad and by foreign investment in Britain; government current spending abroad; and transfer payments such as gifts and pensions paid to people overseas. The net result of these transactions is shown as the *invisible balance* and these details are published quarterly. When the visible and invisible balances are added together we have the Balance of Payments on Current Account.

The UK usually has a comfortable surplus on the invisible account so that the current account can be in surplus in spite of a trade deficit. The balance on current account is of great importance, because it shows whether a country is paying its way in its day-to-day dealings. A surplus on current account enables a country to build up its reserves of foreign currency which are needed (*a*) as a kind of buffer stock to deal with temporary trade fluctuations and other disturbances, (*b*) as a means of adding to overseas investment and (*c*) as a means of repaying foreign debts.

CAPITAL FLOWS

In addition to the current account transactions, there are other flows of money into and out of the country which affect its ability to build up reserves and pay off debts. These are flows of capital coming into or going out of Britain for investment or other forms of lending, both for short and long periods. Money coming in is marked + and money going out is marked —. Capital transactions are carried out by the private and public sectors. Over the years British investment abroad has usually been larger than overseas investment in the UK.

BALANCING ITEM

When the result of all capital transactions is added to the current balance, the total never adds up exactly to the amount of foreign currency the country has gained or lost, which is known precisely by the Bank of England. It is extremely difficult for the statisticians to get a full coverage of all international transactions and so a balancing item is included to give the net effect of all errors and omissions. If the item is a + it means that more foreign currency has come into the country than the recorded transactions indicate.

TOTAL CURRENCY FLOW

The balancing item is added to the current balance and the investment and capital flows to give the total currency flow. This is the second important total in the table since it shows the foreign currency becoming available to the country. Where there is a loss (a minus currency flow) it has to be covered by running down the reserves, or borrowing from the International Monetary Fund, or other sources overseas. A positive currency flow means that foreign currency is available for adding to reserves or paying off foreign debts.

OFFICIAL FINANCING

The last section of the balance of payments table shows how the authorities have covered a net deficit or disposed of a net surplus. Changes in the official reserves, borrowings from and repayments to the IMF and foreign central banks appear in this section. The plus and minus signs may appear rather confusing because a plus sign usually indicates a favourable movement and a minus sign an unfavourable one. In fact the minus sign means that the money is 'going out' to pay off debts or into the reserves and these are favourable transactions. The plus sign means that money is 'coming in' to meet a deficit and since it is coming from the reserves or foreign borrowings it is an unfavourable movement.

Equilibrium in the balance of payments

When is the balance of payments in equilibrium? On the simplest level the concept relates to the current account, and equilibrium may be said to exist when, over the longer term, the value of imports is equal to the value of exports. Such an equilibrium, however, may be achieved by the use of import controls which are suppressing a potential import surplus. It may also be the case that the equilibrium arises because a high level of unemployment is depressing the demand for imports. This would not be considered a satisfactory equilibrium where policy aims included full employment and trade liberalisation as important objectives.

For an advanced country the idea of equilibrium as a mere balance on the current account is not very realistic, since capital movements will be an important feature of its international trade. In particular such a country will be expected to provide economic aid to less developed countries; to build up adequate reserves to meet temporary imbalances; and to increase its investment overseas in order to maintain and increase its invisible earnings. We might say, therefore, that for a country like the UK the balance of payments is in long-term equilibrium where the average current account surplus allows for:

(*a*) some required level of net overseas investment, including debt

repayments and economic aid, and
(b) some required increase in foreign currency reserves,
without having to sacrifice the objectives of full employment and without having recourse to restrictions on imports which violate international agreements on trade liberalisation.

It is not really possible to fully explain the concept of external equilibrium, however, without bringing in the question of foreign exchange and the external value of a country's currency. What has been said above applies to the UK and most other countries when a system of fixed exchange rates is in operation. We shall see later that the situation is rather different where the system is one of floating exchange rates.

Exchange rates

FOREIGN EXCHANGE

The fact that different countries use different currencies gives rise to major complications in foreign trade. Generally speaking, national currencies are only fully acceptable within the territorial limits of each nation, so that a commercial transaction between nations gives rise to two exchanges. There is the exchange of one currency for another and then the exchange of money for a good or service.

The *rate of exchange* is simply the price of one currency in terms of another, and, in the absence of official intervention, it is determined like any other price by the forces of supply and demand. The demand for foreign currencies is largely a derived demand; it is derived from the demand for foreign goods and services. When a British firm wishes to buy an American machine it must first obtain dollars for which it will offer pounds in exchange. This transaction therefore gives rise to a *demand for dollars* and a *supply of pounds* in the foreign exchange market. Similarly an American wishing to spend a holiday in Britain creates a supply of dollars and a demand for pounds in the foreign exchange market. If, at the current rate of exchange, more pounds are being supplied by British importers wishing to buy American goods and services than are being demanded by Americans wishing to buy British goods and services, the price of the pound in terms of dollars will fall. This situation implies a deficit in the British balance of payments with the USA.

We must note that the demand for and supply of a currency on the foreign exchange market depends not only on the flow of trade, but also on the movements of capital, both short-term and long-term. An inflow of capital funds into the UK represents a demand for sterling in just the same way as a foreign demand for British machinery.

Freely fluctuating exchange rates

If the foreign exchange market were a free market and governments made no attempt to influence or control the rate at which their currencies exchanged for one another, the external value of a currency would vary from day to day in accordance with the supply and demand conditions in the foreign exchange market. An increase in the foreign demand for British goods and services would tend to raise the value of the pound, while an increased demand by UK residents for foreign goods would tend to lower the value of the pound.

When the value of a currency is free to fluctuate (or *float*) in the foreign exchange market, there is a kind of automatic adjustment process which will tend to bring about an equilibrium situation in the balance of payments. If, at the current rate of exchange, there is a tendency for the value of imports to exceed the value of exports, the value of the home currency will *depreciate* in terms of foreign currencies. Let us assume that such a tendency causes the value of the pound to fall from £1 = $2·4 to £1 = $2·0. It follows that, in terms of pounds, the prices of American goods have increased. An American machine valued at $4800 will now cost the British importer £2400 as against £2000 before the depreciation. On the other hand, in terms of foreign currencies, the prices of British goods have fallen. A British motor car valued at £1000 will now be available to Americans at a price of $2000 as against $2400 before the depreciation.

These relative price changes are likely to affect the quantity of British exports to the USA and quantity of British imports from the USA. British exports will increase and imports will fall, thus tending to correct the disequilibrium in the balance of payments with the USA.

THE EXCHANGE RATE AND ELASTICITIES OF DEMAND AND SUPPLY

Changes in the exchange rate will cause changes in the volumes of exports and imports, but just how much these volumes change depends upon the elasticities of demand and supply in British and American markets. Let us continue with the assumption of a depreciation of the pound in terms of the dollar.

If the demand for British goods in the US market is inelastic the fall in the dollar prices of these goods will bring about a less proportionate increase in quantities sold, and dollar earnings will fall. If the demand is elastic the volume of sales will increase by a greater percentage than the percentage change in dollar prices. Dollar earnings will rise.

The effect of the depreciation of the pound on British imports is a little more complex. It is the British price of imports which has risen and not the dollar price. If, therefore, there is any fall in the quantities of American goods imported, British expenditure of dollars must fall.

More precisely, if the elasticity of demand for imports is not zero, then dollar expenditure will fall.

But if the British demand for American goods is not very sensitive to price changes (i.e. it is fairly inelastic), the domestic price level will be affected by the dearer imports. This is, of course, especially important where such imports consist of essential raw materials and foodstuffs. The dearer imports might create inflationary pressures of a cost-push nature.

It is also necessary to take into account the elasticities of supply of exports and imports. The increased demand for British exports could well lead to an increase in their prices. If it is not possible to increase the supplies of these goods easily and quickly (i.e. supply is inelastic) the increased demand could lead to higher prices. This is most likely to be the case when full employment conditions exist in the export industries. This domestic price increase will reduce the effect of the depreciation of the dollar prices of exports–they will not fall by the full extent of the depreciation–and the volume of exports will not expand as much as it would have done had the supply been elastic. For example, it was suggested earlier that a depreciation of the pound from £1 = $2·4 to £1 = $2·0 would reduce the overseas price of a £1000 motor car from $2400 to $2000. But this would only be the case if the supply of such cars were perfectly elastic. If this were not so and the increased demand raised the British price to £1100, the effect of the depreciation would be much smaller. The price of the car in the American market falls from $2400 to $2200; a 16·67 per cent depreciation has had only an 8·34 per cent price effect.

Similar reasoning can be applied to the situation with regard to imports. Depreciation, we have noted, raises the sterling prices of imports; it does not change the dollar prices. But where the supply of imports is inelastic, where, for example the foreign supplier cannot find alternative markets and is perhaps extremely dependent upon the UK market, he might decide to accept a cut in his dollar prices in order to maintain the volume of his exports. If he does so, the sterling price of imports will not rise by the full amount of the depreciation and the volume of imports might well be maintained at something near to their previous level–although foreign currency expenditure on them will fall.

SUMMARY

To summarise, we can say that under a system of fluctuating (or floating) exchange rates, a balance of payments equilibrium means that the demand for the currency in the foreign exchange market is exactly equal to its supply at the current exchange rate. Any tendency for the value of exports to exceed the value of imports will cause the currency to *appreciate* (i.e. its foreign exchange value increases), while a tendency for imports to exceed exports will cause it to depreciate. These changes in the external value of the currency will alter the relative prices of exports and imports and cause changes in the quantities of exports and imports demanded which will tend to restore the equilibrium. Just how effectively this automatic mechanism works depends to a great extent upon the elasticities of demand and supply in home and overseas markets.

SOME PROBLEMS WITH FLOATING EXCHANGE RATES

In spite of the fact that fluctuating or floating rates appear to provide a mechanism for the automatic correction of an external disequilibrium, only very rarely have the major international currencies been allowed to float freely. Governments have been loath to leave the external value of their currencies completely at the mercy of market forces for a number of reasons:

(*a*) Factors of production are relatively immobile so that changes in export and import prices could lead to unemployment in those industries adversely affected by price changes. Resources cannot be moved easily and quickly to those industries favourably affected by the international price movements.

(*b*) In a free market the rate of exchange is not only determined by the exports and imports of goods and services; capital movements are also important. Thus, capital movements which may be essentially of a short-term nature could affect the exchange rate and hence the relative prices of exports and imports, although the demand and supply conditions for such goods and services may not have changed at all.

(*c*) The foreign exchange market attracts speculators whose aim is to make a profit by buying a currency at one price and selling it at a higher price. Such speculative activity can increase the instability of the exchange rate, although all speculation is not de-stabilising. Where speculators are operating against current trends they might smooth out variations in the exchange rate.

(*d*) A freely fluctuating rate will add a further degree of uncertainty to international trade. A British importer of cotton, for example, would have to watch not only the dollar prices of his cotton, but also the movements in the pound–dollar rate of exchange. His costs would be affected by changes in the dollar price of cotton *and* by changes in the price of dollars. This added uncertainty would make the placing of large orders and long-term contracts a riskier business than it would be under fixed exchange rates. In practice, however, the risk is diminished because speculators provide a forward market where it is possible for importers to purchase foreign currency for future delivery at an agreed and known price. Recent experience, however, shows that the premiums charged for this service can be expensive and add substantially to costs.

Another argument sometimes advanced against floating exchange rates is that the system allows a freedom of action to governments in carrying out their domestic policies which might be used unwisely. Inflationary conditions at home usually lead to balance of payments problems. If this disequilibrium can be taken care of by easy and frequent adjustments of the exchange rate, there will be some temptation for governments to delay the unpopular corrective measures which must be taken at some time if the inflation is to be brought under control.

Managed exchange rates

The immobilities of domestic resources, the possible damaging effects of speculation and the uncertainties created for importers and exporters appear to have convinced governments of the undesirability of adopting completely flexible exchange rates. One alternative is to allow long-term adjustments in exchange rates while eliminating the unsettling effects of short-term fluctuations. This may be accomplished by making use of stabilisation funds which consist of supplies of the domestic currency, convertible foreign currencies and gold. These funds are used by the monetary authorities to smooth out the day-to-day variations in the market rate of exchange. One such fund is the Exchange Equalisation Account operated by the Bank of England.

If the value of the home currency is falling in terms of other currencies, the monetary authorities will intervene in the foreign exchange market using their fund of foreign currencies to purchase the depreciating currency. This will increase the market demand for the home currency and raise its external value. If the value of the currency is rising, the monetary authorities will intervene to increase the supply, and, by selling the domestic currency, they can replenish their stocks of foreign currency. Thus, by using a stabilisation fund the demand for and supply of a currency on the foreign exchange market can be influenced so as to stabilise its exchange value. It should be obvious that these funds can only be used to smooth out temporary imbalances. Any attempt to use such funds to prevent the depreciation of currency which is due to a persistent balance of payments deficit would soon exhaust the supplies of foreign currencies and gold. It may also be difficult for the authorities to determine the rate at which they should try to stabilise the exchange rate since it may not be easy to discover how much of a deviation in the exchange rate is due to speculative pressures and how much is due to changes in the demands for, and supplies of, goods and services.

Fixed exchange rates

When a country does not allow any short-term variations in the foreign exchange rate, it is said to be on a fixed external standard. If a group of countries maintain a fixed rate of exchange between their currencies and gold (or some other currency such as the dollar), then the rates at which their currencies exchange for one another are also fixed. The merit of such a system is that it removes one of the major uncertainties from international trade–importers and exporters do not have to worry about daily fluctuations in the prices of foreign currencies.

It does not, however, provide any automatic mechanism for bringing about an equilibrium in the balance of payments. Suppose, for example, the UK is experiencing a deficit in the balance of payments so that, at the current fixed rate, the supply of pounds in the foreign exchange market is exceeding the demand for them. The value of the pound will tend to fall and the central bank will be forced to take some action in order to maintain the external value of the currency at the agreed rate. It will intervene in the market by buying pounds, using for this purpose the foreign currency reserves. Thus, under a system of fixed exchange rates a disequilibrium in the balance of payments is reflected in changes in the level of the exchange reserves.

The problem is illustrated in Fig. 36. Initially there is market equilibrium at the fixed rate £1 = \$4. The excess of imports over exports then causes an increase in the supply of pounds which, if allowed to persist, would lead to a free market price of £1 = \$3. At the fixed rate of exchange there would be a surplus of pounds equal to ab. But the authorities are committed to maintaining the rate at £1 = \$4. They have several options open to them.

MAINTAINING A FIXED RATE OF EXCHANGE

In the first instance, as already explained, they will make use of the stabilisation fund (The Exchange Equalisation Account in the case of the UK). By raising the demand from D to D' (in Fig. 36) the rate will be held at £1 = \$4. Although the reserves of foreign currencies used for this purpose may be supplemented by borrowings from abroad there is a limit to such resources. This can only be a short-term measure and if the deficit persists (i.e. the drain of reserves continues) more fundamental measures must be taken.

Price of pounds

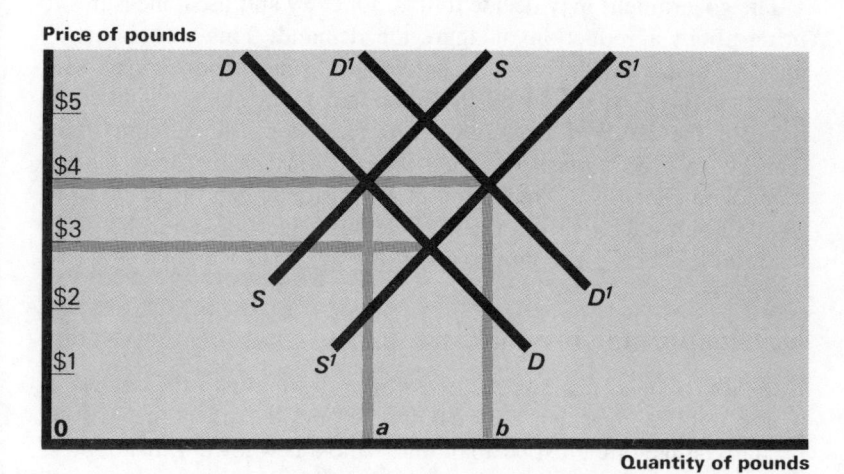

Fig. 36

The monetary authorities can introduce a system of exchange control which would give the central bank a monopoly over the home supplies of foreign currency. Exporters would be obliged to hand over their foreign currency earnings to the central bank which would then ration them out to pay for approved imports. The supply of pounds, in the foreign exchange market is then effectively restricted to $0a$ (Fig. 36). Exchange control is a serious impediment to world trade and international bodies such as GATT and the IMF strongly discourage the use of this measure.

An increase in the rate of interest might be used to attract foreign funds to the domestic money market. There is a large, internationally mobile, supply of short-term capital which moves from centre to centre seeking higher returns or greater security. An inflow of such capital represents an increase in the demand for the home currency in the foreign exchange market. One problem here is that an increase in the rate of interest would tend to restrict investment and consumption with consequent unfavourable effects on national income.

It might be necessary to limit imports by using tariffs and quotas. This would reduce the supply of imports and hence the supply of pounds in the foreign exchange market. The external value of the currency would increase if there were no change in the demand for exports. Unfortunately such actions are likely to provoke retaliation from other countries. Restricting imports also reduces the supply of goods and services on the home market so that there would be some increase in the general price level.

The government may decide to use monetary and fiscal measures to bring about a reduction of aggregate demand. This would restrict imports and provide more incentive for home producers to seek export markets. It would be an unpopular policy since it is likely to increase the level of unemployment. A major switch from home markets to export markets would take a considerable time and the immediate effect of the reduction in aggregate demand is likely to be a fall in output. This would tend to depress investment and have unfavourable effects on economic growth.

Devaluation and revaluation

If the above measures are unsuccessful in dealing with the deficit, or if, for political reasons, they cannot be adopted, then the existing fixed exchange rate must be abandoned and a new lower rate adopted. This procedure is known as devaluation. Whereas depreciation refers to a situation where the external value of a currency falls in a free market, devaluation means a movement from one fixed parity to a new and lower fixed rate of exchange. The opposite movements are known as appreciation and revaluation.

The immediate effect of devaluation is to make exports cheaper in terms of foreign currency and imports dearer in terms of home currency[1]. Whether or not devaluation will be effective in eliminating a balance of payments deficit depends upon the elasticities of demand for and supply of exports and imports, and upon the income effects of the price changes. The appropriate analysis of these features is similar to that already discussed in relation to depreciation (page 204). There are, however, some further points.

Devaluation can only be successful if other nations, particularly major competitors, do not retaliate. If these countries carry out a similar devaluation then the rates of exchange between such countries will be unchanged. If the country devaluing is a major importer, and imports are significantly reduced by the devaluation, there will be unfavourable income effects abroad which may prejudice the expected increase in export sales.

For a country like the UK which is very dependent upon imported foodstuffs and raw materials, the process of devaluation carries a real danger of cost-push inflation. The higher import prices are likely to generate a wage–price spiral. The immediate effects of devaluation are almost certainly bound to be unfavourable. The higher import prices take immediate effect while the lower export prices will mean

---

[1] Devaluation (and depreciation) worsens the *Terms of Trade* since any given volume of exports will now be exchanging for a smaller volume of imports.

reduced revenues for a considerable time – until the volume of exports has increased sufficiently to offset the lower prices. This increased volume of exports can only be supplied if there are idle resources, otherwise supplies must be diverted from the home market. If there is a situation of full employment, therefore, devaluation must be accompanied by measures to reduce home demand.

One of the great problems facing a country which is contemplating devaluation is to decide by how much to devalue. If the present fixed rate has been in operation for some time, and measures such as trade restrictions have been in use to maintain the rate, the true market value of the currency will be largely a matter of guesswork. A devaluation which does not go far enough, so that a balance of payments deficit persists, will provoke massive speculation against the currency. The speculators will gamble that a further devaluation is inevitable and, under a system of fixed rates, speculators are certain of the direction of the change in the exchange rate – the balance of payments position provides a clear indication of which way the rate should go.

Since world exports, by definition, must be equal to world imports, a deficit in one country must be offset by a surplus in other countries. One solution to the problem of a persistent deficit, therefore, might be the *revaluation* of the currencies of those countries experiencing persistent surpluses on their balance of payments. Revaluation increases the foreign prices of exports and reduces the home prices of imports. Hence, after revaluation, the surplus countries would be exporting less and importing more, and, in so doing, making things much more favourable for the deficit countries. Nations experiencing surpluses on their balance of payments are usually very reluctant to revalue, but it might be in their long-term interest to do so, otherwise the deficit countries might be forced to use trade barriers to deal with their deficits. Such measures can only reduce the rate of growth of world trade. West Germany revalued the Deutschmark several times in the 1960s and, in the major adjustment of parities agreed in December 1971, several currencies were revalued in relation to the dollar.

The IMF system

The International Monetary Fund and its sister institution the International Bank for Reconstruction and Development (the World Bank) were set up as a result of agreements reached at a conference held in 1944 at Bretton Woods in the USA. The IMF began work in 1945 and for the next 25 years the code of good conduct set out in the Fund Agreement provided the basis for the international monetary system operated by most of the non-communist world. Membership of the

Fund has increased to 130 from the original membership of 30. The main purposes of the Fund may be summarised as:

(*a*) to promote international monetary cooperation through a permanent institution which provides machinery for consultation and cooperation,

(*b*) to facilitate the expansion and balanced growth of world trade,

(*c*) to promote exchange rate stability and to prevent competitive exchange depreciation,

(*d*) to eliminate foreign exchange restrictions and to work for the full convertibility of currencies,

(*e*) to provide assistance to member countries with balance of payments difficulties so that they do not have to resort to measures which restrict international trade.

THE FUND'S RESOURCES

Each member contributes to a pool of gold and foreign currencies. The size of a country's contribution is determined according to its economic size and its importance as a trading nation. A member country is required to pay the Fund an amount in its own currency equal to 75 per cent of its quota and 25 per cent in gold and foreign currency (the requirement for a contribution in gold was dropped in 1976).

Countries experiencing balance of payments difficulties are able to draw foreign currencies from the Fund in order to help them finance a deficit. These drawings (or, more accurately, purchases, since the country exchanges its own currency for the foreign currency) are essentially short-term loans and the Fund normally requires that they be repaid within 3 to 5 years. The aim is to give deficit countries time to implement economic policies which help to restore external equilibrium without them having to resort to harmful policies such as exchange control, the use of tariffs and quotas, or competitive depreciation of their currencies.

The limits up to which a country may purchase foreign currencies from the Fund are determined by the size of the country's quota. The limit is reached when the Fund is holding a member's currency equal in value to 200 per cent of its quota. Since the Fund starts with a 75 per cent holding of the country's currency it means that foreign currency equal to 125 per cent of the quota may be 'borrowed'. Drawings up to 25 per cent of the quota are unconditional; further drawings may be subject to conditions laid down by the Fund in respect of the economic policies to be pursued by the borrowing country. In exceptional circumstances a country may receive help in excess of these limits. Interest is payable on drawings from the IMF.

The rapid growth of world trade in the post-war period together with the continuous increase in price levels has meant that balance of payments deficits and surpluses have become much greater in monetary terms. Calls for assistance have tended to place great strains on the IMF's resources. To help deal with this problem, members' quotas have been increased several times and a number of other schemes have been introduced to supplement the Fund's facilities.

i. *The General Arrangement to Borrow (GAB)*
This came into being in 1962 when a group of ten major industrial countries (plus Switzerland which is not a member of the IMF) agreed to supplement the Fund's resources in order to finance drawings by any other participant in the arrangement. In 1977 these commitments amounted to some 7·5 billion dollars.

ii. *Foreign currency swaps*
The central banks of the major trading countries have developed arrangements for the swapping of foreign currencies whereby each agrees to lend currency balances for an agreed period of time. This scheme is used mainly as a device for protecting currencies against speculation.

iii. *Stand-by credits*
A stand-by arrangement allows an IMF member to draw on a stated amount of currency from the IMF pool over a certain period of time. If the balance of payments situation quickly improves the stand-by credit may not be drawn but the country has the reassurance that assistance is available should it be needed. This scheme enables the IMF's resources to be used more economically.

iv. *Special Drawing Rights (SDRs)*
In 1970 the IMF introduced this entirely new reserve asset. SDRs were originally described as 'paper gold' since a unit of SDRs could be exchanged for a certain quantity of gold, but with the abolition of the official price of gold the value of an SDR is now expressed in terms of a weighted average of the exchange values of a number of major currencies. In fact, SDRs are simply claims or rights which are honoured by members of the IMF and by the IMF itself. SDRs are allocated to member countries in proportion to their quotas and they can be treated as part of a country's international monetary reserves. A country in deficit may use its SDRs to purchase needed foreign currency from other member countries. SDRs are a genuine addition to the supply of international liquid assets and in 1976 they made up about 5 per cent of total world reserves of such assets.

THE IMF AND EXCHANGE RATES

A basic aim of the IMF is to eliminate foreign exchange restrictions and to secure stability of exchange rates. The expansion of world trade is very dependent upon the freedom of governments, firms and households to convert one currency into another without restriction. If currencies are freely convertible, an export surplus with one country can be used to finance a deficit with another country. If currencies are not convertible then trade becomes bilateral and the volume of trade between any two countries is restricted to the smaller of the two demands. Under these conditions, Country B's ability to buy from Country A is limited to the value of the goods and services which she can sell to Country A. One of the main purposes of the assistance granted by the IMF is to discourage the use of exchange controls (i.e. restrictions on convertibility) as a means of dealing with balance of payments problems.

The belief that stable exchange rates were most conducive to expanding world trade led the architects of the IMF to opt for a kind of modified fixed exchange rate or *adjustable peg* system. Each member was obliged to declare a par value for its currency in terms of gold (more generally expressed in terms of the dollar because at this time the dollar was convertible into gold). The authorities in each country were responsible for maintaining the market value of the currency within 1 per cent of the par value. Thus, if the declared par value of the pound was £1 = \$2·00, the UK would be obliged to maintain the market value of the pound within the limits £1 = \$1·98 and £1 = \$2·02. The par value was not meant to be immutable, but it could only be changed when a member country was experiencing a fundamental balance of payments disequilibrium. Devaluation or revaluation of up to 10 per cent did not require the Fund's permission, but changes of parity greater than this did require permission of the Fund. In fact such consultation did not always take place.

THE IMF SYSTEM AND ITS PROBLEMS

Devaluations and revaluations

The gradual dismantling of the mass of wartime restrictions on the flows of trade and capital together with the gradual achievement of currency convertibility was followed by an unprecedented growth of world trade during the 1960s (averaging about 9 per cent per annum). There is no doubt that the work of the IMF played a major part in these developments. As time went on, however, certain weaknesses in the IMF system were revealed.

One major drawback was the reluctance of governments to revalue or devalue their currencies when they were experiencing a fundamental balance of payments problem. Devaluation was resisted because it came to be regarded as an indicator of the failure of a country's economic policies while revaluation was an unpopular economic measure because home producers saw it as a threat to their home and overseas markets and countries were not anxious to eliminate a surplus on their balance of payments when such surpluses were regarded as indicators of successful economic management.

Countries attempting to avoid devaluation and revaluation held on to fixed parities long after they had ceased to be realistic. This often led to severe speculative pressures from those who believed changes of parity were inevitable. Speculators can, of course, make substantial profits if they sell a currency before devaluation and buy it back after devaluation. Impending revaluation will cause them to buy with a view to reselling. Changes in fixed parities when they did take place after long delays tended to be much greater than would have been the case had they been made earlier. Furthermore there was a tendency for countries to overdo the exchange rate adjustment because they were afraid of underestimating the necessary changes and then finding themselves having to repeat the process in the near future. They also faced the difficulty, already mentioned, of trying to assess the true market value of a currency when a fixed rate of exchange had been in operation for a long time.

The disturbing effects and uncertain results of changes in fixed parities led to strong demands for some modification of the IMF system and most of these demands supported schemes which allowed for a much greater degree of flexibility. One such proposal advocated a *crawling peg* system whereby, in any one year, the parity would be allowed to change by a maximum of, say, 2 per cent. This would perhaps allow the external value of a currency to find its true level gradually and smoothly over a reasonable period of time.

Table 10. *The composition of world liquidity July 1977*

	millions of SDRs
Gold	35 514
Foreign currencies	178 041
SDRs	8 440
Reserve positions in IMF	18 452
	240 447

Source: *International Financial Statistics*

International Liquidity
A further problem for the IMF concerned the supply of international liquidity. International reserves or international liquidity may be

defined as those assets which are generally acceptable to national governments in settlement of international debts. These assets consist of gold, convertible foreign currencies, SDRs, and the unconditional drawing rights in the IMF. Countries require such reserves to finance temporary balance of payments deficits. The supply of world liquidity has not kept pace with the growth of world trade. The ratio of world reserves to world imports declined from about 75 per cent in 1950 to about 25 per cent in 1974, although the reader should appreciate that the significance of these figures is much less when exchange rates are floating than when they are fixed. As Table 10 shows the facilities provided by the IMF account for little more than 10 per cent of total reserves.

It can be seen that gold still accounts for a large proportion of the total stock of international money. The amount of gold held in official reserves has not been increasing because of a rising industrial demand for the metal and increased demands from hoarders (as a hedge against inflation).

The two major reserve currencies are the dollar and the pound sterling, the dollar being predominant. The supply of dollars and pounds in international reserves is determined by the extents of the US and UK balance of payments deficits. If the USA is running a balance of payments deficit then other nations are acquiring dollar claims. These 'unspent' dollars become part of the international monetary reserves. To the extent that foreigners are prepared to hold dollar and sterling balances, they are holding acknowledgements of indebtedness which they are not presenting for payment. Their willingness to hold such currencies depends upon international confidence in them as a store of value.

If confidence in such currencies weakens, serious problems arise. For example, a relatively high rate of inflation in the UK may lead to fears of a serious balance of payments deficit and a substantial depreciation of the pound. Foreign holders of sterling may then present their claims for payment. In other words, they will exercise their right to convert sterling into other currencies and put a serious strain on the UK's holdings of convertible foreign currencies. It is the vulnerability to such movements into and out of sterling and the consequent heavy responsibility to maintain the external value of the pound which has led to such strong pressures for the role of sterling as a reserve currency to be reduced.

The relative weakness of the pound and the dollar in the 1960s and early 1970s together with an expressed determination by the USA and the UK to eliminate their payments deficits led to renewed fears of a dangerous shortage of world liquidity. One suggested remedy was a substantial increase in the official price of gold which, for many years, had been held down well below the free market price. A large increase in the official price of gold would have meant a large increase in the supply of international liquidity since the stocks of gold held in official reserves would then exchange for much greater amounts of foreign currency. Although this proposal was rejected on the grounds that it would give windfall gains to the major gold producers (South Africa and Russia) and that it might increase speculation of further price changes, recent events have led to the virtual abandonment of an officially fixed price for monetary gold. In fact the policy of the IMF seems to be aimed at a drastic reduction in the role of gold as international money. Par values are no longer expressed in terms of gold, the SDR is not linked to gold, members are not required to use gold in transactions with the IMF, international liquidity is now valued in terms of SDRs and the IMF has been selling off some of its stock of gold.

The measures to increase the supplies of international liquidity described on page 213 were adequate to avert any major crisis and the later movement to floating exchange rates (described below) also reduced pressures on the foreign currency reserves.

RECENT DIFFICULTIES AND DEVELOPMENTS

In 1971 the IMF system of fixed parities was in serious disarray. In August of that year several of the world's major currencies were floating. The major cause of this development was the weakness of the US dollar in relation to other major currencies especially the mark and the yen. The US balance of payments was in chronic deficit and the dollar, at its fixed parity, was seriously overvalued. The situation led to large-scale speculative flows of international currencies based on expectations of major devaluations and revaluations. These flows of short-term capital only worsened the situation because speculators were seeking to exchange the currencies of deficit countries for those of surplus countries. These latter countries were also adversely affected since an inflow of foreign currency tends to increase the domestic money supply and increase inflationary pressures. The problems might have been dealt with in several ways.

1. Deficit countries could have used exchange controls, or tariffs and quotas, to restrict imports or they might have devalued their currencies.
ii. Surplus countries could have revalued their currencies.
iii. The countries most affected could have floated their currencies.

In fact the solution adopted was to float the major currencies. At the time the declared intention was to return to a system of fixed parities when exchange rates had settled down to what appeared to be realistic market values. This task was attempted in December 1971 when representatives of the major industrialised countries met at the Smithsonian Institute in Washington. New parities were agreed upon and the permitted band of flexibility was widened from 1 per cent to $2\frac{1}{4}$ per cent on each side of the agreed parity. The agreement did not survive for very long. The system was placed under great strain by massive flows of short-term capital. These funds can be switched very rapidly between international financial centres and countries found it impossible to defend fixed parities in the face of such speculative pressures.

By April 1973 the par value system had been abandoned and most of the major trading countries opted for managed floating exchange rates. The IMF attempted to deal with the problems created by issuing guidelines for exchange rate management so that 'beggar my neighbour' policies would not be adopted by member countries. A further blow was dealt to the plans for the reform of the international monetary system by the unprecedented increases in the price of oil which quadrupled during 1974. This led to the oil-exporting countries achieving huge balance of payments surpluses ($57 billion in 1974 and $32 billion in 1975) while the oil-importing countries incurred huge deficits (aggregating $52 billion in 1974). The size of economies and the levels of economic development in most of the major oil-exporting countries meant that they could not possibly import goods and services to anything like the value of their foreign currency earnings (their abilities to absorb imports were very limited). This meant that a large part of the surpluses earned by the OPEC countries would have to be re-invested abroad, probably in very liquid assets which could be switched from one currency to another in search of higher returns and greater security. This prospect posed an enormous threat to the stability of the international monetary system and further uncertainty was created by the very different rates of inflation being experienced in the developed countries.

The IMF helped to lessen these dangers by arranging a facility to assist members in difficulties arising from the increased price of oil. The oil facility provided resources which were additional to those available under the regular facilities of the Fund. Most of the funds to support this scheme were provided by the major oil-exporting nations so that, in effect, the IMF scheme implied a 're-cycling' of part of the oil-exporter's surpluses. This scheme together with other extensions of the IMF's lending facilities and a considerable degree of central bank cooperation (e.g. the swap arrangements) helped the developed countries to arrange balance of payments finance without severe difficulties.

While the IMF has now accepted the necessity for the current regime of floating rates, it has made considerable progress in obtaining international cooperation on the objectives of reasonable price stability, orderly exchange arrangements, stability of exchange rates, the reduction in the role of gold as a reserve asset, and an increasing role for the SDR.

Fig. 37

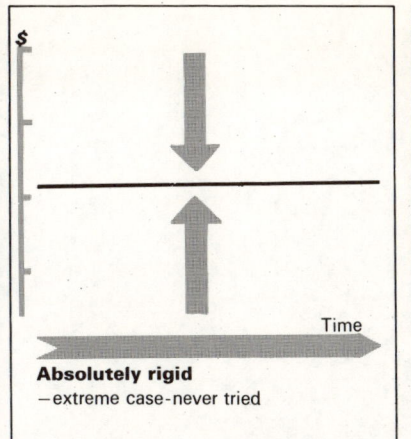

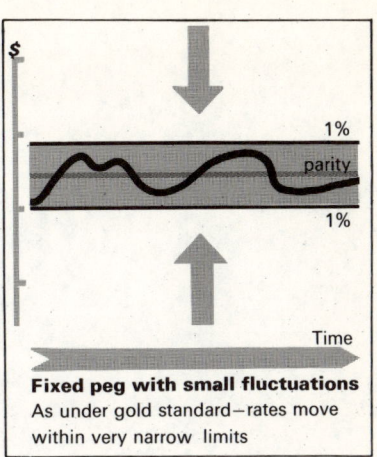

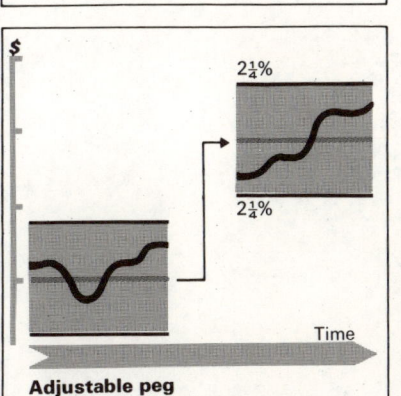

Absolutely rigid
—extreme case-never tried

Fixed peg with small fluctuations
As under gold standard—rates move within very narrow limits

Adjustable peg
—IMF system—rates may move within $2\frac{1}{4}$% of par—but par may be changed

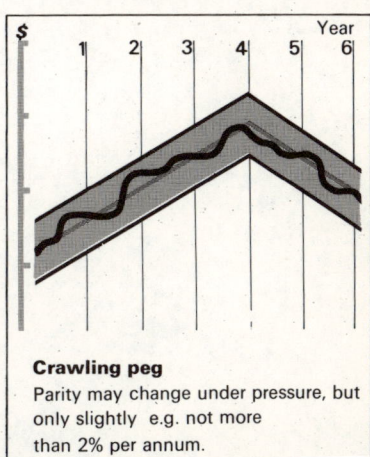

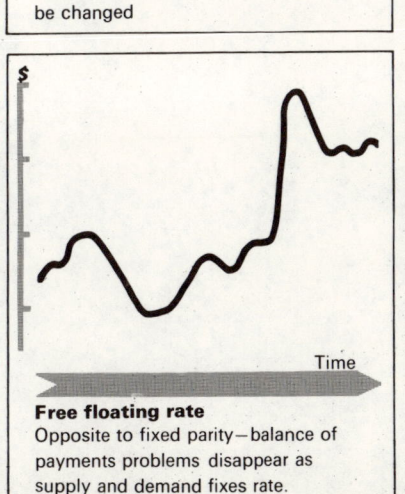

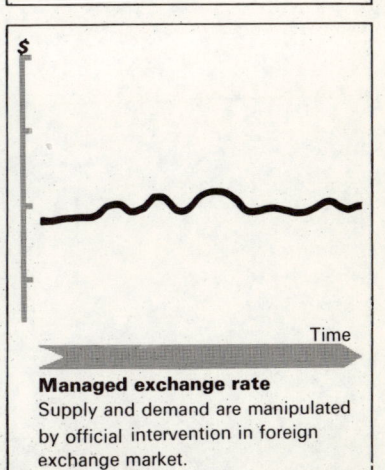

Crawling peg
Parity may change under pressure, but only slightly e.g. not more than 2% per annum.

Free floating rate
Opposite to fixed parity—balance of payments problems disappear as supply and demand fixes rate.

Managed exchange rate
Supply and demand are manipulated by official intervention in foreign exchange market.

19
Economic Growth

The meaning of economic growth

The analysis of income determination presented in the earlier chapters of this book was essentially short-run in character. The size of the population, the stock of capital and the techniques of production were all assumed to be fixed for the time being. In other words, the productive capacity or productive potential of the economy was assumed to be fixed and the analysis concentrated on the determinants of income, employment and prices within this given framework. Output, it was argued, will adapt itself to the level of aggregate demand. Equilibrium may turn out to be at less than full employment, or it may happen that no equilibrium is possible because demand is greater than the current value of full employment output. Ideally equilibrium would provide a situation where the labour force was fully employed and output was just sufficient to satisfy aggregate demand at current prices.

Much of the earlier work on macro-economic theory was carried out against a background of large-scale unemployment and it is not surprising that most attention was devoted to the problem of raising output to provide full employment for a given labour force. Since the Second World War it has become clear that full or near full employment can be maintained by appropriate economic policies and much more attention is now given to the problem of increasing productive capacity. This is the problem of economic growth.

Although the avoidance of unemployment and inflation are most desirable objectives, an economy which maintained a stationary level of full employment output would not satisfy the expectations of its citizens. In the short run, changes in the economy's stock of capital, the size of its labour force and the techniques of production are so small that they can be neglected. The problem for the short run is the extent to which the resources are being utilised. In the longer run, the labour supply will be increasing as population increases, net investment will be increasing the capital stock and technical progress will be improving the quality of the factors of production. This means that with any given rate of employment, output can steadily increase year by year. Economic growth is essentially a long-run concept.

MEASURING GROWTH

Much confusion arises from the use of the term 'economic growth'. Increases in national output which are due to the greater utilisation of existing resources (i.e. a fall in unemployment) do not constitute examples of economic growth. A distinction must be made between a growth of output due to a greater use of existing capacity and increasing output due to a growth of capacity. It is also necessary to restrict the term to movements in *real* income so that, in measuring economic growth, care must be taken to eliminate the effects of price changes.

Economic growth is a subject which attracts a lot of attention, because it is taken as an indicator of the rate at which living standards are changing. Changes in *total* real national income, however, may not be a good indicator for this purpose. We are now concerned with long-term changes and must, therefore, take account of population changes. If output is increasing at 2 per cent per annum but population is growing at a rate of 3 per cent per annum, living standards in general will be falling. When economic growth is measured in terms of *real income per head* we have a better index of movements in living standards.

But the increase in real income per head may be less than the rise in output per person employed, because rising standards of living usually mean that a smaller proportion of the population will be working. It is also likely that the working week will be reduced and the length of annual holidays extended so that each worker works fewer hours per annum. Account must be taken of these developments in assessing changes in the productive capacity of the economy. For the purposes of this discussion we shall take economic growth to mean the increase in the productive capacity per capita over some given period of time.

This view of economic growth is illustrated in Fig. 38. The curved line AB shows all possible combinations of capital and consumer goods available to a nation when all resources are fully employed. The line AB is known as a *production possibility curve*. At the point X there are some resources unemployed and a movement from X to Y (or any other point on the curve) represents an increase in real income: productive potential is unchanged. Economic growth is illustrated by an outward movement of the production possibility curve as shown by the dotted lines. If equal proportional gains in productivity were made in all industries, these production possibility curves will be 'parallel' to one another.

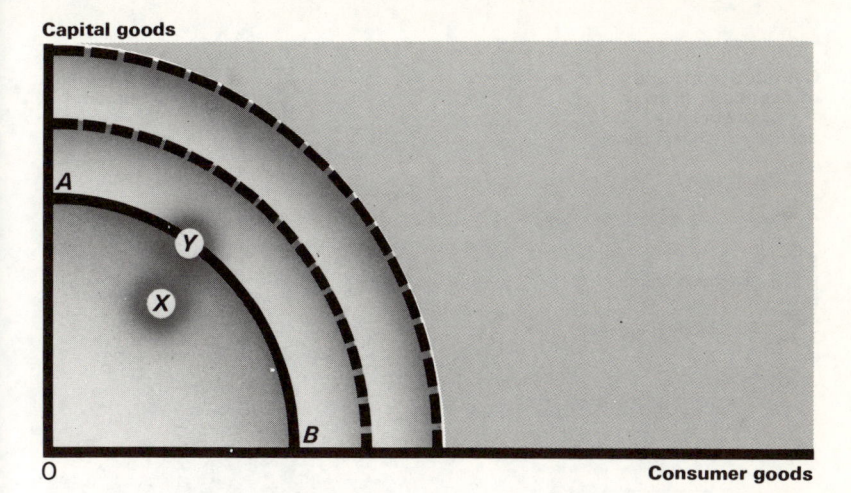

Fig. 38

THE CUMULATIVE ASPECTS OF ECONOMIC GROWTH

One of the most important features of economic growth is its cumulative nature – it is a 'compound interest' type of process. Quite small percentage growth rates have very great absolute effects in the longer term. If real national income grows at 3 per cent per annum, it will lead to a doubling of national output in about 24 years. Quite small discrepancies in national growth rates can lead to very large absolute differences in living standards within a man's lifetime. If Country A is experiencing economic growth at 3 per cent per annum while Country B is growing at 2 per cent, then, assuming that they started at the same level of income, A's income would be twice as great as B's in 72 years.

It is this feature of economic growth which has led to so much publicity being given to international 'league tables' showing rates of growth in different countries with the consequent speculations such as 'How long will it take for Japan to catch up with the USA?', or 'When will the USSR overtake the advanced western countries?'. The cumulative nature of economic growth also helps us to understand why the gulf between the rich and poor countries tends to widen rather than diminish. If two countries at different levels of economic development are growing *at the same rate*, the gap between them, in absolute terms, is growing larger and larger. This particular relationship is illustrated in Fig. 39, where it is assumed that both countries

MACRO-ECONOMICS

are growing (in economic terms) at 4 per cent per annum.

Cumulative effects of economic growth
A 4% growth rate applied to different bases

Developed country
Developing country

National income

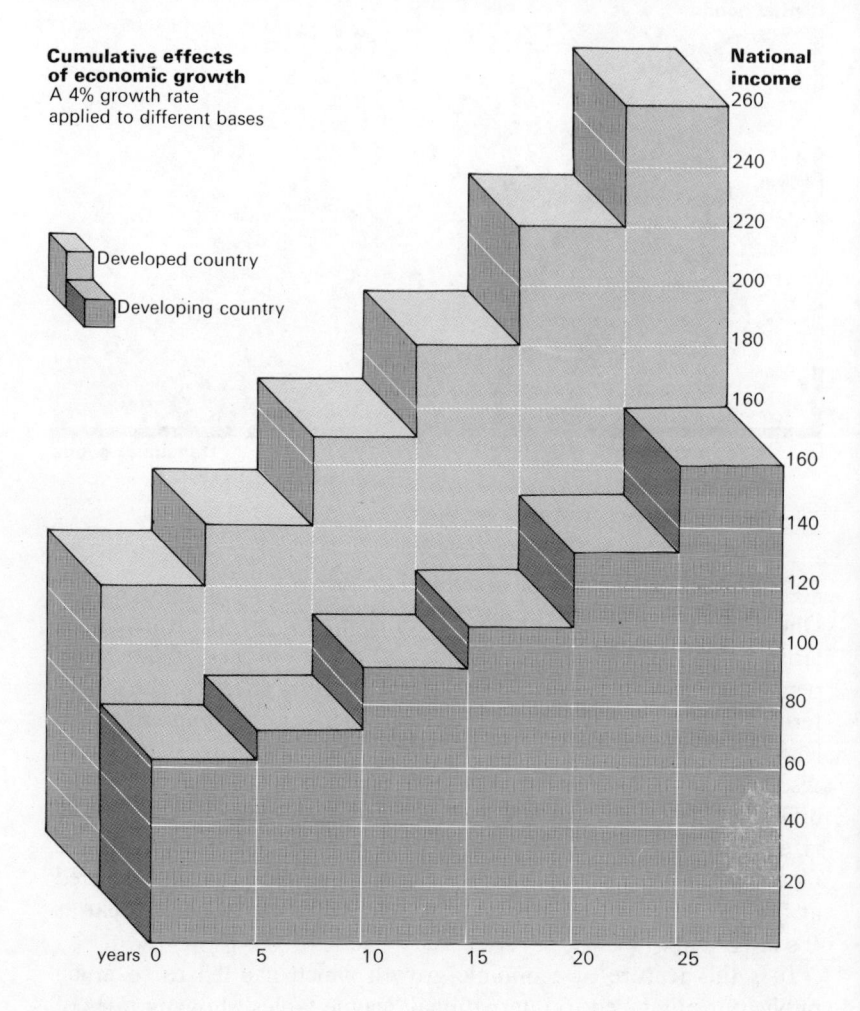

Fig. 39

THE DESIRABILITY OF ECONOMIC GROWTH

It would seem that the desire for faster rates of economic growth is almost universal. This demand for more rapid economic growth has been especially pronounced in the post-war period when growth rates of 5 per cent, 6 per cent or even higher have been achieved fairly consistently by some Western European nations and Japan, as well as Eastern Germany and the USSR. These growth rates are substantially higher than any achieved, consistently, in the past. This rise in real incomes has been greatly publicised and has led to rising expectations in almost every country of the world. There is now a widespread acceptance of the view that a fairly rapid rise in personal prosperity is *possible*.

'Many unfulfilled desires are sharply felt in both the personal and collective sphere ... More social provisions, better education, proper town planning, wider facilities for recreation; more scope for wage increases and tax cuts, which render possible more extensive purchases of durable consumer goods and happier holidays; more free time which can be pleasantly spent only if it is accompanied by higher income. All of these are aspirations which have greatly increased since the war and which make requirements of economic growth'[1].

Economic growth is important because it is the real key to higher living standards. A sustained growth rate of 3 per cent per annum would mean that a man could anticipate a quadrupling of his living standards within his working lifetime (a substantial part of this would undoubtedly be taken in the form of more leisure). It offers the prospect of reducing poverty without having to make some people worse off. Redistribution of income will improve the welfare of the poor at the expense of the better off, but it will be a once and for all gain. Economic growth enables all to gain, and, if redistribution policies are adopted at the same time, the less well off could gain *relative* to the more fortunate. No one need be worse off.

Politically, economic growth is seen as an important instrument for acquiring national power and prestige. Political and military strength are dependent upon economic power.

A SIMPLE GROWTH MODEL

When we introduce the idea of a rising capacity to produce goods and services we encounter a new set of problems. Economic growth refers to a growing capacity *to supply*, but we cannot discuss this subject without reference to changes in aggregate demand. It is no use expanding output if the market for that output is not growing. Equilibrium, in the short run, requires that planned spending at current prices should be just sufficient to absorb full employment output. The problem now is how to ensure that aggregate demand increases at a rate which will just match the growing capacity to produce. If demand is allowed to increase at a faster rate than productive potential there will be demand inflation – if it grows more slowly, there will be unemployed resources. A further problem concerns the stability of the rate of growth. The economic history of capitalism reveals that the economic growth of the

[1] J. Pen, *Modern Economics* Penguin, p190.

industrial nations has pursued a far from steady path. Is it possible to derive the conditions necessary for steady growth at a constant equilibrium growth rate?

The simple model outlined below gives the key role in economic growth to net investment. It is necessary to recognise the dual role of investment. We have dealt with investment largely as an *income-generating force*. While investment projects are being constructed, spending on them creates an injection into the circular flow of income with the appropriate multiplier effects. Once the investment projects are completed, however, they add to the stock of capital and hence increase the productive capacity of the economy. Investment, then, must be seen as a *capacity-generating force*. Thus,

(*a*) Net investment increases productive capacity.

(*b*) *Increases* in investment raise income and demand.

We must now introduce an important new concept – the *marginal capital output ratio* (MCOR). The MCOR describes the relationship between increases in the stock of capital and the increase in output that this capital will yield.

We use I to represent the rate of net investment.

ΔI to represent an increase in the rate of investment.

$\Delta 0$ to represent the increase in output resulting from net investment.

Thus,

$$\text{MCOR} = \frac{I}{\Delta 0} \qquad (1)$$

For example, if £1 000 of new investment causes output to rise by £500,[1]

$$\text{MCOR} = \frac{£1\,000}{£500} = 2$$

Note that the lower marginal capital output ratio the higher the productivity of new investment.

The formula which relates increases in net investment to income is already familiar to us. It is

$$\Delta Y = \frac{1}{\text{MPS}} \times \Delta I = \frac{\Delta I}{\text{MPS}} \qquad (2)$$

We have two formulas. The first gives us the relationship between net investment and new output, and the second tells us how much income will rise as investment increases. We can rearrange the first formula to

[1]. We assume the investment of one time period affects output in the next time period.

tell us the amount by which output increases as a result of the net investment of the previous time period.

From (1),

$$\Delta 0 = \frac{I}{\text{MCOR}}$$

We can now discover by *how much investment must increase in any time period in order to provide the additional income needed to buy the additional output that has been created by the net investment of the previous time period*. To satisfy this condition ΔY must equal $\Delta 0$; i.e.,

$$\frac{I}{\text{MCOR}} = \frac{\Delta I}{\text{MPS}}$$

This is the formula for balanced growth. It can be rearranged as follows

$$\frac{\Delta I}{I} = \frac{\text{MPS}}{\text{MCOR}} = \frac{\text{marginal propensity to save}}{\text{marginal capital output ratio}}$$

This expression tells us what rate of investment is needed to make income payments keep pace with the value of full capacity output. For example, if MPS $= 0.25$, and MCOR $= 2$, the rate of investment must grow (per time period) by

$$\frac{0.25}{2} = \frac{1}{8}$$

in order to create sufficient new income to match the growth of output.

This model indicates that *in a growing economy* the critical amount of investment is not that needed to fill a given deflationary gap, but the *increase* in investment needed to create enough demand to match the growth in capacity.

This is a highly simplified picture which concentrates on one determinant of growth, namely, investment. More advanced models which take account of other determinants such as technical progress, growth of world trade, changes in the supply of labour and changes in the distribution of income are extremely complex. There is no general agreement on why some economies grow faster than others and no settled theory of economic growth. Nevertheless the model presented above does help us to see some of the growth implications of our earlier analysis.

Sources of economic growth

It has already been noted that the growth rates of different countries differ substantially – even where those countries have similar industrial structures. Up to the mid-1950s it was thought that the rapid growth rates of Japan and Western Germany were due mainly to the recovery from wartime destruction and hence might be exceptional and temporary. The continued high rates of growth achieved by these countries has discredited these views. It is extremely difficult to quantify the factors which give rise to variations in growth rates, but it is possible to identify some of the more important contributory factors on the supply side. We must remember, however, that the growth process arises out of the interaction of demand and supply.

THE SUPPLY OF LABOUR

Since we have defined growth in terms of 'full capacity' national product per head, a crude increase in the supply of labour is not, necessarily, a source of economic growth. Population might also be increasing so that output per head remains unchanged. The necessary requirement is an increase in labour input from any given population. This ratio may increase through (*a*) an increase in the average number of hours worked by each worker, or (*b*) an increase in the participation rate – the proportion of the population in the labour force.

The first possibility is not likely to be a cause of economic growth since improved living standards create demands for more leisure. The participation rate, however, is subject to change through changes in the age composition of the population and through changes in social attitudes (e.g. married women at work). This is discussed on page 81. In the more advanced countries a large proportion of married women is already out at work, there are increasing demands for more and longer education and the average working week is tending to fall. There seems little scope for any growth of labour input.

Another important aspect of the supply of labour is the quality of the labour force. An improvement in labour's efficiency due to better education, improved training, good working conditions, adequate housing and health services and so on is equivalent to an increase in the input of labour. This is really a part of the problem of the rate of investment, since these various social services may be looked upon as investment in human capital.

INVESTMENT

Our simple growth model emphasised the role of investment and suggested that an increase in the rate of investment is a necessary requirement for economic growth.

If the population is increasing, an increase in the stock of capital will be needed in order to maintain output per head at its present level. Each new worker must be supplied with tools and machinery so as to maintain the existing ratio of capital to labour. This process, usually described as the *widening of capital*, does not increase productivity – it prevents output per head from falling as the labour force increases.

To achieve economic growth it is necessary to increase the amount of capital with which each worker is equipped. This increases the ratio of capital to labour and is described as a *deepening of capital*. Over the long course of economic development increasing productivity has required the slow accumulation of very large capital stocks per working individual.

Although investment is recognised to be a factor in economic growth, its precise importance and the way in which investment and economic growth are linked is still subject to much dispute. A higher rate of investment in one country than another does not necessarily mean that the rate of growth will be higher. The structure of investment may be almost as important as its total volume.

It may be that political considerations require a large proportion of total investment to be devoted to defence; this does not directly contribute to economic growth. In all countries a large part of investment consists of residential building. The construction of dwellings does not increase the capacity for future growth in the same way as manufacturing, commercial or agricultural investment, as these have a more direct influence on productive efficiency. Differences in growth rates between countries which have similar rates of total investment may be partially explained by differences in the proportions devoted to the various types of investment.

Investment which takes the form of piecemeal modernisation of an industry with an out-of-date structure will be less effective than the same amount of investment devoted to the building of a new industry. Japan and Germany were able to pursue this latter policy after the war, while Britain had the task of modernising several industries which had been established with structures appropriate to the production methods of the 19th century.

REALLOCATION OF RESOURCES

An increase in the productivity of economic resources may be brought about by improved allocation. Where a country is able to direct a major part of its new investment to industries with high growth potential, it will achieve higher growth rates than a country which finds itself obliged to allocate a large part of its investment to declining or static industries in an attempt to alleviate problems of structural unemployment. An important illustration of the effects of reallocating resources is provided by the shifting of resources from agricultural to non-agricultural occupations. Since output per worker in agriculture is generally much less than in other occupations, a transfer of resources out of agriculture provides a source of economic growth. To some extent this accounts for Britain's poor performance relative to other Western European countries in the post-war period. Britain had already 'used up' this source of growth in the 19th and early 20th centuries.

In some industries a reallocation of resources from small scale to large scale production units will lead to significant increases in productivity. These economies of scale become possible when the size of the market expands due to improved techniques of distribution, rising incomes and a greater acceptance of standardised products.

Of critical importance in this question of reallocating resources is the problem of the mobility of the factors of production, especially the mobility of labour. A rapid rate of economic growth calls for a high degree of mobility. Resources must be shifted from declining industries to those with growth prospects. New and improved methods of production can only be fully and quickly exploited by a labour force with a high degree of adaptability, which is prepared to undertake retraining for new tasks, and which displays a readiness to accept changes in traditional working practices. New machines may require fewer men to work them; expensive units of capital equipment may call for 24-hour operation in order to achieve low cost production—this implies an acceptance of shift working; new processes may be indivisible and necessitate the integration of small firms into larger units. Structural changes such as these require a degree of labour mobility which may be harder to achieve in countries where traditional industrial practices have been long established and the rate of change has been relatively slow.

TECHNICAL PROGRESS

The term 'technical progress' can be taken to mean improvements in the quality of the labour force, in the methods of production and in the efficiency of the capital goods themselves. It would embrace such things as the invention and development of new machines and new products; the application of such techniques as work study and method study to improve the performance of labour and capital; improvements in communications; better organisation and management and improved education and training facilities. Research into the causes of economic growth in the USA during the course of this century indicates that improved technology was a more important factor than the increase in the stock of capital.

There are two aspects of technical change, *invention* and *innovation*. Invention is the product of the scientist and takes the form of a new technique or new material produced under experimental conditions.

But economic growth requires someone to make that invention commercially effective. It is often a long, costly and risky journey from the laboratory bench to the commercial production process. This is the role of the innovator. Some inventions have waited many years before a successful innovator came along with a process which made the new product available to the masses. The innovator has been described as the person who translates technological possibilities into technological facts. His role in the process of economic growth is extremely important since innovation raises the marginal productivity curve of capital and provides the necessary inducement for increased investment.

The rate of technical progress depends upon the efforts of pure and applied scientists and the progress of science depends largely on the resources applied to scientific effort. It is quite obvious, therefore, that education plays a vital role in economic development. The resources devoted to education provide an important indicator of the prospects for economic growth – not only because the gifted members of society must be trained in order to ensure the continuing output of new techniques, but the population itself must be capable of adapting to and making full use of the new developments.

Economic growth and population growth

Of great concern to economists at the present time is the relationship between economic growth and the growth of population. It took the world over 18 centuries to increase its population from 250m. to 1000m. At the present time 1000m. people are being added to the world's population every 15 years. The current rate of population growth in many parts of the world, and especially in the underdeveloped regions, have serious implications for countries attempting to achieve satisfactory rates of economic development. It now seems generally agreed that some reduction in the rates of growth of population would greatly improve the prospects for economic development. Some economists argue that in countries such as Pakistan and India investment in birth control would yield higher returns than investment in either industrial or agricultural activities.

There are arguments in favour of a rising population. An increasing population will raise national income and may under certain circumstances lead to faster economic growth. Entrepreneurs, anticipating a rising demand, may be encouraged to increase the rate of investment. A larger population may make possible a more effective use of various economies of scale, and an increasing labour force may also help to offset any tendency towards a fall in the marginal productivity of capital.

On the other hand, some of these arguments lose their force in a world where international trade allows countries to specialise, so that quite small countries can achieve significant economies of scale in their specialised activities. In any case, large markets mean more purchasing power and not simply more people. An increasing labour force needs more capital to work with if output per head is to be maintained, and, if population is increasing rapidly, a country will be forced to devote a large proportion of its total investment just to maintaining the present real income per head. A recent study has shown that in less developed countries over 65 per cent of total investment is being applied to this task, whereas in the more advanced countries the figure is only 25 per cent.

A reduction in the population growth rate could have several important effects on the potential for economic growth. If a country has a capital output ratio of 5 and a population growth rate of 2 per cent per annum, then 10 per cent of the national output must be invested every year to give employment to the new workers. This capital 'widening' will not raise income per head. With no such increase in population, this 10 per cent of the national income might have been applied to the creation of capital for the purposes of improving the productivity of the labour force; that is, capital 'deepening'.

A smaller population brought about by a fall in the birth rate would mean that the national income would be shared by fewer persons. The national income itself will not fall, and, in the short run, may increase. The fall in the population, initially, reduces the number of dependents, not the number of workers. Capital accumulation would probably increase, because a reduction in the number of dependents would increase the ability to save, and the decline in the birth rate would, through better nutrition and education, improve the quality of the labour force. After an interval of about 15 years, however, there will be a negative effect as the fall in the birth rate begins to affect the size of the working population.

It is significant that every country that has become highly developed has experienced a reduction in the birth rate of 50 per cent or more.

In many underdeveloped countries the marginal capital output ratio tends to be high and the propensity to save is low. This is an unfortunate combination as our growth equation indicates. Suppose MPS = 0·1 and MCOR = 6. This gives us a balanced growth rate of

$$\frac{0 \cdot 1}{6} = 0 \cdot 0166$$

or 1·66 per cent. If the growth of population is 2 per cent or more (as it is in many of these countries), the prospects for the growth of GNP per capita are very dismal.

THE COSTS OF ECONOMIC GROWTH

Economic growth defined in terms of productive capacity per capita makes possible several alternative ways of increasing economic welfare. By maintaining the same labour force working the same number of hours, the community may enjoy the fruits of increasing productive potential in the form of a higher real income per head. It might, however, choose to take the gains in the form of a shorter working week and longer holidays. Another alternative is to reduce the proportion of the total population at work by extending the range and coverage of full time education and/or reducing the retirement ages. Another possibility is to devote more resources to improving amenities such as the reduction of pollution or the production of much safer cars. These latter measures would raise production costs and be reflected in a rising GNP although real output by many indicators will not have changed. In fact, it appears that most nations choose to make limited advances on all these fronts. It should be noted that the opportunity cost of a movement in one direction is a reduction of the scope for a movement in another direction.

Nevertheless, in whatever form the benefits are taken the attempt to achieve faster rates of economic growth will require a sacrifice in terms of current satisfactions. We have noted that a higher rate of investment is one of the requirements. This can only be achieved by allocating more resources to the production of capital goods – the opportunity cost being the consumption goods which these resources might have produced. It is true that the policy will lead to a greater output of consumption goods in the future, but it may be many years before any *net* gain is achieved. Is it worth it?

Economic growth gives rise to a variety of *social costs* and this is an aspect of economic development which is attracting more and more attention. Rising incomes lead to the extension of car ownership, but this in turn gives rise to serious problems of traffic congestion and air pollution. Huge modern steel plants, chemical works, oil refineries and generating stations may be very efficient on the basis of a purely commercial assessment, but they also impose costs on the community in the form of river and air pollution and in the destruction of natural beauty. Modern methods of agriculture may be very effective in raising yields per acre, but they may have damaging effects on wild life.

A more personal aspect of social costs arises from the fact that a more rapid rate of economic growth is dependent upon a continuous stream of new techniques and products. Machines and production methods will be subject to a fairly rapid rate of obsolescence. But the same will be true of labour – the changes which make economic growth possible also make labour redundant. Programmes of retraining with supporting financial grants can deal with this problem to some extent, but there still remains a social cost in the form of the disruption and often unpleasant breaks in a person's working life. The trouble is that the impact of growth which is supposed to benefit all is not evenly spread. Instead of everyone reducing their working week by a small fraction, a few find themselves made redundant.

20
Managing the Economy

The purpose of this chapter is to provide a link between the concepts and theories which have been used to explain the important macro-economic relationships and the everday issues of economic policy. In some cases no more than a summary of earlier discussions is required because matters of economic policy have been introduced at various points in the text. The major instruments of economic policy–fiscal and monetary measures–were explained in Chapters 9 and 14, while aspects of economic policy were dealt with in the sections on Money, Banking, Employment and Economic Growth.

An account of economic policy usually begins by setting out the targets or objectives of that policy. These objectives are based on *value judgements*. The desirability of full employment, price stability and economic growth are determined according to the value judgements of society as a whole and given expression through the political system.

In order to achieve these objectives, the authorities must have some devices for operating on the macro-economic variables (investment, consumption, etc.). These devices are the *instruments* of economic policy. But the use of these instruments implies an understanding of how the economic system works. It is necessary to have some idea of how the economic system is likely to respond when the instruments are used. This understanding of the functioning of the economic system is the role of *analysis*–to which the major part of this book has been devoted. Fig. 40 illustrates the relationship between these various aspects of economic policy.

The instruments of economic policy

We can define an instrument as anything which a government may use in order to achieve its objectives. These instruments can be divided into five categories: (1) Fiscal; (2) Monetary; (3) Exchange rate; (4) Direct controls; and (5) Institutional changes.

Objectives (e.g. control of inflation) → **Analysis** (Excess demand) → **Instruments** (Monetary, Fiscal) → **Measures** (Increase rate of interest, Reduce banks' reserve assets) (Increase taxation, Reduce government spending)

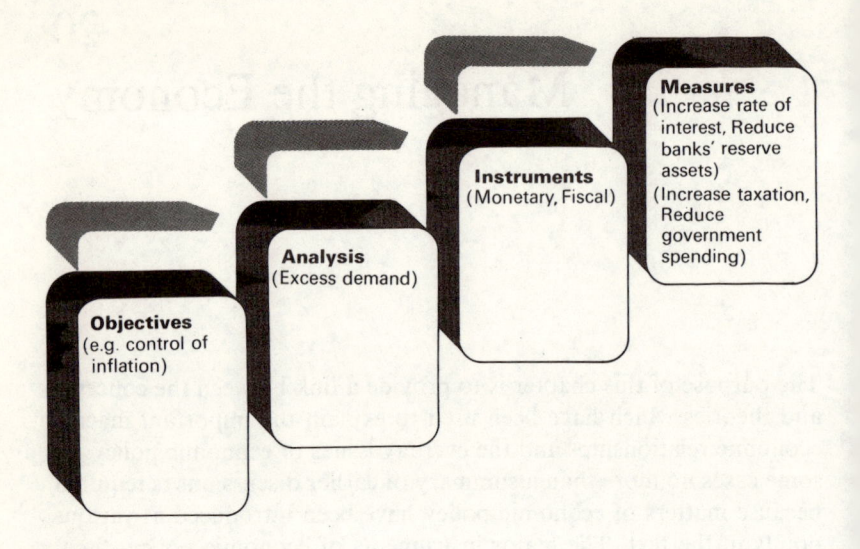

Fig. 40

1. FISCAL INSTRUMENTS

The major instrument of fiscal policy is the Budget and the measures consist of planned variations in government income and expenditure, although fiscal systems may have built-in automatic stabilisers. Fiscal measures were explained in Chapter 9.

2. MONETARY INSTRUMENTS

Monetary instruments act upon the money supply and the price of credit (i.e. the rate of interest). Again this subject has been dealt with in the sections on Money and Banking (see Chapter 14).

3. THE EXCHANGE RATE

Chapter 18 deals at some length with the use of the exchange rate as an instrument of policy. The movement from fixed to floating rates has meant that the management (or non-management) of the exchange rate has become an important feature of government policy. In 1977, for example, the UK government intervened to dampen down the rate of appreciation of the pound in order to prevent UK exports from becoming too uncompetitive in world markets.

4. DIRECT CONTROLS

These can take many forms and be used for a variety of purposes. The essential difference between this instrument and the others is that it seeks to achieve the objective by directly controlling the economic variables, whereas the other instruments seek only to influence the way in which the variables behave. Direct controls are likely to be used in wartime and in immediate post-war periods. The rationing of foodstuffs, other essential consumer goods and raw materials is a common feature of such national emergencies. Another example of direct controls is a statutory control of prices, which invariably accompanies the use of rationing, although price controls may operate long after rationing has been abandoned.

Direct controls may be used to influence the location of industry and commerce. In the UK controls have been used to restrict the building of industrial and commercial premises in the more prosperous areas. The level of imports may be controlled by the use of quotas or by the rationing of foreign currency.

A direct control by its very nature tends to be a negative instrument. It can be used to restrict building in certain areas or to reduce imports. It has not been used to force firms to build in other areas or to force firms to export. In the UK financial inducements are used for these latter purposes.

5. INSTITUTIONAL CHANGES

Economic policy may take the form of establishing specialised institutions to achieve particular objectives. The Monopolies Commission and the Restrictive Practices Court are good examples of such institutions. They were established for the specific purpose of increasing the extent of competition in the British economy. Some of these institutions such as the Restrictive Practices Court may have legal powers, but the majority only have advisory functions.

In a society which tries to allow a large measure of freedom of choice to producers and consumers, the government is obliged to make some use of exhortation and persuasion in trying to achieve its objectives. Advisory bodies such as the Monopolies Commission, the National Board for Prices and Incomes (now disbanded) and the National Economic Development Council have an important role in this respect. Their investigations and subsequent reports are widely publicised and provide a useful means of focusing attention on, and improving the general understanding of, national economic problems.

Another type of institution is one which is given executive powers. The National Enterprise Board has powers to acquire shares in both profitable and unprofitable companies and to take such companies into public ownership where necessary. Its aim is to encourage the restructuring of industry.

Nationalisation provides another example of institutional change, although this may be carried out for non-economic as well as economic reasons.

The objectives of economic policy

Although there is very little conflict over the main aims of economic policy, there is considerable disagreement over the means by which these objectives might be achieved and over the priorities to be accorded to the various objectives.

The major problem of economic policy arises from the incompatibility of particular objectives. It seems that all the aims of government economic policy cannot be achieved simultaneously; some aims must be modified in order to make progress towards others. Society is faced with a problem similar to that which confronts the individual with a limited income. The individual with limited means cannot satisfy all his wants, he must choose, from the enormous variety available, that combination of goods and services which will maximise his satisfactions. Society must somehow choose between apparently incompatible objectives so as to maximise collective economic welfare. It is this choice between alternatives which forces governments to 'trade off' one objective against another. These practical problems of policy are discussed later in the chapter.

FULL EMPLOYMENT

We have already discussed the concept of full employment and the difficulties of measuring the extent of unemployment (Chapter 8). There are sound economic, social and political reasons why full employment is accepted as a major objective of government policy. Unemployment represents a waste of resources and a permanent loss of output. Socially, unemployment creates hardship for the families of the unemployed and has damaging effects on the morale of those out of work. These social effects generate feelings of bitterness which are reflected in political attitudes long after the unemployment problem has been dealt with.

There are two aspects of a full employment policy. The first concerns the level of aggregate demand. This must be maintained at a level which ensures that the number of jobs is equal to the numbers seeking work. The second problem is that of matching the demand for and supply of labour both occupationally and geographically. For most of the postwar period it has been this second aspect of employment policy which has created the greatest difficulties in the UK.

Demand deficiency unemployment

The most serious type of unemployment in the advanced industrial countries has been cyclical or mass unemployment. This is the unemployment associated with the trade cycle and resulted in unemployment rates in the UK varying from 2 per cent (boom) to 8–10 per cent (slump) before the First World War, and from 10 per cent (boom?) to 22 per cent (slump) in the inter-war period. Heavy and general unemployment of this type is clearly the result of inadequate spending; there is a deficiency of aggregate demand. Fig. 17 on page 78 illustrates this particular condition although the aggregate demand function illustrated is that for a two-sector economy.

The policy aim must be to raise aggregate demand by acting on the variables on the right hand side of the equilibrium equation

$$Y = C + I + G + X - M.$$

Monetary policy may be used for this purpose and, by using the measures described in Chapter 14, it will be the task of the government to bring about lower interest rates and an increase in the availability of bank credit. Open market purchases, a release of special deposits and a lowering of market rates of interest would be appropriate measures. But in slump conditions will consumption and investment spending be sensitive to easier and cheaper credit? When businessmen have idle machinery and excess capacity it is doubtful whether investment spending will be stimulated simply because loans are easier to obtain and interest rates are lower. If there is heavy unemployment, it is also doubtful whether easier credit terms will have much effect on consumption spending. The cheap money policy, however, will facilitate any borrowing by the public sector. Monetary measures are more likely to be effective if they are accompanied by fiscal measures (tax cuts and more public spending) which will help to revive business confidence.

Fiscal policy in conditions of general and persistent unemployment calls for reductions in direct and indirect taxes and an increase in public spending. The appropriate measures for raising aggregate demand are described in Chapter 9.

Although we know which way to alter the monetary and fiscal variables in order to stimulate spending, it is extremely difficult to know *how much* to alter them. The nature of the relationships between the monetary and fiscal weapons and the level of aggregate demand is known, but the precise *quantitative* relationships are not known. The measures used are likely to be insufficient or excessive, and progress towards full employment is likely to be erratic.

Structural and frictional unemployment

Although the government has the means of manipulating the level of aggregate demand so that it is sufficient to match the aggregate supply of labour, it has proved much more difficult to equate the demands for, and supplies of, labour in the different labour markets at levels which provide full employment in each and every market. There are several reasons for this. The basic reason is that the world is always changing. Fashions and tastes change, new production techniques are always coming into use, new products supersede the older ones, economic and political changes alter the structure of overseas markets and so on. Some industries benefit from these changes whilst others are adversely affected so that the demands for some types of labour will be increasing and the demands for others declining. This continually changing pattern of demand for labour skills gives rise to *frictional unemployment*. This type of unemployment will exist even when the aggregate supply of jobs is equal to the total supply of labour. It arises because the unemployed workers do not have the right skills or are not in the right place to take up the available jobs. Frictional unemployment then is due to the occupational and geographical immobilities of labour. This is a type of unemployment which cannot be dealt with by an expansion of aggregate demand. All this would do is to create even more excess demand for those industries already short of labour. The policy objective must be to reduce or remove the barriers to the mobility of labour.

Some of this mobility may be due to ignorance of the conditions in the labour market. Where there is no effective market mechanism for bringing together those seeking work and those seeking workers there is bound to be some element of frictional unemployment. The removal of this particular market imperfection is the function of the Labour Exchanges (now being replaced by the new Job-Centres).

The major problem, however, is one of retraining the redundant workers so that they can take up new jobs in expanding industries, and, most important, to change the social attitudes to labour mobility. Economic change is a necessary feature of economic growth, but the victims of such changes are those who are thrown out of work. Changes which cause redundancy are bound to be resisted unless those affected are convinced that their interests are being safeguarded. In the UK the government has established retraining centres where workers can learn new skills. Financial assistance in the form of training grants is provided for those attending these centres. Workers losing their jobs because of changes in demand qualify for redundancy payments and unemployment payments are related to previous earnings for several weeks following dismissal. Modification of apprenticeship schemes by making them multi-craft instead of single craft, or by shortening the training period would also help labour mobility.

Frictional unemployment may also be due to geographical immobility. Jobs of the right kind may be available but not in the areas where men are unemployed. The UK government provides financial assistance for men travelling in search of work and grants are available to meet removal costs. Geographical immobilities are discussed under Regional Problems.

Persistent and heavy unemployment may exist in a localised or concentrated form even when the national average rate of unemployment is low. This type of unemployment is defined as *structural unemployment*. It arises when there is a permanent shift in demand away from the products of a major industry. It is particularly severe when the industry is heavily localised, since local multiplier effects can force unemployment rates well above the national average.

The fall in demand may be due to technological change (e.g. coal being replaced by oil and natural gas; rail transport by road transport) or a loss of overseas markets (e.g. the UK cotton and shipbuilding industries). The problem is magnified when the newer expanding industries choose locations in other areas. The UK has this problem since the newer industries (cars, radio, television, food processing, etc.) chose locations in the South East and the Midlands while the older industries are located in the North of England, Scotland and South Wales.

Regional problems

Providing there is no deficiency of aggregate demand the problem of structural unemployment is one of immobilities. If the industry affected is widely dispersed the measures to deal with occupational immobilities are those described above. Where, however, the unemployment takes on regional characteristics it is a problem of geographical immobility. Workers cannot, or will not, move to those areas which are short of labour. A shortage of houses, the reluctance to break family or social ties, and the problems of interrupting the schooling of the children are major barriers to the geographical movement of labour. But even if such movement were possible, it might create other problems. The more prosperous areas would tend to become congested and factor prices, particularly the price of land, would be subject to strong upward pressures. Society would have to provide large amounts of new social capital (houses, schools, hospitals, etc.) in the areas attracting labour while the social capital in the depressed areas may be underutilised. The age composition of the population in the areas losing labour would become unbalanced since the more mobile groups would tend to be the younger members of the working age groups.

Persistent interregional differences in the level of unemployment create the need for a specific regional policy. The existence of surplus resources in some areas represents a loss of potential output in a situation where there is a manpower shortage in other areas. Moreover, when demand rises, inflationary pressures are quickly encountered in the low unemployment areas, and this calls for restrictions on demand while spare capacity exists elsewhere.

In the UK current policy accepts the difficulties and undesirability of achieving a large geographical movement of labour and has chosen instead to stimulate the geographical mobility of capital—'taking work to the workers rather than workers to the work'. Fiscal policy may be used for this purpose. Substantial investment grants may be offered to firms in development areas (i.e. those with higher than average unemployment). Alternatively, such firms may be offered attractive tax allowances on capital expenditures. Since these policies tend to favour capital-intensive industries it may be necessary to devise instruments which favour firms in labour-intensive industries. The British Regional Employment Premium was one such device. Employers in the development areas were paid a weekly premium for each worker employed. In this particular case the scheme was restricted to manufacturing industry. Monetary measures might include the provision of loans at favourable rates of interest and the exclusion of firms in the development areas from the effects of any credit squeeze measures. Other measures designed to attract firms to areas of high unemployment have included grants to assist with the movement of key personnel and capital equipment; training grants to assist with the retraining of local labour, and government-built factories made available at artificially low rentals. In planning its own spending the government may deliberately allot a disproportionate share of its orders to firms in depressed regions, and it could bias location decisions affecting the nationalised industries so as to favour these areas.

This wide range of inducements may be supported by direct controls in the form of severe restrictions on expansion in the prosperous areas. In the UK an Industrial Development Certificate or Office Development Permit must be obtained from the Department of Trade and Industry before any factory or office building can be undertaken (other than very small extensions). These certificates are readily available for projects in the development areas, but may be more difficult to obtain for other regions.

A fundamental criticism of the kind of measures outlined above is that firms, if left alone, will choose minimum-cost locations and any interference may only result in a loss of efficiency and a reduction in the attainable level of output. The magnitude of the inducements which have been offered to firms to persuade them to relocate their enterprises does seem to indicate a fairly strong reluctance to move. In most cases the policy measures come into effect when a firm has applied for permission to expand its existing capacity. In such cases it is very likely that an expansion of existing facilities is a more economic proposition than the alternative of establishing a fairly remote branch. On the other hand it is argued that, for many industries, location itself has little influence on average costs of production. It is also pointed out that, given time, sufficient new industry might be established in the development region for location advantages such as trained labour, subsidiary firms offering specialised services, and so on, to develop in that region.

Whether the UK government's regional policy has worked is questionable. There seems to have been little tendency for regional unemployment rates to come into line with the national average. But, in the absence of such measures as have been applied, the divergence could well have widened. It is interesting to note that much more attention is now being given to the possibilities of increasing the geographical movement of labour. The obstacles are great, but it is pointed out that interregional migration already occurs on a much larger scale than is commonly supposed.

Seasonal unemployment

In some industries the demand for labour has a marked seasonal pattern. In agriculture and building this is due to climatic factors while in the tourist trade, demand varies according to the time of the year. Little can be done to alleviate this problem, although technical progress has now enabled building to proceed throughout the year by making use of materials less susceptible to frost damage, and the replacement of labour by capital in agriculture has drastically reduced the extent of the winter lay-off. In tourism there are moves to extend the season by encouraging people to take holidays in less popular months.

PRICE STABILITY

The maintenance of a stable price level has been a major objective of post-war British economic policy and the idea that governments should control or influence the level of prices goes back a long way into history. It is difficult to define exactly what is meant by price stability. In an economy with changing conditions of demand and supply it is inevitable that the prices of individual goods and services should change. In macro-economics, price stability refers to the general price level as measured by some price index, usually, the Index of Retail Prices. Stable prices as a policy objective does not mean that the index of prices should remain absolutely stable. Prices in general are inflexible in a downward direction so that changes in supply and demand usually mean a gradual increase in the price level (see Table 8). The policy objective therefore is to restrict the annual rise in prices to some moderate average percentage – although what percentage this should be is rarely stated.

We have already noted that a rapid rise in prices gives rise to some undesirable effects, but since inflation is often associated with prosperity, opinions are divided as to whether inflation is as great a problem as it is sometimes made out to be. Some economists argue that a small annual increase in prices promotes growth since the expectations of rising prices provides firms with an incentive to invest. Others argue that even a mild inflation should be checked to prevent it accelerating into rapid price inflation. This fear of acceleration is undoubtedly one of the factors which prompts governments to adopt anti-inflationary policies.

Policies to deal with inflation must take account of the type of inflation being experienced. If the government is faced with excess demand inflation, the aim must be to eliminate the excess demand by cutting spending plans. The appropriate fiscal measures will consist of cuts in public spending and increases in taxation. These are described in Chapter 9, but attention is drawn to the problems of cutting public expenditure and the secondary effects of raising the rates of taxation which are discussed on pages 98/9. Monetary policy in inflationary circumstances will aim to raise the level of interest rates and reduce the supply of money. These measures are described on pages 160/2. Again we must note the limitations of monetary policy (see pages 164/8). We must also bear in mind that fiscal and monetary measures are interlinked. Fiscal measures designed to eliminate demand inflation will produce a budget surplus and hence reduce the spending power of the private sector. If the surplus is used to reduce the national debt by the purchase of privately held securities, the money supply would increase and if the recipients use the money to buy goods instead of securities, planned spending would rise – just the opposite of what is required.

The control of cost-push inflation would appear to present a much more difficult problem. The essential features of this type of inflation have been described on pages 189/194. The main characteristic appears to be the refusal of income recipients to accept any cut in, or slowing down in the growth of, their real incomes. A possible solution, but one which no government is likely to pursue, would be to reduce aggregate demand and create sufficient unemployment to reduce the bargaining powers of the different income groups. Under modern conditions it would be necessary to create unemployment on a massive scale and this could only mean political suicide for any government attempting such a policy. Some compulsory control of incomes and prices would seem to be one way out, but in a democracy it is difficult if not impossible to impose such controls except in dire emergencies. A voluntary incomes policy is another alternative but subsequent discussion (pages 254-261) shows that this too has not had much real success.

EQUILIBRIUM IN THE BALANCE OF PAYMENTS

It has already been explained that this particular objective does not necessarily mean that the target is an exact balance of receipts and expenditures on foreign account. It may be necessary for a government to aim at a current surplus over the longer period. Policies to deal with a disequilibrium in the balance of payments are dealt with in Chapter 18.

ECONOMIC GROWTH

This fourth objective of economic policy is probably the most disputed, for there has been increasing criticism of the growth objective in many advanced countries. The argument is that growth creates social costs which outweigh the benefits to be gained. Nevertheless it remains a major objective of economic policy since governments see it as the key to the problem of bringing material benefits to the millions who still experience poverty. Many authorities hold that it is only when the overall standard of living is increasing that the government can intervene really effectively to redistribute income towards the less well off. The growth objective is also the one which is most often sacrificed so that the other objectives can be achieved. Inflationary pressures and/or balance of payments difficulties call for restrictions on home demand which will have the effect of inhibiting growth, but the short-term objective will be given priority over the long-term objective.

It is doubtful whether enough is yet known about the causes of growth for a government to establish the conditions necessary to achieve some given growth target. All that can be done is to encourage those developments which are conducive to growth – greater mobility, more investment in growth industries, a faster rate of technical progress, improved education and training and so on.

OTHER POLICY OBJECTIVES

Full employment, price stability, balance of payments equilibrium and growth are the most important aims of economic policy. In addition to these, governments have many other economic objectives, although in most cases these may be seen as part of the general policy to achieve the four major objectives already dealt with.

The improvement of conditions in particular regions is a major objective. This has been discussed as a feature of full employment policy, but it also has relevance to growth policy. There are, of course, strong social grounds for such a policy.

Improving the allocation of resources is another objective of policy. We have already noted that the British government has established a variety of institutions to promote competition and industrial reorganisation as a means of getting a more efficient utilisation of resources. Again this can be seen as a feature of growth policy.

Reducing inequalities in the distribution of wealth and income may also claim to be an important objective of economic policy. The use of the taxation system and the provision of a wide range of social services are means to this end, which may be regarded, perhaps, as a social rather than a purely economic objective.

Policy problems

One of the major problems of economic policy, that of the incompatibility of objectives, has already been mentioned several times. Probably the most debated issue is the apparent conflict between the objectives of full employment and price stability. If there is some inverse relationship between movements in the rate of unemployment and movements in the general price level, what degree of inflation should be tolerated in order to maintain full employment? – or what degree of unemployment should be accepted in the interests of price stability? It might be agreed, for example, to accept a degree of inflation of, say, 5 per cent per annum as the price of keeping unemployment below 3 per cent. But this rate of inflation may lead to an import surplus and balance of payments difficulties.

Some of the most intractable policy difficulties arise in dealing with a balance of payments deficit. Actions which are designed to reduce home demand in order to restrict imports and possibly stimulate a greater export effort will tend to raise unemployment and provide a check to economic growth. Policies designed to switch expenditures will also produce problems. Tariffs and quotas could lead to retaliatory actions abroad which will reduce exports. Devaluation when carried out against a background of full employment will require supporting measures to reduce home demand. These again will probably produce some unemployment and restrict growth – unless exports respond very quickly to the fall in their foreign prices.

Plans to speed up the rate of economic growth might lead to stockbuilding programmes which create an import surplus. A faster rate of economic growth also calls for improvements in productivity, in management and particularly it seems in the techniques of marketing. Such improvements in technical and commercial efficiency call for a more positive attitude towards innovation and for better individual performances. These, in most cases, are unlikely to be forthcoming without some financial incentives in the form of higher rewards. Such incentives, however, will probably increase the extent of inequality in the distribution of income, or at any rate, upset the existing income differentials.

The policy of providing social services on a large scale is a means of redistributing income. Some of these services, notably education and health, have a large positive income elasticity of demand. The demands for such services grow more than proportionately as income increases. When these services are provided free and financed almost wholly from taxation, the government has a number of unpleasant alternatives to consider. It can continue to allocate sufficient resources to meet the growing demands for such services and meet the increasing cost by increasing the burden of taxation. This will not be popular and might have some disincentive effects on effort and enterprise, or, under conditions of full employment, cause cost-push inflation as people try to restore their real income. It might, alternatively, choose to limit spending on such services to some fixed percentage of the national income and hence keep the tax burden constant. But this policy is likely to be unpopular and offend contemporary ideas of social and economic justice, since the better-off members of the community will be able to take advantage of the restrictions on the public services, and purchase, privately, much superior education and health services. This example helps us to see why economic growth is likely to remain an important economic objective.

Just why governments have been unable to achieve their objectives simultaneously is difficult to explain. Some part of the explanation lies in the inadequacy of the analysis of the working of the economic system. Although our understanding of macro-economic forces has improved greatly since the 1930s, we must acknowledge that theories of economic behaviour are subject to constant change as evidence becomes available to test them. Economics as a science is still in its infancy and some of the deficiencies of economic policy stem from a still inadequate understanding of the workings of the economic system.

Even when the authorities have a clearly defined objective and the appropriate instruments are available, there are still the critical questions of *when* to act, and by *how much*, to be answered. Econometrics is steadily increasing our knowledge but we still know relatively little about the quantitative relationships between the economic variables. Consider the position of the Chancellor of the Exchequer who is committed to maintain unemployment at some target level. Unemployment begins to increase above this level. When should the appropriate fiscal and monetary measure be applied? Is the rise in unemployment a seasonal or temporary deviation due to some exceptional factors? Once the action has been decided upon, how much stimulation should be given to aggregate spending? How long will it be before the measures begin to take effect? How long will the measures be needed? Should they be tapered off as private spending begins to rise or will this provide a further blow to business confidence? These questions should suffice to show the great extent of uncertainty in economic decision-taking.

One major cause of this uncertainty is the difficulty in getting an accurate assessment of the *present* problem. The decision taker has to contend with the inevitable lag of statistics behind the events. The Chancellor's problems are clearly illustrated in this quotation: 'Most of the data necessary for the construction of national income estimates relate to a period of at least one month ago, and often, three months ago. The quarterly figures which give the most comprehensive picture of the economic situation appear three months or more after the event. This means that when the February forecasts are being prepared in advance of the Budget, the latest available national accounts relate to the third quarter, i.e. the quarter centred on August. Obviously a lot can happen in the seven months between August and April' [i.e. when the Budget is presented].[1]

Quite apart from this time lag in the presentation of statistics, there is also the question of reliability. Some of the preliminary estimates, which might have to serve as the bases for decisions, are subject to considerable amendment in the light of later information. As one economist has put it, 'The hardest thing to know is where you are *now*'.

The problems of economic management are formidable. They consist of an amalgam of economic theories, forecasting problems, the creation and selection of suitable instruments, the quantification of the measures to be applied, and the time lags before the measures achieve any results.

---

1. Cairncross, Sir Alec, *Essays in Economic Management*, Allen & Unwin.

Questions on Chapters 18–20

ESSAY QUESTIONS

1. What limitations are there to fiscal policy as an instrument of stabilisation? **(JMB)**

2. Assume that as a result of the next Budget the government's budget deficit will be substantially reduced. Analyse the expected effects on the growth of output, the volume of bank deposits and the price level. **(O & C)**

3. Discuss the use of fiscal policy as a means of reducing aggregate unemployment. **(L)**

4. What is meant by regional policy? How can it contribute to the future economic development of the UK? **(L)**

5. 'Direct taxes are deflationary, indirect taxes are inflationary. Discuss. **(L)**

6. Explain what is meant by Full Employment. What is its connection with inflation? **(L)**

7. What is the economic justification for government intervention in the location of new industries? In what respects can the policy be carried too far? **(W)**

8. By what methods can a government seek to restore balance of payments equilibrium? What are the relative advantages and disadvantages of these methods? **(O & C)**

9. 'A devaluation will improve a country's balance of payments in the long run if the demand for and supply of her imports and exports are sufficiently elastic'. Discuss. **(L)**

10. How do you account for fluctuations in the foreign exchange rate? What is the case for trying to stabilise the rate? How is this done officially in this country? **(W)**

11. Comment on the following statement: 'Devaluation leads to a deterioration in the terms of trade and therefore a fall in the standard of living'. **(JMB)**

12. Does deflation always improve the balance of payments? **(C)**

13. Evaluate the role of the International Monetary Fund in the post-1945 world economy. **(L)**

14. Why is it difficult to reconcile a policy of price stability, with full

employment and economic growth? **(C)**

15. 'Growth depends at least as much on investment in human beings as on investment in physical capital'. Explain and discuss. **(L)**

16. Concern has been expressed about the slow rate of growth of the British economy. What are the reasons for this slow rate of growth? **(JMB)**

17. What is the relationship in an economy between capital formation and economic growth? **(O & C)**

18. What are the main problems involved in operating a national incomes policy? **(JMB)**

19. Is an incomes policy possible in a market economy? **(C)**

20. Set out the main items in the United Kingdom's Balance of Payments. How would fiscal policy affect these items? **(L)**

MULTIPLE CHOICE QUESTIONS

Questions 1, 2 and 3 refer to the following measures:
  (*a*) Devaluation.
  (*b*) Tax concessions to firms in Development Areas.
  (*c*) An increase in social welfare benefits.
  (*d*) The introduction of a scheme for Redundancy Payments.

Which of the above policies would be *most likely* to:

1. Bring about an immediate increase in consumption spending?

2. Lead to some increase in the general price level?

3. Reduce the incidence of structural unemployment?

4. The government increases direct taxation by £1m. and at the same time increases its own expenditure by £1m. The marginal rate of leakage is 0·4. What will be the effect on national income?
  (*a*) It will remain unchanged.
  (*b*) It will rise by £1m.
  (*c*) It will fall by £1m.
  (*d*) It will rise by £600 000.

5. Suppose full employment income at current prices is estimated to be £20 000m. The present level of income is £15 000m. To achieve full employment, government spending must be increased by,
  (*a*) £5 000m.
  (*b*) £5 000m. times the multiplier.

250

(c) £5000m. divided by the multiplier.
(d) £20000m. divided by the multiplier.

6. If the monetary authorities pursued an 'easy' monetary policy, it would tend to:
    (a) Raise the investment schedule and lower national income.
    (b) Raise both the investment and savings schedules and leave national incomes unchanged.
    (c) Lower the investment schedule and raise national income.
    (d) Raise the investment schedule and raise national income.

Questions 7 and 8 refer to the following policies:
   (a) A successful savings campaign.
   (b) A deflationary monetary policy.
   (c) An increase in indirect taxation.
   (d) An effective incomes policy.

7. Which policy in aiming to deal with demand-pull inflation might give rise to cost-push inflation?

8. Which policy might deal effectively with demand-pull inflation, but seriously impede economic growth?

Questions 9, 10 and 11 relate to the following developments:
   (a) An unfavourable movement in the terms of trade.
   (b) A favourable movement in the terms of trade.
   (c) An unfavourable movement in the balance of trade.
   (d) A favourable movement in the balance of trade.

9. Which of the above is an inevitable result of devaluation?

10. Which of the above is an inevitable result of revaluation?

11. Which of the above, given that the demands for and supplies of both exports and imports are elastic, is a likely consequence of devaluation?

Questions 12, 13 and 14 refer to the following terms:
   (a) Fiscal policy.
   (b) Monetary policy.
   (c) Exchange controls.
   (d) Exhortation.

Into which of the above categories would you place the following measures?

12. A subsidy to exporters.

13. A reduction in the travel allowances for holidays abroad.

14. A 'Buy British' campaign designed to reduce imports.

Questions 15 and 16 are based on the following terms:
(a) Unconditional drawing rights in the IMF.
(b) SDRs.
(c) Convertible foreign currencies.
(d) International liquidity.

15. Which of the above is referred to as the 'gold tranche'?

16. Which of the above embraces the other three?

17. Under a system of freely floating exchange rates which of the following changes would tend to cause a depreciation of the pound sterling?
(a) An increase in the foreign tonnage carried by British ships.
(b) A major change in the drinking habits of the British people leading to an increased consumption of wine.
(c) An increase in the overseas business of British insurance firms.
(d) A decline in the number of British citizens taking foreign holidays.

18. Which of the following conditions is *not* favourable to a country carrying out a policy of devaluation?
(a) The supply of exports is inelastic.
(b) The demand for exports is elastic.
(c) The demand for imports is elastic.
(d) The supply of imports is elastic.

19. The question is based on the following data.
National income £10 000m. Capital stock £50 000m. (ACOR=MCOR).
Rate of population growth 2 per cent per annum.
What proportion of the national income must be devoted to capital formation in order to maintain income per head?
(a) 2 per cent.
(b) 5 per cent.
(c) 10 per cent.
(d) 20 per cent.

Questions 20 and 21 refer to the following policy measures:
1. A proportional income tax.
2. A pension scheme in which pensions are directly linked to the Retail Price Index.
3. National Insurance contributions which vary inversely with the level of unemployment.

4. Unemployment benefits which vary directly with the level of unemployment.

20. Which of the above measures will act as built-in stabilisers?
    (*a*) 1 and 2.
    (*b*) 1 and 4.
    (*c*) 3 and 4.
    (*d*) 2 and 3.

21. Which of the above is likely to have the most inflationary tendencies?
    (*a*) 1.
    (*b*) 2.
    (*c*) 3.
    (*d*) 4.

Questions 22, 23 and 24 contain an Assertion and a Reason. Answer
    (*a*) If both assertion and reason are true statements and the reason is the correct explanation.
    (*b*) If both assertion and reason are true statements, but the reason is not a correct explanation.
    (*c*) The assertion is a true statement, but the reason is false.
    (*d*) The assertion is false, but the reason is a true statement.
    (*e*) Both assertion and reason are false statements.

Assertion	*Reason*
22. An increase in wage rates will always lead to inflationary pressures.	In most industries wages are a major item in total costs.
23. Other things being equal, an increase in liquidity preference will raise interest rates.	An increase in liquidity preference means an increase in the demand for securities and hence security prices will rise.
24. Under conditions of full employment, other things being equal, an increase in exports will be inflationary.	Exports generate income to domestic factors of production, but reduce home supplies of goods and services.

Appendix
Incomes Policy

The problem of cost inflation [1]

For some two decades after the Second World War most Western governments used demand-management techniques with a large measure of success. Full or near-full employment was maintained for most of this period while, at the same time, inflation was held at relatively low levels (1%–5% p.a.). In the late 1960s, however, problems emerged which did not seem capable of solution by the use of the traditional demand-management techniques. The association of rising unemployment and rising prices presented governments with a serious dilemma. While few doubted that the pace of inflation (which in many countries was running at much higher levels than those of the early post-war period) *could* be reduced by cutting aggregate demand, it now appeared that the extent to which demand would have to be contracted in order to achieve the objective would prove politically and socially unacceptable. In order to bring inflation down to acceptable levels (2%–3% p.a.?), the UK government, for example, would have had to reduce demand by an amount which would clearly have seriously worsened an already unsatisfactory employment situation. On the other hand, an attempt to improve the employment situation by increasing aggregate demand would have caused an escalation of the rate of inflation.

The problems of cost-push inflation, it seemed, could not be handled in a satisfactory manner by using the familiar Keynesian demand-management techniques. What was wanted was some way of reducing inflation whilst avoiding the economic and social costs of unemployment. Many governments turned hopefully to incomes policy as a solution to their problems.

The principles of an incomes policy

The major aim of an incomes policy is to achieve a close relationship

[1] See also pages 189–94.

between movements in output per head and movements in incomes. Advocates of incomes policy see it as the most effective way of diminishing the cost-push pressures which arise when incomes are rising faster than output. Incomes policies, however, usually have additional objectives. They are seen as a legitimate means of protecting the interests of those income groups with weak bargaining powers. Since governments will be brought into the bargaining processes which determine incomes, the state can use its influence to prevent any serious redistribution of income towards those groups which have very powerful bargaining positions. An incomes policy may also be seen as an important instrument in economic planning. It ensures that the national interest is brought into the processes of wage settlements. A system of perfectly free collective bargaining is uncoordinated and leads to the determination of wage rates in many thousands of separate negotiations where narrow sectional interests are the dominant forces. By focusing public attention on the need to raise productivity in order to achieve any significant increase in real income, an incomes policy may lead to a greater public awareness of the need for improvements in industrial and commercial efficiency.

There are three basic requirements in formulating an incomes policy:

1. To decide the 'norm'; that is, the permitted annual increase in total incomes.
2. To decide how this permitted increase in total incomes should be distributed.
3. To devise some effective machinery for making the policy effective.

The first of these tasks calls for an estimate of the rate of growth of output per head over the time period under consideration (usually one year). If the permitted growth in money incomes is limited to the growth rate of output per head there should be little danger of cost inflation. In several cases the projected growth rate for the UK economy proved far too optimistic and even if incomes had been restrained within the norm there would have been some inflationary pressures.

The second task is much more difficult to achieve. If the norm is, say, 5 per cent, it is not the intention that all workers should receive annual pay rises of 5 per cent. Such a procedure would freeze existing wage differentials and a major incentive to labour mobility would be destroyed. Differentials must be allowed to change if workers are to be persuaded to move, in accordance with changes in demand, from low-growth industries to those with a high growth potential. It is also accepted that incomes policy should make provision for other exceptional cases. Pay increases above the norm might be allowed where workers have made a real contribution to an increase in productivity; where the remuneration of a particular group is considered too low to maintain a reasonable standard of living, or where wages have got seriously out of line with rates of pay for similar work elsewhere. Some of these exceptional cases will offend accepted views of what is 'fair' since they will mean a movement away from existing differentials. Even more difficult will be the problem of balancing these 'above-the-norm' increases by getting other groups to accept increases below the norm.

The third fundamental feature of incomes policy also presents great problems. While the objective of the policy is quite clear, the statement of an objective does not tell us how to achieve it. How do we make incomes policy effective? There seem to be three possibilities.

(*a*) Ideally, the policy would operate on the basis of voluntary cooperation between employers, unions and government. Voluntary restraint, however, has not proved very effective in practice except in times of very serious crisis. Unions are very reluctant to surrender their right to negotiate the best possible bargains for their members. Employers short of labour will be tempted to evade the restraints of incomes policy by providing 'hidden' pay increases in the form of additional fringe benefits, 'paper' promotions and bogus productivity agreements. Since wages are increasingly negotiated at factory level the policing of an incomes policy is a formidable task. An incomes policy must embrace all forms of personal income so that it is also necessary to maintain some kind of official supervision and control over profit, interest and rent payments.

(*b*) It is also possible to operate an incomes policy by means of statutory controls on incomes and prices. Except for short periods when there is some kind of crisis it has proved very difficult to use legal controls in a democratic society and the major political parties in the UK have now stated that they will not use legal sanctions.

(*c*) A third possibility is to operate the policy by making use of fiscal measures. Movements in disposable income may be controlled by removing, in the form of increased taxation, a proportion, perhaps 100 per cent, of all increases above the norm.

INCOMES POLICY IN THE UK

The first attempt at an incomes policy in Britain was probably during the Second World War when the government appealed to unions and employers to cooperate in stabilising the cost of living. This policy was successful in so far as the official cost of living was only a few points higher in 1947 than it was in 1941. But conditions during this time were exceptional; subsidies, price controls, rationing and compulsory savings all played a part in holding down prices. There was at this time a good deal of suppressed inflation in the economy.

In the immediate post-war years the government made further

appeals for wage restraint with recommendations that the level of personal incomes should not increase faster than the volume of production. Certain exceptions were allowed–mainly where some 'essential' industry was undermanned and higher wages were needed to attract labour. These appeals were fairly successful up to the middle of 1950. One factor in this success was the desire of the trade unions to cooperate with what was the first effective Labour government.

Voluntary wage restraint began to break down towards the end of 1950 as price increases resulting from the 1949 devaluation began to take effect. Prices received a further upward thrust as a result of the large stockbuilding on the outbreak of the Korean War.

After the change of government in 1951 incomes policy was in abeyance for some time although a voluntary and temporary pause was attempted in 1956. The policy of exhortation was continued with the appointment of a Council on Prices, Productivity and Incomes in 1957. This body was superseded in 1962 by a National Incomes Commission. The role of these bodies was to keep under review changes in prices, productivity and the level of incomes, publicising the relationship between them and making recommendations as to desirable future changes. They were not very effective because the trade unions refused to cooperate with them. A White Paper on incomes policy published in 1962 laid down a recommended norm of $2\frac{1}{2}$ per cent. This was raised to $3\frac{1}{4}$ per cent as the result of a report by the recently established National Economic Development Council on growth prospects for the UK economy.

The Labour government which took office in 1964 instituted a voluntary incomes policy in which both sides of industry (the TUC and the CBI) agreed to cooperate. Each group was to examine the price and wage behaviour of its members and advise on whether it was in the national interest. In 1965 the government established a National Board for Prices and Incomes to investigate and report on the wage and price decisions of individual firms. A White Paper published in the same year gave details of the criteria which the Board was to use in making its judgements. It proposed an appropriate norm of $3-3\frac{1}{2}$ per cent for wage rises and gave indications that certain exceptions would be allowed although increases above the norm were to be balanced by increases elsewhere below the norm. In November 1965 the government established an early warning system under which employers and unions were to notify the government of any proposed increases in wages and prices so that they could be considered before they were put into effect. The TUC established a special committee to examine pay claims and unions were expected to wait until they heard the TUC's views before pursuing the claim.

MACRO-ECONOMICS

Earnings continued to rise faster than the recommended norm and in July 1966, faced with a severe balance of payments crisis, the government introduced a standstill on prices and incomes which was to run for one year. During the first six months there was to be a freeze on all prices and incomes. The next six months was to be a period of severe restraint in which the norm for pay increases was to be zero and only specified exceptional cases would be allowed to exceed this norm. The Prices and Incomes Act passed in August 1966 gave the government compulsory powers to enforce the standstill and restraint policies. Part II of the Act contained a compulsory early warning system and powers to delay the implementation of any increase in pay or prices while it was being considered by the NBPI. Part IV of the Act empowered Ministers to make orders directing that specified pay or prices should not be increased and any unjustified increases implemented since 20 July 1966 could be reversed. The powers taken under this Act were to expire in August 1967. Ministerial orders under Part IV were signed 14 times. These measures were successful in restraining the rise in money incomes although increasing unemployment during the period may have made the government's task easier.

In August 1967 another Prices and Incomes Act became law. The compulsory powers of Part IV of the 1966 Act were not retained, but the compulsory early warning system was. The norm for the next twelve months was to remain at zero and the Act gave the government power to hold up proposed pay and price increases for a total of seven months subject to a reference to the NBPI. The government, therefore, could delay but not prevent a wage increase. These delaying powers were later extended to twelve months but were abandoned at the end of 1969 when reliance was placed on Part II of the 1966 Act. The recommended norm for 1968 and 1969 was $3\frac{1}{4}$ per cent.

Throughout the period of the Labour government's incomes policy, earnings rose consistently by more than the norm. In the twenty months before the freeze of July 1966 they had been rising at $7\frac{1}{2}$ per cent per annum. During the period of the zero norm, earnings rose at an annual rate of 6 per cent per annum, in 1968 they rose by 6·8 per cent, in 1969 by 7·4 per cent, and in 1970 by 12 per cent.

The change of government in 1970 brought a change of policy in so far as the Conservatives announced that they were not intending to impose any statutory incomes policy nor indeed lay down any norms or detailed wage criteria. The government wound up the National Board for Prices and Incomes, but later made it clear that it was prepared to consider proposals for some kind of voluntary incomes policy. In fact, the accelerating pace of inflation during the latter part of 1972 forced the government to adopt a statutory prices and wages policy. A 90-day standstill on pay and prices was followed by a period of strict controls on pay, prices, rents and dividends. Two new agencies, a Price Commission and a Pay Board were established to enforce the new legislation.

Price increases were limited to cover only the rise in 'allowable' costs which included only half of any increase in wage costs. This policy collapsed because of a very marked increase in the rate of inflation which was due to an enormous increase in world commodity prices and the government's expansionary policy at home (an attempt to increase the rate of growth). The miners' strike led to a change of government in 1974 and the new Labour administration abandoned statutory wage controls. It replaced them with a voluntary agreement known as the Social Contract, but price controls were retained.

This agreement between government and unions promised legislation desired by the unions in return for the unions' promise to moderate their wage claims. In fact wages continued to rise very rapidly and this, together with the restrictions on prices, severely squeezed profits, caused many bankruptcies, and increased unemployment. In July 1975 the government adopted a more formal pay policy with a norm of £6 per week for the next twelve months and followed this with a recommended maximum rise of £4 for a further twelve-month period. These limits on pay increases were voluntary but the government did threaten to use sanctions[1] against firms which breached the pay code. Great hopes were placed on an agreement with the unions which declared that wage settlements should be twelve months apart (the twelve-month rule). This rule was seen as the major barrier against escalating cost-push inflation.

From July 1975 to July 1977 the voluntary policy was successful in reducing both the rate of increase in wage rates and the rate of inflation, although other factors such as the recovery in the external value of the pound also had some influence. A major problem, however, was that a policy which had made use of a series of flat-rate wage increases had seriously eroded the traditional differentials between the pay of skilled workers and the pay of semi-skilled and unskilled workers. This caused serious dissatisfaction in certain industries and perhaps, by reducing the incentive to train, prejudiced the future supply of skilled workers. Proposals for further stages in incomes policy envisaged some restoration of these differentials.

EFFECTIVENESS OF INCOMES POLICIES

Some important lessons have emerged from attempts to operate incomes policies in industrial countries. It does seem that for a limited period, legal wage and price controls can be effective, but it is difficult to

---

[1] e.g. a refusal to place public contracts with firms which breached the pay code.

maintain a standstill on prices and wages for more than a few months because such controls frustrate the function of the price mechanism in allocating resources. In addition such controls tend to bring the trade unions into conflict with the government and unions will not surrender their rights to negotiate on behalf of their members for any extended period of time. A further problem of operating a system of tight controls on wages and prices is that once these controls are relaxed there tends to be a flood of wage claims and price increases which may very soon bring both wages and prices back on their former trend.

It also seems that an announcement by the government of an annual norm is not very helpful. It often becomes no more than a negotiating minimum. On the other hand the announcement of a norm might serve to lower the level of expectations of those seeking increases in wages and other incomes.

There is a great deal of evidence that the most important pre-condition for acceptance of an incomes policy by labour is some degree of price stability. As far as British experience is concerned it seems that wage and price controls when firmly applied do work for a time, but they break down when prices are forced upwards by non-wage factors. The increases in prices brought about by the 1949 devaluation, the 1967 devaluation, the heavy increase in indirect taxes in 1968, and the massive increases in world commodity prices in 1972–1974 were important factors leading to the breakdown of incomes policies.

A major problem with the operation of a longer-term incomes policy is how to embody some measure of flexibility into the restrictions. There must be some kind of incentive for workers to increase their productivity, but above-the-norm payments for such increases will be strongly resented by workers in industries where productivity cannot be easily measured or where technical and physical factors make it very difficult to increase productivity. Similarly some changes in wage differentials will have to be permitted if labour mobility is to be encouraged, but, in periods of general wage restraint, such 'special cases' will be criticised as 'unfair' by those who do not benefit from the exceptional increases which might be allowed to industries short of labour. An incomes policy which applies to millions of workers and which has to be administered by many thousands of firms must be easy to understand and simple to apply. This requirement together with a desire to help the lower paid led UK governments to apply norms in the form of flat-rate wage increases with the consequences mentioned earlier.

Another difficulty arises when an incomes policy is introduced. In countries like the UK, wage bargaining is a continuous process and wage settlements in different industries are made at different times throughout the year. A policy of wage restraint must have some starting date and when it is introduced there will be some 'lucky' groups (those who have just completed a wage settlement), and some 'unlucky' groups (those who were in the process of reaching a settlement). This problem was dealt with in the UK by the adoption of the twelve-month rule mentioned earlier. An argument has been put forward in favour of more centralised wage bargaining with all or most industries settling their wage claims simultaneously. This would mean, it is said, that more account would be taken of the national interest and it would be so much easier to make comparisons between different industries.

There have been many other proposals for dealing with cost-push inflation. One of these, the taxation of wage increases above the norm has already been mentioned. This proposal would tax the recipient of the increased wage, but another suggestion is that the tax penalty should fall on the firm which pays increases above the norm. The idea of tying wages to the cost of living index has also been suggested and, indeed, formed part of a British incomes policy in 1973–74 when workers were allowed an extra 40 pence per week for each 1 per cent rise in the Index of Retail Prices. This policy of *indexation* received much support because for most of the 1960s and 1970s wages were rising faster than prices and in these circumstances a direct link between wages and prices should moderate the rate of growth of wages. Inflation would be reduced by indexation if workers could be persuaded to accept smaller basic settlements because they know that their real incomes are being protected. Opponents of the scheme point out that it would shorten the period between an increase in prices and the resulting wage increase and hence might speed up the rate of inflation.

Another suggestion is for annual increases for all workers based on the national average increase in productivity. The essential feature of this proposal is that the increases would be automatic and would not require claims or strikes by workers in order to get them. It has appeal on grounds of equity since it seems reasonable that the gains from increased national efficiency should accrue to the whole population. Increases in productivity most often result from technical progress, more investment, better management and economies of scale, and there seems no good reason why the whole of the gains from increased productivity should go to the workers in the industry concerned.

Index

Acceleration principle 62–4
Acceptance houses 137, 147
Active balances 154, 165
Adjustable peg 214, 218
Aggregate Demand
  and employment Chap. 8
  and equilibrium Chap. 4, Chap. 7
  and foreign trade Chap. 10
  and government sector Chap. 9
  and prices Chap. 16
  in two-sector economy Chap. 7
Aggregate Supply 37–8, 67
  and price level Chap. 16
Appreciation 206
Automatic stabilisers 94–5
Autonomous demands 39, 62, 64, 75–6, 99, 106, 186–7
Average propensities (defined)
  to consume 43–8
  to import 105
  to save 43–8

Balanced Budget multiplier 99–100
Balance of Payments 4, 5, 104, 107, 187–8, 196, Chap. 18, 245–8
Balance of Trade 201
Balancing item 201
Bank assets Chapters 11, 12, and 13
Bank deposits 122–3, 126–33
  cash base theory 127–33
  reserve ratios 132, 141
Banknotes
  development 124–6
  in money supply Chap. 12
Bank of England 125, 126, 127, 129
  and control of money supply Chap. 14
  and exchange rate 207
  functions of 135–7
  role in U.K. banking Chap. 12
Bank rate 139
Banks in U.K. Chap. 12

Base rate 144
Beveridge, Lord 84
Bill of exchange 137
Budget, 36, 87, 94, 97–100, 187, 244, 248
  (see also Fiscal policy)
Building societies 122, 146

Cambridge version (of quantity theory) 175
Capital
  deepening 229
  fixed and circulating 12
  flows (balance of payments) 201–3
  formation (investment) Chap. 6
  goods 11, 51–3
  marginal efficiency 58–61
  marginal productivity 55, 59, 60
  output ratios 226–7, 232
  widening 229
Cash base theory 127–33
Cash ratio 126–33, 141, 147, 167
Ceilings 162
Central bank, see Bank of England
Certificates of deposit 148
Chicago school 177–8
Clearing banks 129, 135, 140–5
Clearing house 129, 140
Commercial banks 129–33, 140–5
Competition and credit control, (1971 measures) 141, 167–8
Consumer goods 11, 41, 51
Consumption 32–3
  and aggregate demand Chap. 4
  and circular flow Chap. 3
  and disposable income 89
  and equilibrium Chap. 7
  and taxes 92
  function Chap. 5
Controls (direct) 5, 236–7, 242, 244, 260
Control of money supply Chap. 14
Convertibility
  banknotes 124

foreign currency 213, 215
Cost-benefit analysis 54, 60
Cost-push inflation 189–96, 210, 244, 254
Costs
  and investment decision 53–61
  and output 180–2
Currency flow 201

Deflationary gap 77
Demand for money Chap. 13
Demand-pull inflation 185–9, 191–6, 244
Depreciation
  capital 12, 20, 25, 52
  foreign currency 204–6
Devaluation 193, 210–12, 214–5
Direct controls 5, 236–7, 242, 244, 260
Direct taxes 88–92, 96, 98, 99, 239
Discounted cash flow 57
Discount Houses 137–40, 142, 148, 161, 167
Discounting 56–8, 138–9
Disposable income 49, 65, 89, 92
Double counting 19

Economic development, see Economic growth
Economic growth 4, Chap. 19, 245–6
Economic models 6–7
Economic policies 2–5, Chap. 20 (See also, Monetary policy, Fiscal policy, and Foreign exchange)
Economic theory 6–7
Elasticities of demand and supply 88, 204
Employment 39, Chap. 8
  policy 238–43 (See also Full employment, and Unemployment)
Equation of exchange 174
Equilibrium 31, 33, 34, 36, Chap. 4
  and balance of payments Chap. 18
  and economic growth 221
  and employment 80–4
  and foreign trade Chap. 10
  and government sector Chap. 9
  and output 157–8
  and price level Chap. 16
  and two-sector economy Chap. 7
Eurodollars 148
Ex ante and ex post 33
Excess demand 79, 186–7
Exchange control 209, 212, 217
Exchange Equalisation Account 135, 207, 208

Exchange rate 196, Chap. 18
Expectations,
  and consumption 49
  and growth 225
  and investment 61
  and liquidity preference 156
Expenditure
  and demand 38–9
  and liquidity preference 156–8
  and national income Chap. 2
Exports 18, 34, Chap. 10, 187–8, Chap. 18

Fiduciary issue 125
Finance houses 145–8, 163, 167
Financial intermediaries 146–9
Fiscal policy 4, 87, 94–102, 166, Chap. 20
Fisher, Irving 175
Fixed exchange rates 208–13, 218
Flexible exchange rates 204–7, 217–18
Floating exchange rates 204–7, 217–18
Fluctuating exchange rates 204–7, 217–218
Foreign exchange Chap. 18
  reserves 213–16
Foreign trade 18, Chap. 10, Chap. 18
  multiplier 106
Frictional unemployment 83–4, 239–43
Friedman, M. 177–8
Full employment 3, 38
  and exchange rate 205
  and growth 221
  and price level 181, 186, 189
  meaning and measurement 80, 83–4
  policies 238–43, 246–8
Funding 161

General Agreement of Tariffs and Trade (GATT) 209
General Arrangement to Borrow 213
Gold 123–5, 213–15, 216–17
Gold tranche 212
Government
  policy 2–5, 17, 35, Chap. 20
  sector and level of income Chap. 9
  see also Economic policies
Gross Domestic Product 20, 22, 25
Gross National Expenditure 22
Gross National Product 20, 22, 25
Growth Chap. 19

Hire purchase 48, 162
Hyper-inflation 188

263

Idle balances 152, 157, 165, 177
Imports 18, 19, 34, Chap. 10, 188–9, Chap. 18
Income
  and consumption Chap. 5
  and foreign trade Chap. 10
  and government sector Chap. 9
  and growth Chap. 19
  and investment 62–4, Chap. 7
  as a flow 15–17
  measurement of N.I. 10–25
  types of income 13–15
Incomes policy 193, 254–61
Income velocity of circulation 175
Indirect taxes 21, 88–92, 98–9, 189, 193, 239
Induced demand 39, 42, 76
Industrial Development Certificates 242
Inflation 5, 38, Chap. 17
  cost-push 189–94, 254
  demand-pull 185–9, 195–6
  effects of 194–6
  and incomes policy 254–61
  policy 243–8
Inflationary gap 79
Injections Chapters 3, 7, 9, and 10
Innovations 230
Instruments of policy 235–7
Insurance companies 17, 146
Interest *see* Rate of interest
International liquidity 215–17
International Monetary Fund 167, 202, 211–18
Inventions 230
Investment 12, 13, 16, 18, 25, Chap. 6
  abroad 202
  autonomous 39, 62, 64, 76, 99, 186
  and fiscal policy 96–7
  and growth 225–30
  and income 62–4, 157
  and inflation 187–8
  and rate of interest 54–60, 157–8
  and savings Chap. 3, Chap. 7
  gross 12, 22, 25, 63
  induced 39, 62, 76
  motives 53–4
  Multiplier 71–5
  net 12, 25, 52, 63, 226–7
  public 52, 54, 60, 80–1
  types 51–2
Invisible trade 201

Keynes, Lord 3, 58, 61–2, 77, 94, 151, 163, 176–8

Labour,
  demand for 82
  supply of 81, 228
  (*see also* employment and unemployment)
Leakages Chapters 3, 7, 9, and 10
Liquid assets 121, 127, 140–1, 144, 147, 167
Liquidity 121
  and IMF 213–17
  and monetary policy 164–8
  and profitability 141, 144
  and quantity theory 174–8
Liquidity preference theory Chap. 13, 177, 188
Local authority finance 142, 143, 147
Location of industry 241–3
London Clearing House 129, 140
London Money Market Chap. 12

Managed exchange rates 207
Managing the economy Chap. 20
Marginal capital output ratio 226, 232
Marginal efficiency of capital 58–61
Marginal productivity of capital 55, 59, 60
Marginal propensities
  to consume and save 43–8, 90–4, 226–7, 232
  to import 105
Mathematical notation 7–9
Merchant banks 137, 148
Minimum lending rate 139, 140
Monetary policy 4, 163–7, Chap. 20
Money 12, Chap. 11
  demand for Chap. 13
  evolution 123–6
  functions of 120–1
  liquidity preference 154–8
  quantity theory Chap. 15
  supply 122, Chap. 14
Money at call 138–9, 142–3, 161
Money market 137–40
Multiplier
  bank deposits 131–3
  income 71–5, 90–2, 105–6

National Board for Prices and Incomes 257–8
National debt 100–2, 135, 161, 165–6
National Economic Development Council 257
National Giro 146, 148
National income Chapters 2–10
  and standard of living 25–7, Chap. 19

and value of money 175
identities 15
measurement 18–21
  real and money 21–5
  tables 22
Near money 122
Net National Product 20

Open market operations 160, 168, 239
Output,
  and demand Chap. 4
  and employment Chap. 8
  and national income Chap. 2
  and prices Chap. 16

Paradox of Thrift 75
Parallel money markets 146–9
Participation rate 81
Pay Board 259
Phillips' curve 191–4
Planned and realised values 33, Chap. 7, 89
Population and growth 31, 231–2
Precautionary demand for money 151–2
Present value 55–8
Prices 3
  and inflation Chap. 17
  and liquidity preference 156
  and output Chap. 16
  and quantity of money Chap. 15
  index of 24, 261
  stability of 243–5
Prices and Incomes Act 258
Price Commission 259
Production possibility curve 222–3
Productive potential 182
Productivity 182, 221
  and inflation 189–96
Profits 13, 15, 20, 32, 184
  and inflation 195
  and investment 53, 55–7, 60
  and output Chap. 16
Propensities
  to consume and save 43–8, 90–4, 226–227, 232
  to import 105
Property income from abroad 20, 21, 15
Public expenditure 17, Chap. 9, Chap. 20 (*see also* Government)
Public investment 52, 54, 60, 80–1 (*see also* Government)

Quantitative controls 162, 167
Quantity of Money Theory Chap. 15

Quasi money 122
Quotas 209, 217
Radcliffe Committee 164
Rate of interest,
  and inflation 188
  and investment 57–62
  and liquidity preference 152–7
  and monetary policy 163–8
  and money market 137–40
  and money supply 159, 177–8
  and national debt 100–2
  and quantity theory 176–8
  policy 161
  structure of rates 158
Rationing 237
Realised saving and investment Chap. 3
Real national income 21–5, 37, 39, 222
Real rate of interest 166
Regional Employment Premium 242
Regional problems 241–3
Regulator 98
Reserve assets ratio 127, 132, 141–3
  and control of money supply 159–62, 167–8
Revaluation 210–12, 214–5

Savings 16, 17, 104–5
  and consumption Chap. 5
  and equilibrium Chap. 7
  and growth 226–7
  and inflation 187–8
  and investment Chap. 3
  and multiplier 72–5
  function 46
  institutions 146–9
Seasonal unemployment 243
Secondary money markets 146
Shares 51
Social costs and benefits 54, 60, 233
Social services 17, 95, 98, 247
Special deposits 144, 162, 168
Special drawing rights 213–15
Speculation (foreign exchange) 206, 211, 215, 217
Speculative demand for money 152–5
Stabilisation funds 207–8
Stabilisers 94–5
Standard of living 25, Chap. 19
Sterling certificates of deposit 148
Stock appreciation 19, 21
Stocks 12, 13, 21, 38, 51, 61, 64
Strikes 194
Structural unemployment 239–43
Subsidies 21, 25
Supplementary special deposits 168
Supply (aggregate) Chap. 16

265

Supply of money   Chap. 11, Chap. 14
Supply price   180–1, 184

Tariffs   209, 217
Taxes   21, 25, 35, Chap. 9, 239
   and inflation   189–93
   types of   87–8
Technical progress   230
Terms of trade   210
Thrift   75
Trade unions   188–96
   and incomes policy   254–61
Transactions demand for money   151, 188
Transactions velocity of circulation   175
Transfer payments   17, 21, 35, 85–6, 93–5, 100
Treasury Bills   127, Chap. 12, 138, 140, 142

and monetary policy   Chap. 14

Unemployment   81–4
   and inflation   191–4
   policy   239–43

Value added   18
Value of money   21, Chap. 15, Chap. 17
Velocity of circulation   164–5, 174–8
Visible trade   201

Wages   13, 15, 16, 80–1, 99, 179, 180, 187, 191
   and inflation   189–96
   and incomes policy   254–61
Washington agreement   217
Wealth   12, 49, 119

Answers to questions

Questions on Chapter 2.
1. (d)   2. (c)   3. (a)   4. (a)   5. (a)   6. (c)
Problem: 935

Questions on Chapters 3–10.
1. (b)   2. (c)   3. (c)   4. (d)   5. (c)   6. (b)   7. (d)   8. (d)   9. (a)
10. (d)   11. (b)   12. (b)   13. (a)   14. (d)
Problems.
1. 1·43 approx.
2. (i) £625m.   (ii) £250m.   (iii) deficit £25m.   (iv) deficit £25m.

Questions on Chapters 11–14.
1. (c)   2. (d)   3. (a)   4. (c)   5. (a)   6. (b)   7. (a)   8. (c)   9. (c)
10. (c)
Problems.
1. (1) fall by £50m.
   (2) fall by £500m.
2. 5 per cent.

Questions on Chapters 15–17.
1. (m)   2. (v)   3. (t)   4. (b)   5. (a)   6. (b)   7. (d)   8. (c)

Questions on Chapters 18–20.
1. (c)   2. (a)   3. (b)   4. (b)   5. (c)   6. (d)   7. (c)   8. (b)   9. (a)
10. (b)   11. (d)   12. (a)   13. (c)   14. (d)   15. (a)   16. (d)   17. (b)
18. (a)   19. (c)   20. (c)   21. (b)   22. (d)   23. (c)   24. (a)